Proceedings

Seventh International Workshop on Research Issues in Data Engineering

High Performance Database Management for Large-Scale Applications

Proceedings

Seventh International Workshop on Research Issues in Data Engineering

High Performance Database Management for Large-Scale Applications

April 7 – 8, 1997

Birmingham, England

Sponsored by

**IEEE Computer Society Technical Committee on
Data Engineering**

Edited by

Peter Scheuermann

IEEE Computer Society Press
Los Alamitos, California

Washington　•　Brussels　•　Tokyo

IEEE Computer Society Press
10662 Los Vaqueros Circle
P.O. Box 3014
Los Alamitos, CA 90720-1264

IEEE Computer Society Press Order Number PR07849
Library of Congress Number 97-70592
IEEE Order Plan Number 97TB100122
ISBN 0-8186-7849-6 (paper)
ISBN 0-8186-7851-8 (microfiche)

Additional copies may be ordered from:

IEEE Computer Society Press	IEEE Service Center	IEEE Computer Society	IEEE Computer Society
Customer Service Center	445 Hoes Lane	13, Avenue de l'Aquilon	Ooshima Building
10662 Los Vaqueros Circle	P.O. Box 1331	B-1200 Brussels	2-19-1 Minami-Aoyama
P.O. Box 3014	Piscataway, NJ 08855-1331	BELGIUM	Minato-ku, Tokyo 107
Los Alamitos, CA 90720-1264	Tel: +1-908-981-1393	Tel: +32-2-770-2198	JAPAN
Tel: +1-714-821-8380	Fax: +1-908-981-9667	Fax: +32-2-770-8505	Tel: +81-3-3408-3118
Fax: +1-714-821-4641			Fax: +81-3-3408-3553
Email: cs.books@computer.org			

Editorial production by Regina Spencer Sipple
Cover design by Joseph Daigle/Studio Productions
Printed in the United States of America by Technical Communication Services

 The Institute of Electrical and Electronics Engineers, Inc.

Table of Contents

Preface

RIDE '97 is the seventh in the series of annual workshops held in connections with the IEEE International Conference on Data Engineering. This year the topic of the workshop is High Performance Database Management for Large-Scale Applications. The Internet and its organizing infrastructure, that is, the Web, is restructuring the way in which we interact with service providers — banks, retail stores, government agencies and professional and social organizations. Large-scale applications today involve complex decision making and/or finding of relevant patterns, such as those found in data mining and data warehousing, which requires efficient access to billions of bytes coming from many sources. We hope that this workshop will serve as a forum for the exchange of promising ideas in this field among researchers, developers, and practitioners.

The workshop program consists of five sessions of regular papers, a session with work-in-progress, and two invited talks and a panel. The topics covered in the regular sessions are: Databases and the Web, Data Mining and Warehousing, Electronic Commerce and Workflow Management, Challenges in Scalability of Database Systems, Distributed File Structures, and Multimedia Servers. We are very happy to have two of the best known experts in the field give invited talks: Avi Silberschatz on "Storage and Retrieval of Multimedia Objects" and Martin Kersten on "The Database Engine for the Next Decade." Furthermore, we have assembled a session of work-in-progress reporting on joint university-industry team projects funded by the European Community.

For this workshop we received 36 regular paper submissions and all papers were reviewed by at least three members of the program committee. The final paper selection was made in a round of e-mail discussions. We chose 14 of the papers for presentation.

We would like to express our gratitude to the people who put together the technical program: the members of the program committee for their timely and thorough reviews of the papers; the international coordinators, Chris Clifton, and Ian Gorton, and especially Michael Arentoft for his help in setting up the work-in-progress session with projects sponsored by the EC; Arie Shoshani for organizing the panel on data warehousing and OLAP.

It is our pleasure to thank Innes Jelly and Radek Vingralek for doing such an excellent publicity job in the UK and the US; Jim Griffioen for his handling of the financial affairs; Alan Sexton for his work coordinating the local arrangements with ICDE; Sharad Mehrotra for his help with the proceedings, and Marey Garvey for registration. Special thanks are also due to the members of the RIDE steering committee, and particularly, Ahmed Elmagarmid and Marek Rusinkiewicz for their advice and support during all stages of the workshop organization.

We gratefully acknowledge the support of the IEEE Computer Society and its Technical Committee on Data Engineering and recognize Regina Sipple for her outstanding job supervising the production of these proceedings.

No workshop is a success without the authors who present the papers and the attendees who engage in thought-provoking discussions during and after the sessions. We hope that you will all enjoy the setting of this workshop and we thank you for contributing to its success.

Yuri Breitbart	Jon Kerridge	Peter Scheuermann
General Co-Chair	*General Co-Chair*	*Program Chair*

Committees

General Co-Chairs

Jon Kerridge, *Napier University, Edinburgh, Scotland*
Yuri Breitbart, *Bell Laboratories, USA*

Program Chair

Peter Scheuermann, *Northwestern University, USA*

Program Committee

Serge Abiteboul, *INRIA, France*
Daniel Barbara, *Bellcore, USA*
Azer Bestavros, *Boston University, USA*
Stephen Blott, *ETH, Switzerland*
Michael Carey, *IBM Almaden, USA*
Stefano Ceri, *Politecnico di Milano, Italy*
Misbah Deen, *Keele University, UK*
Klaus Dittrich, *University of Zurich, Switzerland*
Shahram Ghandeharizadeh, *USC, USA*
Jiawei Han, *Simon Fraser University, Canada*
Mathias Jarke, *RWTH-Aachen, Germany*
Martin Kersten, *CWI, The Netherlands*
Masaru Kitsuregawa, *University of Tokyo, Japan*
Simon Lavington, *University of Essex, UK*

Witold Litwin, *University of Paris, France*
Kia Makki, *University of Nevada, USA*
Patrick O'Neil, *University of Massachusetts, USA*
Tamer Ozsu, *University of Alberta, Canada*
Nikki Pissinou, *Univ. of Southwestern Louisiana, USA*
Rajeev Rastogi, *Lucent Bell Labs, USA*
Nick Roussopoulos, *University of Maryland, USA*
Doron Rotem, *Lawrence Berkeley Lab, USA*
Timos Sellis, *Nat'l Technical Univ. of Athens, Greece*
Oded Shmueli, *Technion, Israel*
S. Sudarshan, *ITT Bombay, India*
Gerhard Weikum, *Univ. of Saarbrucken, Germany*
Yelena Yesha, *NASA CESDIS, USA*
Clement Yu, *Univ. of Illinois at Chicago, USA*

Steering Committee

Ahmed Elmagarmid, *Purdue University, USA*
John Urban, *USA*
Yahiko Kambayashi, *Kyoto University, Japan*
Marek Rusinkiewicz, *MCC, USA*

Publication Chair

Sharad Mehrotra, University of Illinois at Urbana-Champaign, USA

Publicity Co-Chairs

Innes Jelly, Sheffield Hallam University, UK
Radek Vingralek, Northwestern University, USA

Industrial Coordinator

David Parsons

American Coordinator

Chris Clifton

European Coordinator

Michael Arentoft, *European Commission, DG Industry*

Far East Coordinator

Ian Gorton, *CSIRO, Australia*

Local Arrangements

Alan Sexton, *University of Birmingham, UK*

Financial Chair

Jim Griffioen, *University of Kentucky, USA*

Registration Chair

Mary Garvey, *University of Wolverhampton, UK*

List of Additional Reviewers

Y. Breitbart
S. Chee
B. Fordham
D. Jonscher
S. Gatziu
W. Gong
H.-J. Lenz
F. Korn
K. Kalpakis
M. Kamber
S.A.M.Makki
M. Nakano
M. Rabinovich
I. Radev
L.L. Yan
D. Tombros
R. Vingralek

SESSION : 1

DATABASES AND THE WWW

PRIME-GC. A Medical Information Retrieval Prototype on the WEB.

M. Mechkour, P. Mulhem, F. Fourel & C. Berrut

CLIPS-IMAG

BP 53, 38041 Grenoble cedex 9

France

{mourad.mechkour, philippe.mulhem, franck.fourel, catherine.berrut}@imag.fr

Tel : (33) 4 76 63 59 76,

Fax : (33) 4 76 44 66 75.

Abstract

We describe in this paper a prototype [1], PRIME, of a multimedia medical information retrieval system. The documents managed by PRIME are patient records, which are composed of administrative data, textual reports, and Magnetic Resonance Images. PRIME is developed on top of the object oriented DBMS O_2, and its interface can be any WWW-navigator (Netscape, InternetExplorer, ...). The retrieval engine of PRIME is based on Sowa's Conceptual Graph Formalism structures and operations.

Keywords : Multimedia modeling, Conceptual Graphs, Object Oriented Database, Knowledge Base, Information Retrieval, Image Retrieval, html, hypermedia.

1 Introduction

PRIME is a medical application developed on top of the OODBMS O_2 and devoted to the management of a collection of multimedia records, including structured data, textual reports and Magnetic Resonance Images (MRI). Potential users are mainly students and physicians analyzing previous disease cases.

PRIME implements multiple original points compared to existing multimedia information retrieval systems :

- PRIME combines information retrieval and navigation approaches to get the most effective process of searching for particular documents in an organized base.

- The document representation is based on a semantic model, where documents and queries are represented by conceptual structures, and not simple independent terms. The retrieval engine used to evaluate user queries is based on a semantic matching function, which does not limit the set of relevant document to those exactly matching the query.

- PRIME is available on the WEB where a very large medical community can access it and benefit from the collection of medical records, using an easy to learn and widely available interface, which can be any W3-navigator (Netscape, InternetExplorer, etc.).

This PRIME description is organized in two main parts. In the first part we present a general description of PRIME, including the document structure and content, the functionalities provided and the architecture of the PRIME prototype. The second part is devoted to the details of two main components of PRIME, which are the user interface for querying and browsing in the document base, and the retrieval facility of PRIME which is composed of the Conceptual Graph Framework, the indexing model and the matching function.

2 PRIME description

2.1 The documents

We depict now the documents that are managed by PRIME. In the following, all the elements that we describe are related to Fig. 1. This figure shows, using the BNF notation, the overall structure of these documents.

In the context of the medical application we focus on, the data on patients (rule 1 of Fig. 1) managed by an Hospital are of two kinds: administrative data and medical data. The administrative data (rule 2 of Fig. 1) are related to non-medical general information about patients, like birthday, name, address, ... The medical data (rule 3 of Fig. 1) are themselves split into general medical data, and single examination data. The general medical data bears on medical

---

[1]This work has been funded by the EEC under Basic Research Action FERMI, n 8134.

```
1.<Record>      ::=<Adm. data> <Med. data>
2.<Adm. data>   ::=<Id> <first name> <last name>
                   <address> <sex> <birthplace>
                   <birthday> <nationality>
3.<Med. data>   ::={<chronic disease>}
                   { <allergy> }
                   { <medical antecedent>}
                   { <other medical remark>}
                   (<date of examination>,<Examination>)
                   { (<date of exam> , <Exam>)}
4.<Examination>::=<asking physician> { <asking physician>}
                   <specialist> { <specialist>}
                   <Report> <Series> { <Series>}
                   [<index>]
5.<Report>      ::=<text> [ <index>]
6.<Series>      ::=<MRI> { <MRI> }
7.<MRI>         ::=<physical view> [ <logical view>]
```

Figure 1. The PRIME Data Model

characteristics of a patient that are of general interest for all physicians. Parts of the general medical data are chronic diseases and allergies. The examination data is related to each examination that a patient is subject to.

In PRIME, we address the management of the data related to Magnetic Resonance examinations. Records of such examinations involve multimedia data. In this context, the examination data (rule 4 of Fig. 1) comes from scanning based on magnetic resonance (MR), the examination is composed of one textual report (rule 5 of Fig. 1) and of several MR image series (rule 6 of Fig. 1) that contain between 3 and 20 MRI (rule 7 of Fig. 1).

The figure 1 sums up the elements described above. The Id of rule 2 is a unique identifier (corresponding to a social security number) for each patient. In the rule 4 (examination), we store data on the physician(s) who is asking for an examination, and we also handle data on the specialist(s) that makes the examination. The index non-terminal symbol is described in the following part.

2.2 The functionalities

Because we are focusing on linking information retrieval techniques to hypermedia navigation, we use IR index that correspond to a representation of the semantic content of documents managed by PRIME.

From the IR point of view, the data on which retrieval makes sense are the MR images, the textual reports and the whole medical reports. So, the data that have to be indexed are the examinations (rule 4 of Fig. 1)), the reports (rule 5 of Fig. 1) and MR images (rule 7 of Fig. 1).

The navigation is provided along the structural composition links described by the non-terminal tokens of the Fig. 1.

We also define navigation between images of the same series, series of the same examinations, examinations of the same patient to ease the analysis and the evolution of the disease of a patient.

One innovative point comes from the mixing of the navigation and IR data. This mixing takes place at two levels:

- the navigation provided along the raw medical data integrates also the presentation of parts of their indexes. This point enlarges the vision of the data by helping the physician to focus on important points of the data.

- the PRIME system takes into account the structure of the medical data when presenting query results. The results provided usually by IR systems are flat (in term of structure of composition), and the use of the structure of the medical data ease the access to data that are related to the rough query results.

These points will be developed in parts 3.1.2 and 3.1.3.

2.3 The architecture

Figure 2 shows the principle components of the PRIME prototype. In this schema each module groups the set of class definitions implied in the achievement of a particular task, and does not correspond to a process, since PRIME is implemented as a database schema for the O_2 OO-DBMS.

The choice of an OO-DBMS is mainly motivated by its ability to provide secure storage and access to large amount of data, which is a really important point in PRIME document collection. And the object oriented approach handles quite well the complexity of the relationships between the medical data.

The basic components of PRIME are on one side the Conceptual Graph framework, described in 3.2.1 and the documents manager which is developed on top of a multimedia extension to O_2. This extension offers the main image processing functions, that are not available in the OODBMS. The link between these two modules is done via the index manager which associates with each PRIME documents its index.

The matching function is concerned about the estimation of the relevance degree of a document to a given query.

Since PRIME is available on the WEB, we can use any WWW-navigator as a user interface. The interface part in PRIME is concerned about the generation of the adequate HTML pages to be viewed by the chosen WWW-navigator.

We describe in the following the details of the two main components of PRIME, and which are the retrieval facility and the interface.

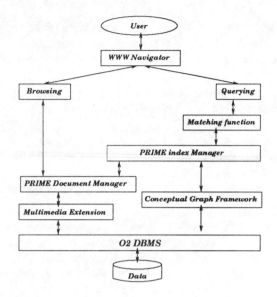

Figure 2. Architecture of the PRIME prototype.

3 PRIME components

3.1 The user interface

The interface to PRIME is any WWWnavigator. The choice of the WEB interface is motivated by three main reasons :

- the WEB servers can provide interactive access to large amounts of complex, multimedia and distributed data;

- the WEB is widely used by different user communities to browse through Internet and search for particular documents they interested in, so PRIME can be used without prior learning;

- it is easier to develop an application interface for the web (writing the programs that generates the html pages for displaying PRIME elements) compared to X/Motif based interfaces.

We describe in the next sections what is the gateway between the O_2 DBMS and the WEB, the querying interface and then the browsing interface and facility.

3.1.1 O2web

O2Web depicted in the Fig. 3 is the utility from O_2 company that provides WWW Clients with the ability to browse the rough hypermedia information stored in any O_2 database. The information presented to the client is a view of the objects of the database, that can be manipulated using

their associated functions and methods. The PRIME interface is then developed as a set of methods associated to the displayed elements (MRI, examination, query, ...), and a set of functions for guiding the interaction and processing user queries.

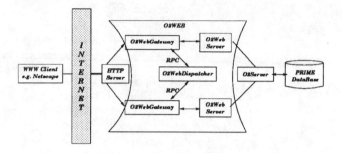

Figure 3. O2Web Architecture.

3.1.2 Browsing

The set of PRIME medical records is organized as an hypermedia, where the nodes correspond to elements of the record like examination, MRI, series (see fig. 1), and the links between nodes (navigation path) correspond to two types of relations between linked elements.

1. Structural relations linking a complex element to its components and to the element that contains it. For example, an examination is linked to the textual Report and to the set of MRI series that compose it, and to the Medical Data element. Fig. 4 shows the display of an examination (DMS in French) where the navigation through the components can be done by clicking on their corresponding anchors (**Le CRM** for the textual report, and **Série 1, Série 2, Série 3** for the MRI series), and to display the Medical Data we click on the left arrow in the top-right corner.

2. Set relation linking the elements of the same type that belong to the same list. Using this link we can travel in the list by going from an element to its previous and following elements. For instance, we can travel along all the images of the same series, series of the same examination, and examinations of the same patient. Fig. 5 shows the display of a MRI, from a series, and we can see the previous and following MRI in the same series, just by clicking on the corresponding arrow in the top-left of the display.

Note that both link types are bi-directional.

Each element of the record in PRIME is displayed as an HTML page, and an html page is always presented in the same way :

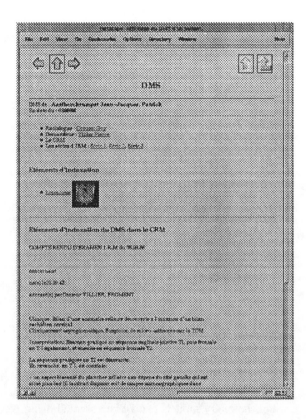

Figure 4. Example of the Examination element display.

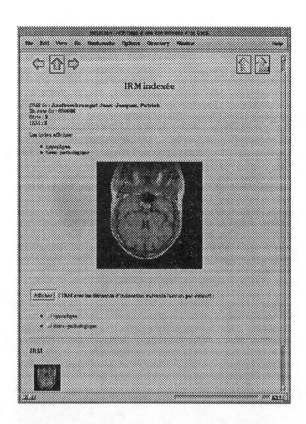

Figure 5. Example of the display of a MRI.

- In the top of the page we have the different buttons that are used for the browsing. At the left the three buttons corresponding to the hypermedia links of the set type, and to the right the buttons that permits to go up in the hierarchical structure of a Patient record.

- In the middle part of the page we put the identifying information of the element presented. In Fig. 5 we can see that a MRI is identified by the patient's name, the examination date, the series and the MRI numbers.

- In the bottom part of the display we put the description of the content of the elements, along with anchors that permits to reach its components, and the one that reach the indexing elements associated with the displayed element. In Fig. 5 we can see two buttons corresponding to the objects indexing the MRI, by choosing one of them or both user can see on the MRI where these objects are located.

3.1.3 Querying

The scope of this section is to give a brief description of the querying functionality of PRIME. We first describe the three ways to access documents, than we focus on the content queries with a query formulation screen example (figure 6).

In addition to the browsing aspect, PRIME supports three ways to retrieve documents :

1. Querying by name of the patient,

2. Querying by patient identifier,

3. Querying by Content on examinations, textual reports and MR images.

We use the functionalities of the O_2 DBMS [12, 13] to handle the query by name and query by identifier, and we have developed an interface and a specific process dedicated to the query by content.

In RIME, the content of the components of the documents is represented by conceptual graphs according to a model including many features of the documents (structure, spatial relationships, symbolic content, ..., see 3.2.2). Content queries can be formulated by specifying any combination of terms and relationships between terms.

The interface is divided into three regions (due to to the lack of space, we only give two of them in the figure 6) in a WEB page : the current query area, the query builder and a third area to correct the query.

5

The content of the current query is displayed in the first area : terms and relationships between terms. To discriminate the terms that appear many times we concatenate an identifier (_n) to the terms. The Search button allows to evaluate the query. The results of a content query are displayed on a new page containing the links to explore the retrieved documents. Into this result page, the retrieved documents are ranked according to "qualitative measure" of their relevance to the user query. The elements of the result are organized in relevance classes and we indicate the qualitative level of the retrieved documents by the use of colors.

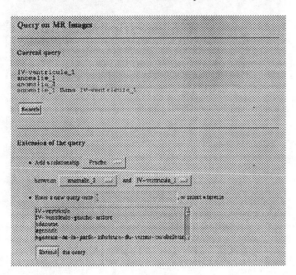

Figure 6. Query Formulation Screen

A content query is composed in the query builder. In this area, the user can extend the query in two ways : he adds a relationships between terms or he adds a term to the query. In the first case, the user has to choose relationships in a pre-defined list (see [8] to know the list), and the related terms among the terms of the current query. To add new terms in the query, the user enters a term in the editable text area or selects one among the list of terms in the scrolling window. There exist three lists of terms, one for each type of document searched. These lists contain the terms used to index the documents. When the user clicks on the Extend button the term or the relationships is added to the query and appear in the current query area.

The third area allow to delete terms and/or relationships in the current query. In this area the user can also choose the type of searched documents and he can erase the query.

In the figure 6, we give a content query example to retrieve MR images with two "anomalies", one of the anomaly is in the 4th ventricle (expressed by the Dans relationship). The localization of the second one is not specified in the current query. Therefore, the user specifies in the query builder that the second anomaly must be near (the

Proche relationship) the 4th ventricle. The user has to extend the query by clicking on the Extend button and than execute the complete query using the Search button.

3.2   The PRIME retrieval facility

The document model and the correspondence model definitions are key problems in Information Retrieval development. We describe in this section the original solutions adopted for both problems, suitable for image retrieval, and extensible to other media types.

Sowa's Conceptual Graph (CG) formalism has been adopted as an operational model of PRIME. Two principal reasons motivated this choice:

- First, the multi-level description in our model is based on a set of concepts (image objects, spatial objects, symbolic descriptors, ...) and a set of relationships (composition relation, spatial relations, events, ...) which are also the basic component of a conceptual graph [9].

- The second reason is that the CG formalism can represent all components of an IR system: the document and the query models can be represented using conceptual graphs, the general domain knowledge that can be reduced to ontologies is represented using concept type and conceptual relation type lattices, and the correspondence function is implemented using an extension of the projection operator, [4].

We describe briefly in the following sections the CG framework developed for the management of CGs, the document indexing model and the matching function implemented.

3.2.1   The conceptual graph framework

The prototype developed is composed of two main parts, PGGC kernel which is concerned about the CG internal representation and operations, and the low level interface. We describe in the following the CG model implemented, the set of operations available, and the linear form of CG's used in the interface.

a. CG model implemented :
Sowa's CG basic formalism have been modified in our framework. Some restrictions are introduced to get a simple and more efficient implementation, and two new notions have been introduced into the prototype.

1. Restrictions

- The first restriction concerns the conceptual relations, that are all binary relations. Note that this restriction is not so constraining since we can easily transform an n-ary relation ($n > 2$) into a set of binary relations, see [5] for examples,
- and in PGGC we do not consider the abstraction nor type definitions, i.e. all concepts are simple elements.

2. Extensions

- The canonical basis is minimal, [4], and PGGC keeps this assertion true after the insertion of a new graph into the canonical basis,
- and the concepts and conceptual relations are uncertain, [15].

b. PGGC functionalities :

PGGC is intended for the management of knowledge bases (KB) based on Sowa's conceptual graph formalism. A KB is defined by a set of canonical conceptual graphs, corresponding to the facts of a particular domain, and a canon, that controls the construction of the graphs. The canon insures a certain coherence (canonicity) of the facts described by the graphs of the KB. Each KB in PGGC is defined by the triplet :

- KB = [name, canon, { graphs }]

PGGC offers a set of operations to access and manipulate the components of a KB. These operations are classified in different categories and described briefly in the following.

The first category includes operations for manipulating the collection of KBs. It permits the creation of a new KB, the deletion of an existing KB, the display of the KB components, and the selection of the working KB.

The second category includes all operations on the components of a particular KB, they are executed on the working KB. Three main groups of operations are proposed.

1. Canonical operations is the basic set of canonical operations defined by Sowa, along with some variants.

- The copy of a canonical graph.
- The join of two canonical graphs; here we propose two variants of the join operator : in the first the join is made on one concept found in the graphs, and the second is a maximal join which combines a set of external joins and internal joins.
- The restriction replaces in the canonical graph all the concepts which are generic to the given concept.

- And the simplification which removes any redundant conceptual relation between two concepts.

2. General operations include all operations defined on the canonical graphs of the KB, we offer :

- insert a new canonical graph in the KB,
- check the validity of a canonical graph (see [5]),
- projection of one graph on an other graph,
- compute all projections of a graph on another graph.

All the graphs of the graph base are canonical. A new graph is inserted in the graph base only if it is canonical according to the reference canon.

3. Canon operations

In this group we consider the operations that manipulate the canon of a KB. It offers :

- the insertion of a new basic graph in the canonical basis,
- the insertion of a new concept and/or conceptual relation type,
- checking the canonicity of a graph.

The canonical basis is minimal. Each operations on the canon should keep this proposition true, so a new graph is inserted in the canonical basis only if it is not canonical.

Deleting a concept type or a conceptual relation type from the lattices implies the deletion from the canonical basis and from the graph base of all graphs that were referencing the deleted concepts or relations.

c. PGGC interface : graph linear form :
PGGC functions are accessible via a menu based interface n the O_2 DBMS. The user can select the function to execute and enter the graphs using a language like representation.

- For example a black and white image whose author is "Nadar" containing a man and a woman represented by the following conceptual graph :

$$
\begin{array}{c}
[\text{Woman} : \#1] \\
\uparrow \\
(\text{Contains}) \\
\uparrow \\
[\text{Black\&White}] \leftarrow (\text{Type}) \leftarrow [\text{Image}] \rightarrow (\text{Author}) \rightarrow [\text{Nadar}] \\
\downarrow \\
(\text{Contains}) \\
\downarrow \\
[\text{Man} : \#2]
\end{array}
$$

- is defined in PGGC using the following linear form :

[Black&White]←(Type)←[Image:@im]

[Image:@im]→(Author)→[Nadar]

[Woman:#1]←(Contains)←[Image:@im]

[Image:@im]→(Contains)→[Man:#2]

The referent @im of the image concept is equivalent to the generic marker *. It is introduced to indicate that the generic concepts of type Image in the two subgraphs correspond to the same concept in the whole graph.

3.2.2 The document indexing model

To represent the PRIME element content for the best retrieval we developed an image model, called EMIR[2] [8, 11, 10], and we used simple concepts for the Examination and Textual reports. These representations are then translated in the conceptual graph formalism.

In EMIR[2] an image is considered as a complex and multi-facet object. An image is described using an homogeneous structure grouping a set of facets relevant to the image contents description. In EMIR[2] we consider a physical view of the image, and a logical view that groups different interpretations of the image content. In this view we combine four basic views :

- the structural view that deals with the complex aspect of the objects in the image,

- the spatial view (Spa), that deals with the shape of objects and their relative positions in the image,

- the perceptive view, that deals with the visual attributes of the image and/or image objects (texture, color, brightness),

- and a set of symbolic views (Sym) that associates semantic descriptions to the image or to image objects.

This image model and its query language have been formalized using a general mathematical formalism, and an operational model has been implemented using the framework described in section 3.2.1 above.

For example the MRI of Fig. 5 that shows a pathological tissue beside the hypophysis, is represented in our image model EMIR[2]-CG [11] by the following conceptual graph. In this graph we indicate basic objects in the image (#21 and #22), their symbolic descriptions (hypophysis and pathological-tissue), their spatial descriptions (rectangles), and the spatial relation between the objects.

[Object:#22]←(COMP)←[Image:#2]

[Image:#2]→(COMP)→[Object:#21]

[Rectangle:#21]←(Spa)←[Object:#21]

[Object:#21]→ (Sym)→[hypophysis:#21]

[Rectangle:#22]←(Spa)←[Object:#22]

[Object:#22]→ (Sym)→[pathological-tissue:#22]

[Rectangle:#22]→(Touch)→[Rectangle:#21];

3.2.3 The matching function

The matching function compares two conceptual graphs, one of them being an element of PRIME record (document) and the other the query, and estimates the similarity degree between them, [9]. In PRIME, we combine in the query all the elements defined in the

document indexing model to state retrieval criteria. The function developed uses a modified version of Sowa's projection operator [5] to implement the similarity function between a query and a document.

The result of this function for textual and Examination queries is a list of elements of the query type that are completely relevant to the query. But for MRI queries this function could provide six levels of relevant MRI. To each level, we specify some particular views of the model to be checked. The first level of result, that contains the most relevant MRIs, is obtained by checking all the views of the model by the matching function. The next levels only check some views defined in the query. For instance a document could answer a query according to its structural and symbolic views. So the spatial view is not taken into account in the matching process. This approach mixes the information that comes from the views and gives more importance to some views, for instance in our application, the symbolic view is the most important. This approach allows to extend the results, and provide more flexibility even if some of these retrieved documents do not match completely the query, but part of it.

4 Conclusion

We described in this paper a multimedia medical retrieval system. All the functions described have been implemented, but we are still working to solve two main problems : the lack of efficiency of the matching function (which based on an exponential algorithm), and the process of image indexing which is human driven. The former problem will be faced in the future by the study of conceptual graphs signatures. The second problem will be addressed by integrating signal processing during the indexing process.

We should think about a real experimentation of the prototype in a medical environment where students and scholars can use it to search the huge collections of medical records they have in the archives.

References

[1] Catherine Berrut, Philippe Mulhem, and Pascal Bouchon. Modelling and indexing medical images : the rime approach. In *HIM 95 (Conference Hypertext, Information Retrieval, Multimedia), Konstanz, Germany*, pages 105–115, April 1995.

[2] Gardarin C. and Valduriez P. *SGBD avancés : bases de données objets, déductives, réparties*. Hermès, 1992.

[3] Lecluse C. and Richard P. Langages orienté-objet et bases de données : l'expérience o². In *5ème journées Bases de données avancées, septembre 1989, Genève*, 1989.

[4] Jean-Pierre Chevallet. *Un Modèle Logique de Recherche d'Informations appliqué au formalisme des Graphes Conceptuels. Le prototype ELEN et son expérimentation sur un corpus de composants logiciels*. PhD thesis, Université Joseph Fourier, Grenoble, 1992.

[5] Sowa J. F. *Conceptual structures : information processing in mind and machine*. Addison-Wesley publishing company, 1984.

[6] Sowa J. F. *Principles of semantic networks : exploration in the representations of knowledge*. Morgan Kaufmann, 1991.

[7] Mugnier M. L. and Chein M. Characterization and algorithmic recognition of canonical conceptual graphs. In *Proceedings of the First International Cobference on Conceptual Structures, ICCS'93. Quebec City, Canada*, August 1993.

[8] Mourad Mechkour. A conceptual graphics model for information retrieval. In *Work Part 3 Deliverable: A Model for the Semantic Content of Multimedia Data*. ESPRIT BRA Project No. 8134 - FERMI, 1995.

[9] Mourad Mechkour. Emir2. an extended model for image representation and retrieval. In *Work Part 3 Deliverable: A Model for the Semantic Content of Multimedia Data*. ESPRIT BRA Project No. 8134 - FERMI, 1995.

[10] Mourad Mechkour. A multifacet formal image model for information retrieval. In *MIRO final workshop, Glasgow, UK.*, 18-20 september 1995.

[11] Mourad Mechkour, Catherine Berrut, and Yves Chiaramella. Using conceptual graph framework for image retrieval. In *International conference on MultiMedia Modeling (MMM'95), Singapore*, pages 127–142, 14-17 November 1995.

[12] Deux O. and al. The o2 system. *Communications of the ACM*, 34(10):34–48, October 1991.

[13] O2. The o2 user manual, version 4.6. Manual, O2 Technology, january 1996.

[14] Gerard Ellis Robert Levinson, editor. *Proceedings of the second interbational workshop on PEIRCE : A conceptual graphs workbench*, August 7 1993.

[15] Wuwongse V. and Manzano M. Fuzzy conceptual graphs. In *Lecture Notes in Artificial Intelligence.*, volume 699. Springer-Verlag, August 1993. Proceedings of the First International Conference on Conceptual Structures, ICCS'93, Quebec City, Canada.

[16] Kim W. and Lochovsky F. H. *Object oriented concepts, databases, and applications*. Frontier series. ACM Press, Addisson Wesley Publishing Company, 1989.

Caching of large Database Objects in Web Servers

Divyesh Jadav
ECE Department
Syracuse University , Syracuse, NY 13244
divyesh@cat.syr.edu
http://www.cat.syr.edu/~divyesh

Monish Gupta
Seetha Lakshmi
Informix Software, Inc.
Menlo Park, CA 94025.
{mgupta, seetha}@informix.com

Abstract

The popularity of the World Wide Web has been increasing at an exponential rate of late. As such growth was unanticipated, the infrastructure is increasingly experiencing problems. The combination of increased network bandwidth demand and overloaded servers results in increased data retrieval latency for the end-user. Caching data at appropriate points in the Web helps alleviate this problem. Almost all previous and existing web servers use a flat file approach to store data, with use of database management systems (DBMSs) rudimentary, if extant at all. Storing pages in a file system may result in faster retrieval, but storing them in a DBMS gives the user greater administrative control. The use of a DBMS in a web server, and the concomitant implication of frequently changing data, complicates the caching problem in Web-based applications. The Illustra Object Relational DBMS provides a flexible and user-friendly environment for building Web applications where all the server data is stored in the DBMS. In this paper, we develop a caching scheme for large objects in the Web DataBlade module of the Illustra ORDBMS. Implementation details and preliminary performance results are presented.

1. Introduction

The ease with which diverse data types (text, audio, video, etc) can be incorporated into a document, user-friendliness and client-server model-based computing are the main reasons for the exponential growth in the user community of the World Wide Web (WWW). The increasing use of the Web results in increased network bandwidth demand, straining the capacity of the underlying networks. It also leads to more and more web servers becoming "hot spots", sites where the high document access rate exceeds the capacity of the server to

retrieve and supply requested documents. The combination of increased bandwidth demand and overloaded servers eventually results in increased document retrieval latency experienced by users, leading to disillusionment with the Web. For this reason, it is often said that the WWW has/will become a victim of its own popularity.

The WWW is a continuously evolving infrastructure. Web technology can be classified into three generations [2]. We briefly review these three generations in terms of the architecture and characteristics of each. Figures 1, 2 and 3 show the three generations of web sites. The common feature in each generation is that multiple types of clients connect to multiple types of web servers. The difference lies in the mechanism employed by the servers in storing and retrieving web pages.

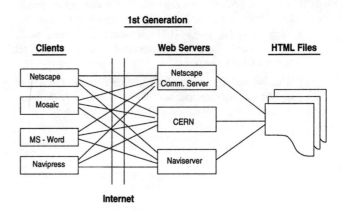

Figure 1. First generation web site

The first generation web sites (figure 1) are characterized by static HTML pages, lack of access to databases and storage of multimedia assets in the file system. Storing content in the file system (as opposed to in a database) may yield better performance (in terms of data rtrieval time), but there are several drawbacks of this architecture : backup and recovery is file system based, there is no referential integrity guarantee for the data and global changes require huge amounts of work.

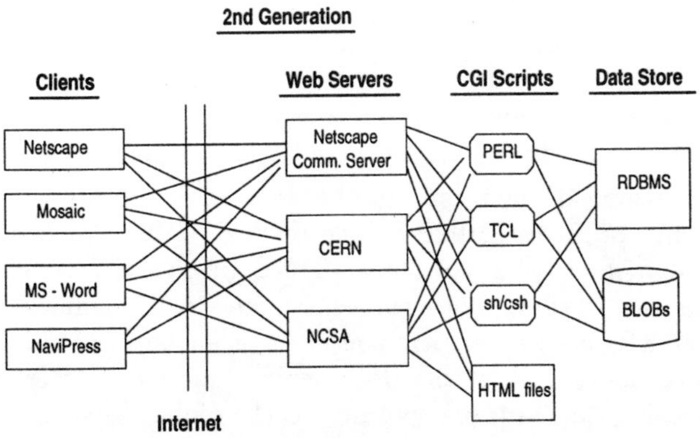

Second generation web sites (figure 2) improve on some of the drawbacks of the first generation sites. Database access is provided by CGI (Common Gateway Interface) programs; the CGI program driven approach provides some measure of access to dynamic data. However, multimedia assets are still stored in the file system; thus content is stored in multiple places (file system and database). Moreover, most CGI-based servers use a scripting paradigm and this has its own problems : script maintenance is complicated and performance is slow due to the interpreted nature of scripting languages. Lastly, backup and recovery is partially file system based.

Figure 2. Second generation web site

The third generation of web sites allow users completely dynamic database generated HTML pages and storage of all data assets (text, video, audio, etc) in one place (the database). An example of a third generation web site is a web server connected to an Illustra [10] database server augmented with the Illustra Web DataBlade module [11] (figure 3). The advantages of the third generation web site over the previous two generations are manifold : backup and recovery is database driven, central control of all types of data assets, no need to learn new scripting languages, and ease of use and maintenance.

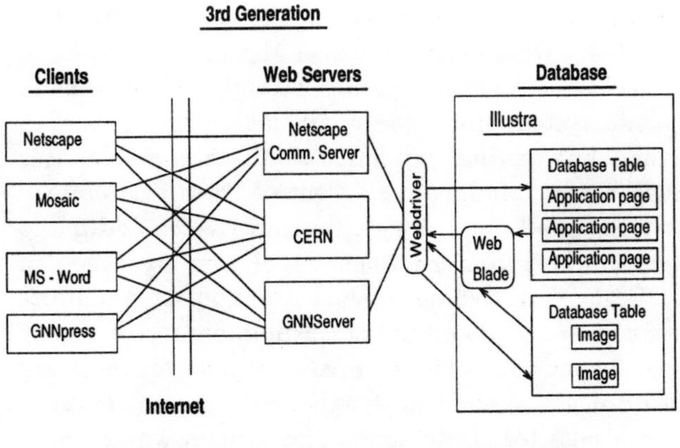

Given the fact that trying to scale network and server bandwidth to keep up with client demand is not an economically viable option in alleviating the performance problems caused by the exponential growth of the WWW, various caching techniques have been proposed and used as an alternative. Caching effectively migrates copies of popular documents from servers closer to clients. Web clients see shorter delays when requesting documents, network managers see less web traffic, and web servers see lower request rates. Most of the caching approaches proposed to date have been developed in isolation from the generations of web technology described above. Third generation web sites introduce an extra level of access, and hence retrieval latency, on account of the presence of the database server. In this paper we propose a caching approach for third generation web sites that addresses the additional performance hit caused by the architecture of such sites.

Figure 3. Third generation web site

2. Related work and research contributions

Due to the performance problems caused by the exponential growth of the WWW, considerable effort has been spent investigating the caching of WWW data. A cache can be used on a per-client basis, within networks used by the Web, or on web servers [12]. Most commercially available browsers do per-client caching. Such caching, while improving the latency for frequently accessed documents by the *same client*, does not exploit frequent access to documents by *multiple clients*. Since the benefits of caching grow with the number of clients sharing the same cache, the *caching proxy* was developed [14]. The primary use of proxies is to allow access to the Web from within a firewall. A proxy is a special Web server that typically runs on a firewall machine. The proxy waits for a request from inside the firewall, forwards the request to the remote server outside the firewall, reads the response and sends it back to the client. In the usual case, the same proxy is used by all the clients within a subnet. This makes it possible for the proxy to do efficient caching of documents that are requested by a number of clients. Many of the documents are retrieved from a local cache once the initial request has been made. The advantages of a caching proxy can be summed up as follows [6] : reduces latency on requests for cached pages, reduces overall network load and remote server load, and provides availability when a remote server is unavailable. It suffers from the disadvantage of all caching schemes : the possibility of returning stale versions of a page when the remote version has changed and the cache does not know it. One of the first implementations of the caching proxy was the CERN HTTP server [4]. In early 1995, support for the caching proxy was added to the Netscape server [16]. Various studies of the effectiveness of the caching proxy have been done. An implementation by [6] found a cache hit rate of 30-50 %, and a cache hit supplies a page in 1/4 to 1/6 the time of retrieving the page from the network. [1] used traces of Web access from a university environment to simulate the effectiveness of a caching proxy for documents retrieved by the HTTP, GOPHER, FTP and WAIS protocols using WWW browsers. The cache hit ratios obtained were similar to those reported in [6]. This study also reported the ineffectiveness of classic Least Recently Used (LRU) cache replacement policy for WWW data. An implementation of a caching proxy in a production environment is being used at HENSA Unix [7].

Each of the servers referred to above merely acts as a simple proxy with a cache of pages to improve performance. Other projects have developed proxy servers that attempt to go even further; the most notable of these is the Harvest Object Cache [3]. The Harvest cache is a proxy designed to operate in concert with other instances of itself. Harvest allows a single cache to interact with neighbour and parent caches in a cooperating tree-like hierarchy. The neighbours are usually on networks that the cache has good access to. When a server receives a request for data and suffers a cache miss, it can call upon its neigbours and parents in the tree to find if any of them have the data cached.

Caching of data can also be done at a web server itself. [15] investigated caching of WWW data in the main memory of a web server. Trace-driven simulation was used to show that even a small amount of memory (512 KB) used as a document cache is enough to hold more than 60 % of the documents requested. After exposing the inadequacy of LRU cache replacement for WWW data, a dynamic cache management algorithm was proposed and evaluated.

In summary, efforts at using caching techniques for WWW data have been directed at the inter-web server level, intra-web server level, and at the intranetwork level. Most of the literature on caching of WWW data pertains to static (read-only) data. One of the request classes that were classified by [6] as being unlikely to cache successfully was database lookups. Database connectivity is an inherent characteristic of third generation Web sites (figure 3). This paper addresses the issue of caching certain types of data when all data content is stored in a database. We develop the motivation for caching these data types. We propose a simple caching strategy for caching frequently accessed, infrequently changing, large objects stored in the Ilustra Object-Relational Database Management System, (ORDBMS). As stated earlier, storing Web content in the file system may give good data retrieval performance, but storing content in a DBMS gives the user much better administrative control. Retrieval latency for large sized data objects (example video and audio files) can be a concern when the objects are stored in a DBMS; our caching scheme attempts to maximize performance while retaining the administrative advantages for such objects. There are two ways for accessing such objects, static and dynamic. We present preliminary results for static access and explain why caching is difficult for dynamic access.

The rest of this paper is organized as follows : in section 3 we briefly review the features of the Illustra ORDBMS and DataBlades. In section 4 we focus on the Web DataBlade module of the Illustra ORDBMS, and the architecture of applications built using it. In section 5 the concept of large objects in Illustra, and the motivation for caching them, is explained. In section 6 we explain the web server-based caching scheme, and report preliminary results. Section 7 discusses related issues, and section 8 concludes the paper.

3. Illustra ORDBMS and DataBlades [IAG95, ITI95, IUG95]

One of the weaknesses of SQL-92 (Structured Query Language-92) is that a column of a database table is restricted to be of one of a predefined set of data types : integer, floating point, fixed or variable length character string, date and time, time interval, numeric and decimal. SQL-92 defines a precise (and hard-coded) collection of functions and operators that are available for each data type. If a SQL-92 user requires data types that are not in the language, then the user must simulate the new data types with those that are available. Similarly, if operations that are not in SQL-92 are required, then they must be simulated using ones that are available, or data must be retrieved to a user program and the required operation done using user logic. The Illustra Object Relational Database Management System (ORDBMS) is a powerful data management tool that allows programmers to define new object classes, or types, and new methods, or functions, that operate on them. By taking advantage of the architectural support provided to programmers, they can extend the database manager with knowledge about new kinds of data and ways of manipulating it. The Illustra term for these extensions is *DataBlade modules*.

An Illustra DataBlade module is a collection of data type definitions, code, and supporting objects that extend the Illustra server to manage new kinds of data. A particular DataBlade module may contain some or all of these pieces, but most include at least data type definitions and a collection of functions that operate on the new types. DataBlade functions may be written in C or SQL. A typical DataBlade module provides specialized support for some application domain. For example, Illustra sells DataBlade libraries that provide two and three dimensional spatial objects as native database types. These libraries support geographic and geometric applications by providing new types such as circles and polygons, and functions on them, such as distance and containment.

Illustra's support for DataBlade module extensions to the server gives it several advantages over more conventional database management systems. Application programs are simpler to write, since they take advantage of the server extensions. Access to data is more efficient, since the database manager can optimize user requests for data to find the fastest strategy for sat-

isfying them. Finally, users can add support for new kinds of data or new analysis techniques as they are discovered. The database system can grow to meet new demands.

4. Illustra Web DataBlade module [IWD96]

4.1. Introduction

The Web DataBlade module allows users to create Web Applications that incorporate data retrieved dynamically from an Illustra database in HTML pages. In typical non-Web database applications, most of the logic is in gateway application (Common Gateway Interface, or CGI) code written in Perl, Tcl or C. The CGI application connects to a database, builds and executes SQL statements, and formats the results. The Web DataBlade module eliminates the need to develop a CGI application to dynamically access database data. Instead, the user creates HTML pages, called Application pages, that include Web DataBlade tags and functions to dynamically generate SQL statements and format the results. The types of data that can be retrieved include traditional data types, as well as HTML, image, audio and video data, all stored in the Illustra database. The Application pages are also stored directly inside the Illustra database. The salient features of the Web DataBlade module are as follows :

- Web DataBlade tags provide the ability to embed SQL statements directly in HTML pages.

- Web DataBlade tags provide error handling, conditional statements, and other advanced query processing and formatting techniques.

- Webdriver, Illustra's CGI driver, allows users to customize Web applications based on information obtained from a configuration file, the CGI environment, URLs and HTML forms.

- Webdriver provides an interface to the Illustra DBMS and allows users to customize Web applications without additional CGI programming

4.2. Architecture of Web DataBlade-based applications

The software architecture of a Web DataBlade-based application consists of four main modules (figure 4):

1. The **client browser**,

13

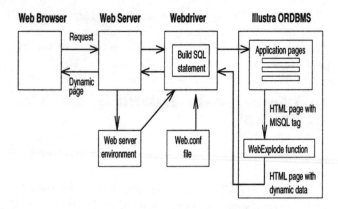

Figure 4. Web DataBlade Architecture

2. The **Web server**, which receives incoming page requests from clients,

3. The **Webdriver**, which is a thin (light-weight) CGI driver program that builds the SQL statement necessary to retrieve the Application pages from the Illustra database, connects to an llustra database, and returns the HTML resulting from the *WebExplode* function to the Web server.

4. The **WebExplode function and the Illustra database** : The *WebExplode* function parses, dynamically builds, and executes SQL statements embedded in HTML pages and returns the results of those SQL processing instructions to Webdriver.

Figure 4 shows the sequence of events involved in retrieving a page in a Web DataBlade-based application. The Web browser makes a request to the Web server to invoke Webdriver. Based on configuration information, Webdriver composes the SQL statement to request an application page from the *WebExplode* function. *WebExplode* retrieves the application page from the Illustra database, executes the SQL statements within that page (by expanding the Web DataBlade tags), and formats the results. *WebExplode* returns the expanded page to the Web server, which returns the page to be rendered by the Web browser.

5. Illustra Large Objects, and motivation for caching them

The architecture outlined in the previous section for Web Datablade-based applications means that all four modules could exist on the same computer, on the one hand, or the client browser may execute on one machine, the web server and Webdriver live on a second machine and the WebExplode function and the database exist on a third machine, on the other hand. We focus on the latter scenario. At first glance, it seems logical for the web server, Webdriver, WebExplode and the database to be installed on the same machine. However it makes sense for the web server and database server to exist on different machines because the web server may be serving documents stored locally (rather than in the database), and the database server could be home to databases other than the web database, for example, employee database, payroll database, etc. Consequently, it might be desirable for load-balancing purposes that each server be installed on a separate machine. Another reason why the two servers may reside on separate machines is security : the web server would be outside the security firewall, while the database server is within it. In practice, many corporate users of the Illustra Web DataBlade module indeed use such an architecture [5].

We now introduce the notion of *large objects* in the Illustra server, and explain how retrieval latency for such objects can be improved in Web DataBlade-based applications. Data larger than approximately 8 KBytes must be stored as either external files or *large objects* in the Illustra database [10]. An external file is just a UNIX file that is accessible from an Illustra table. The Illustra server imposes no structure on an external file. External files are useful for situations where an object, such as a picture or video, is created and accessed frequently, but rarely or never updated through the data manager. External files can be accessed quickly, but the cost of this speed is that they have no support for transaction rollback, crash recovery, and multi-user protection. External files can also be accessed by applications other than Illustra applications.

A large object is an object stored using the Illustra DBMS facilities. It has all the database properties of an Illustra object, such as transaction rollback, crash recovery, and multi-user protection. However, once created, it cannot be overwritten or appended to. In other words, the only permissible operations on large objects are creation, selection, copying and deletion. A large object is accessed by a unique identifier called a *handle*. A handle is a character string, such as 'I010982029384', which represents the large object.

Consider now the following access pattern for a class of large objects : Most of the content on the Web these days is of text type. There is some content of image type and very little content of continuous data types (audio, video). The main reason for this is that files of continuous data types typically have very large size (of the MByte range), and bandwidth limitations and traffic volume make the existing Internet very slow at downloading files of such size. However, the scale of

14

embedding of continuous objects in web pages is bound to increase as the web becomes more interactive. Examples of hyperlinks pointing to continuous media objects that will become more pervasive in the foreseeable future are :

1. Video and audio clips embedded in interactive computer-based training documents.

2. Video and audio clips of third-party endorsement of a company's product on the web page of that product.

3. Commercials of a company product on the web page of that product

4. Previews of movies being screened in theaters, available in video stores, video games, etc

Observe that the files for all of the above examples are of a read-only nature. Existing web-browsers typically perform client-side caching. The Web DataBlade implies a three-tier architecture, with the web server being between the client and the database server. However, no caching is done at the web server. This does not imply a significant performance degradation for text-only pages retrieved from the database. Moreover, some pages query the database in order to determine the contents of the retrieved pages. Hence it is imperative that the data be "current". However, for read-only accesses to large objects of the type described above, caching of the large objects can be done at the web server.

Large Objects are accessed in the Web DataBlade module using Webdriver. The following variables must be initialized to specify a large object and its output MIME type :

- LO: large object handle.

- type: MIME [17] type and subtype used to export the large object.

We classify queries for retrieving large objects into two classes : static and dynamic. A *static* query for a large object has the large object handle hardwired into the query. In a *dynamic* query, the value of the large object handle is obtained at run-time.

Figure 5 shows an example of each type of query. The figure also shows how a client accesses pages/data stored in the database from a web browser. Consider first the static query. When the query is entered by the client, the large object corresponding to the handle specified (in this case a 'GIF' image), is retrieved from the database and will be displayed on the client browser. A static query can also be embedded in a

```
               Static query :

http://mymachine:port/cgi-bin/
       Webdriver?LO=I010782263&type=image/gif

     OR

<HTML>
<HEAD>
<TITLE> Welcome Page </TITLE>
</HEAD>
<BODY>
<H1> Welcome to my world </H1>
<IMG SRC=http://mymachine:port/cgi-bin/
       Webdriver?LO=I010782263&type=image/gif>
</BODY>
</HTML>

               Dynamic query :

<HTML>
<HEAD>
<TITLE> Welcome Page </TITLE>
</HEAD>
<BODY>
<H1> Welcome to my world </H1>
<?MISQL SQL="select image from web_images
          where name='welcome';">
<IMG SRC=$WEB_HOME?LO=$1&type=image/gif>
<?/MISQL>
</BODY>
</HTML>
```

Figure 5. Static and dynamic queries for large objects in a Web DataBlade-based application

HTML page, as shown in the example following the 'OR' in figure 5. Consider now the dynamic query. Note that dynamic queries must be embedded in a HTML page, since there is no way that a dynamic query can fit in one line, unlike a static query. The MISQL tag indicates to the *WebExplode* function of the Web DataBlade some SQL processing that needs to be done. In this case, the text following <?MISQL> selects the row whose *name* attribute is 'welcome', and returns the value stored in the *image* column of that row, from the *web_images* table stored in the Illustra database. The value of the *image* attribute happens to be the handle of the corresponding image, and the line beginning '<IMG SRC=..' retrieves and displays that large object (a 'GIF' image) on the client browser. [1]

We restrict ourselves to static queries for the time being. We explain below the caching scheme and present preliminary results. We then explain the issues in doing caching for dynamic queries.

6. The web server-based caching scheme, and preliminary results

In order to prove the potential gain due to caching for static queries, we conducted a simple experiment. For the case of web server and database server installed on separate machines, the experimental setup we used was as depicted in figure 6. We used two Sun Sparc 20 machines - hurley.informix.com and lark.informix.com on the same subnet, with the software installed as shown in the figure. We measured the retrieval time for three

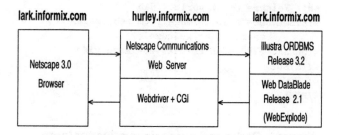

Figure 6. Block diagram of the experimental setup

large objects (MPEG [13] video clips) in two scenarios :

- **Case 1 :** Data is stored in the Illustra database as a large object, and retrieved from there for

---
[1] The entry '$WEB_HOME' in the dynamic query example is an environment variable that can be configured to point to the full pathname of Webdriver - in this case : http://mymachine:port/cgi-bin/Webdriver

each request.

- **Case 2 :** Data is stored on the web server and retrieved from there for each request.

Let the $t1$ and $t2$ denote the respective retrieval times, where retrieval time is the time interval between the client browser issuing the request and the client browser receiving all the requested data. The retrieval time for each file was measured twenty times, and the average was taken of those twenty trials. We did not eliminate any values that might be considered statistical extremes, since seemingly abnormal results are typically due to bursts of uncontrollable network activity, which are an important aspect of the environment and should be taken into consideration. Another important point to note is that in all our experiments, client browser caching was disabled. Table 1 shows the results of the first experiment. We note that the files were retrieved from the web server in 44 % to 62 % of the time it took to retrieve them from the database. This clearly establishes the performance hit in the Web DataBlade module when the web server and database server reside on different machines. Clearly, it would be beneficial to cache large objects at the web server.

File Size (MB)	Retrieval Time from Database (t1) (sec)	Retrieval Time from Web Server (t2) (sec)	t2/t1 as %
3.59	14.6893	6.4621	44.0 %
8.54	23.0431	14.5098	63.0 %
14.2	39.2691	24.3699	62.0 %

Table 1. The time to download 3 files for the two scenarios

We investigated whether the database performs any (main memory) caching at all of large objects. Table 2 shows the timings for two consecutive retrievals of the same file. While the second retrieval did take less time, the difference is not substantial enough to conclude that it is due to caching at the database.

File Size (MB)	Retrieval Time from Database (t1) (sec)	Retrieval Time from Web Server (t2) (sec)	t2/t1 as %
3.59	14.1434	13.6082	96.2 %
8.54	22.4527	21.5227	96.0 %
14.2	36.3375	35.5436	97.8 %

Table 2. The effect of database caching

Having established the benefits to be accrued by web server-based caching for large objects, we now describe details about the caching scheme.

Two ways in which a client could invoke static queries were shown in figure 5. We restrict ourselves to the case where a client explicitly requests a large object i.e. not as part of a page. For example, either by clicking on a hyperlink, or by opening a URL. An example of the former kind would be as follows : the page from which the large object is requested would have an entry of the form :

<a href=http://hurley.informix.com/cgi-bin/
Webdriver?LO=I010782263&type=video/mpeg>
video of a sailing ship </a>

An example of the second type of static query that we consider would be opening of a URL of the form :

http://hurley.informix.com/cgi-bin/Webdriver?
LO=I010782263&type=video/mpeg

For implementation purposes, no syntax changes could be done at the client end. At the server end, we chose to build on top of the existing binary distribution for a proof-of-concept prototype. We wrote a new program, Webcache, that is external to Webdriver and caches large objects retrieved through Web DataBlade queries. This allowed us to run existing Web DataBlade applications without modifying any code. Figure 7 shows the sequence of steps when the Web DataBlade module is augmented with our caching scheme. Clients now invoke Webcache instead of Webdriver, so that the query above would become as shown in figure 7. Webcache parses the client query and determines if a large object is being requested [2]. If the query is indeed for a large object, Webcache checks to see if the requested large object is stored locally (on the web server). If so, it can be delivered from the local copy. If not, a cache miss has occurred; Webcache invokes Webdriver, passes it the query, and the normal (i.e. in the absence of caching) sequence of events for retrieving the large object is then followed. Moreover, when the data is returned by the database, it is cached on the web server's disk by Webcache for satisfying further requests for the large object. Similarly, when the client request is not for a large object, Webcache invokes Webdriver and passes it the original query.

Tables 3, 4 and 5 show the preliminary results of using web-server based caching of large objects for the setup shown in figure 6. The tables correspond to the three cases considered : database connectivity using the Web DataBlade but no caching (table 3), no database connectivity (i.e. serving files directly out of the web server) (table 4) and database connectivity using the Web DataBlade augmented with large object caching (table 5). The same three files were used. Note that the entry in table 5 for the first file is a cache miss;

Query : http://hurley.informix.com/cgi-bin/Webcache?LO=I010782263&type=image/gif

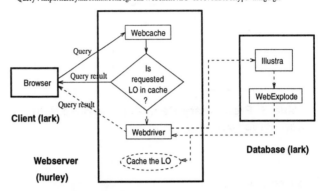

Figure 7. Operation of the caching scheme.

for this reason the retrieval time is almost the same as the retrieval time without caching. The times for the other two files are for a cache hit, and clearly show the benefit of caching. An improvement of about 50 % over the case of no caching is observed. An interesting point is that when caching is used, the retrieval time is less than the case when the file is served from the web server and there is no database (the second column). One reason for this is that the Webcache program does file I/O in 64 KB chunks, and also sends data to the client in chunks of this size. We observed that the web server packetizes and sends data in about 1.4 KB chunks, leading to higher packetizing overhead.

	DB & No Caching	
File Size *(MB)*	*Time* *(sec) (t1)*	*Percentage* *of t1*
3.59	14.6893	100.0 %
8.54	23.0431	100.0 %
14.2	39.2691	100.0 %

Table 3. Preliminary Results : database and no caching

	No DB	
File Size *(MB)*	*Time* *(sec) (t2)*	*Percentage* *of t1*
3.59	6.4621	44.0 %
8.54	14.5098	63.0 %
14.2	24.3699	62.0 %

Table 4. Preliminary Results : no database

---

[2]the syntax for retrieving pages is different than that for retrieving large objects in the Web DataBlade module

| File Size (MB) | DB + Web Server Caching | |
	Time (sec) (t3)	Percentage of t1
3.59	13.9329*	95.0* %
8.54	13.0049	56.4 %
14.2	19.4408	50.0 %

Table 5. Preliminary Results : database with web server caching

7. Discussion

The advantages of the proposed approach are clear : faster retrieval of frequently accessed, infrequently changing large objects, potentially reduced network traffic between the web server and the database server, reduced workload on the database server, and minor modification to existing syntax and code.

As with any caching technique, the biggest disadvantage of the proposed approach is the danger of delivering stale (cached) data to clients. However,

- The assumption is that the data that is being cached changes rarely, if at all. As stated earlier, a large object cannot be modified : it can only be created, copied (to a new large object), retrieved or deleted. This restricted set of operations on large objects reduces (but does not eliminate) the probability of serving stale data.

- The client can bypass caching totally, as described below.

- Even in the absence of caching, the client can be looking at stale data; for example, suppose some data changes in the database while the client is browsing it. Unless the client reloads/retrieves the page afresh, the data being browsed will be stale.

The client can be provided a facility to *bypass* the caching mechanism i.e. even if the requested large object exists at the web server, Webdriver will retrieve it from the database server. This ensures that the retrieved copy is up to date. This would require a minor modification to the above syntax :

 < a href=http://hurley.informix.com/cgi-bin/
 Webdriver?LO=I010782263&type=video/mpeg
 &copy=original>video of a sailing ship </a>

In other words, the client would be able to specify whether or not cached copies are to be used.

An important question that arises is that of integrity of the cached data : how is it possible to ensure that the

```
create alerter inspect_cache
    (mechanism = 'callback',
    support = cache_invalidate);

create rule LO_update as
    on update to multimedia_data.large_obj
    do
    alert inspect_cache;
```

Figure 8. Using alerters for cache invalidation

cached large objects in the web server have not been deleted in the database ? This can be done by using *alerters* provided by the Illustra database. Alerters are special rules. If a read or write operation meets the user-defined criteria, an alerter notifies interested parties. A client indicates interest in an alerter by issuing the **listen** statement. Any number of clients can listen for the same alerter, and a client can listen for multiple alerts. A client listening for one or more alerters can simultaneously execute queries and run transactions. Any database client can register interest in an alerter. When an alerter fires, all interested listeners are notified. There are two notification mechanisms : poll or callback. In the context of the Web DataBlade, the web server can be configured to be alerted when a large object is deleted from the database. For example, figure 8 creates an alerter, *inspect_cache*, and a rule, *LO_update*. The alerter is created with callback notification, and also specifies the name of a *support* function, *cache_invalidate*, which defines the semantics of the alerter. Since deleting a large object involves changing the large object handle in the corresponding table row, the alerter is fired whenever an update occurs in the *large_obj* column of the *multimedia_data* table. The *cache_invalidate* support function can be appropriately written to invalidate cached copies of the deleted large object.

A web-server based caching similar to the one described in this paper (developed independently by a different team) has been implemented in the Web DataBlade module Release 2.2 (July 1996) of the Illustra server. The issue of data staleness is addressed in the released product through a user-configurable parameter called *MI_WEBCACHELIFE* which is applicable for all cached objects. The value of this parameter denotes the time-to-live of a cached object. After the specified time has elapsed, the cached copy is deleted from the web server, whether or not the original large object in the database has been deleted.

In this paper we did not address the issue of caching large objects when they are accessed using dynamic queries. The reason for this is as follows : dynamic queries are always embedded in a HTML page, within MISQL tags. Webdriver/Webcache receives the client query for a page or a large object, hence caching can be done for static queries. Dynamic queries are always parsed, processed and formatted by the *WebExplode* function, which resides on the database server. If caching were to be implemented for dynamic queries, network traffic would be added between the database and the web server after the query has been processed. This is overhead. We are investigating whether the penalty due to this overhead is comparable to the benefit to be gained if caching were to be extended to dynamic queries.

8. Conclusions

Most caching schemes for Web data reported to date have been developed in the context of first and second generation web sites. The Illustra Web DataBlade module is a powerful tool for users to build applications centered around a third generation web site, where all the server data is managed transparently by the Illustra ORDBMS. In theory, as well as in practice, many web sites built using the Web DataBlade module and the Illustra ORDBMS would have the web server and database server installed on two different machines, separated by a network. A DBMS-based web site allows users transparent access to changing data and the ability to dynamically query the database. While this is an advantage, we identified several user access patterns that are likely to access frequently requested, infrequently changing server data objects. When the web server and database server reside on separate machines, accessing such objects from the database server for each request leads to network traffic and extra load on the database server. In this paper, we developed a scheme for caching such objects on the web server in the Web DataBlade module Release 2.1 of the Illustra ORDBMS. Preliminary performance results show a 50 % improvement in data retrieval latency for the cached objects. We are investigating the efficiency of the caching policy in a production environment.

References

[1] M. Abrams et al. Caching Proxies : Limitations and Potentials. *Proc. of the 4th Intl. World Wide Web Conference*, Boston, December 1995.

[2] *Building Illustra-Based Web Applications*, course offered by Illustra Information Technologies, Inc., Oakland CA 94607, March 1996. *http://www.illustra.com*

[3] A. Chankhunthod, et al. A Hierarchical Internet Object Cache. *Proc. of USENIX 1996 Annual Technical Conference. http://excalibur.usc.edu/cache-html/cache.html.*

[4] CERN httpd as a Proxy Server. *http://info.cern.ch/hypertext/WWW/Daemon/Proxies /Proxies.html.*

[5] J. Gaffney (*gaffney@illustra.com*). *Email communication to the authors*, August 1996.

[6] S. Glassman. A Caching Relay for the World Wide Web. *Computer Networks and ISDN Systems, 27(2)*, November 1994. Also appeared in *Proc. of the 1st Intl. World Wide Web Conference*, Geneva, May 1994.

[7] HENSA, The UK National Web Cache at HENSA Unix. *http://www.hensa.ac.uk/wwwcache/.*

[8] *Illustra Developers' Kit Architecture Guide, Release 1.1*, Illustra Information Technologies, Inc., Oakland CA 94607, March 1995. *http://www.illustra.com*

[9] *Introduction to Illustra*, Illustra Information Technologies, Inc., Oakland CA 94607, August 1995. *http://www.illustra.com*

[10] *Illustra User's Guide, Release 3.2*, Illustra Information Technologies, Inc., Oakland CA 94607, October 1995. *http://www.illustra.com*

[11] *Illustra Web DataBlade Module : User's Guide Version 2.1*, Illustra Information Technologies, Inc., Oakland CA 94607, March 1996. *http://www.illustra.com*

[12] T. Kwan, R. McGrath and D. Reed. User Access Patterns to NCSA's World Wide Web Server. *NCSA and University of Illinois Computer Science Technical Report*, 1994.

[13] D. LeGall. MPEG: A video compression standard for multimedia applications. *Communication of the ACM*, Vol. 34, No. 4, April 1991.

[14] A. Luotonen and K. Altis. World-Wide Web Proxies. *Proc. of the 2nd Intl. World Wide Web Conference*, Chicago, October 1995. *http://www.w3.org/hypertext/WWW/Proxies/.*

[15] E. A. Markatos. Main Memory Caching of Web Documents. *Proc. of the 5th Intl. World Wide Web Conference*, Paris, June 1996.

[16] Netscape Proxy Server. *http://home.netscape.com/comprod/proxy_server.html.*

[17] RFC 1341: Multipurpose Internet Mail Extensions.

Knowledge Discovery from Users Web-Page Navigation*

Cyrus Shahabi[†], Amir M. Zarkesh[‡], Jafar Adibi[†], and Vishal Shah[†]

[†] Integrated Media Systems Center and
Computer Science Department
University of Southern California
Los Angeles, California 90089
[shahabi, adibi, vishalsh]@usc.edu

[‡] Quad Design Technology
Camarillo, California 93010
azarkesh@qdt.com

Abstract

We propose to detect users navigation paths to the advantage of web-site owners. First, we explain the design and implementation of a profiler which captures client's selected links and pages order, accurate page viewing time and cache references, using a Java based remote agent. The information captured by the profiler is then utilized by a knowledge discovery technique to cluster users with similar interests. We introduce a novel path clustering method based on the similarity of the history of user navigation. This approach is capable of capturing the interests of the user which could persist through several subsequent hypertext link selections. Finally, we evaluate our path clustering technique via a simulation study on a sample WWW-site. We show that depending on the level of inserted noise, we can recover the correct clusters by %10-%27 of average error margin.

1. Introduction

The orthodox view on the web-pages assumes a uni-directional flow of information from the server to the client. In this view, the flow of information in the other direction is possible only if the client chooses to respond through e-mail or web-page forms. The previous studies on the design of the web-pages are also concentrated on how to make this uni-lateral flow more efficient to the client. In this paper, we discuss a broader view in which the servers also could continuously receive useful information from the clients.

Capturing the characteristics of the users of a business web site is an important task for their marketing department.

The *navigation path* of the web-page users, if available to the server, carries valuable information about the users interests. In this paper, we propose a technique to detect the navigation path rather accurately up to the restrictions set by the current Internet security protocols. Our technique detects *link* hits and viewing time per page. This is a superset of information on the order of page hits. It basically encodes the entire user navigation path. Our profiling approach has crucial advantages over existing commercial and academic profilers. The main advantages include: 1) it requires no modification at the client site (e.g., hacking the browser source code), 2) it complies with the current state of the HTTP protocol and its packet structure (i.e., requires no modification and/or extension to the protocol), and 3) it does not require any manual modification at the server side, as the entire process is automated (i.e., the one-time process of modifying a large web-site to make it available for profiling takes less than an hour). Subsequently, a systematic approach, called *path-mining* [24], is explained. This approach is well suited to capture similarity among the orders of the accessed pages in the navigation paths. The merit of our approach in probing the similarity among users interests is shown in a detailed analysis of a test site in Sec. 5.

We start by describing the structure of users navigation profile and set the notation in Sec. 2. The structure of a sample site is also described there. In Sec. 3, we discuss the challenges involve in the construction of the user profile: accurate capturing of the web-page viewing time, detecting client cache hits, and obtaining hypertext links information. We describe the design of our profiler as a *remote agent* which can accurately construct the users profiles. In Sec. 4, we discuss a systematic method to cluster the users navigation paths. First a similarity measure on the feature space of the navigation paths is presented. This similarity measure is capable to detect similarity in the order of the navigation links. The behavior of this measure is shown in a detail analysis of some paths in the sample site. As the second step, many

*This research has been funded in part by the Integrated Media Systems Center, a National Science Foundation Engineering Research Center with additional support from the Annenberg Center for Communication at the University of Southern California and the California Trade and Commerce Agency.

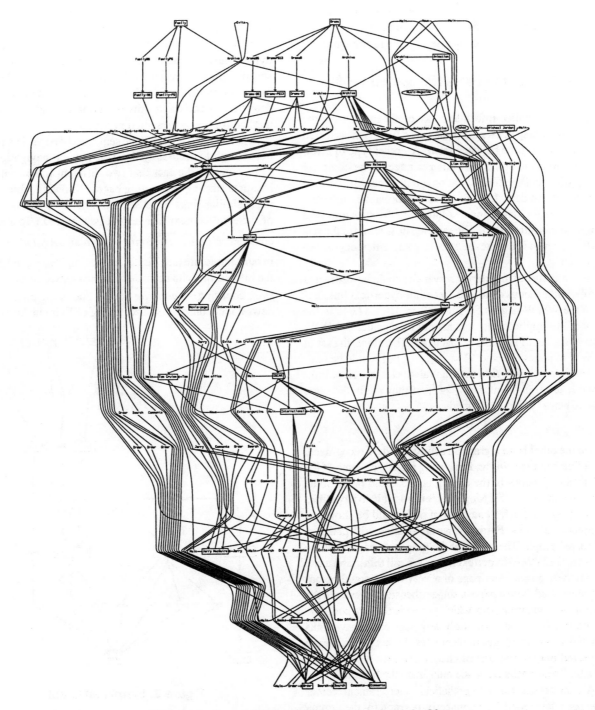

Figure 1. Connectivity Graph for the Sample Site

21

classical data mining approach can be used for the classification based on the given similarity metric. In Sec. 5, a big set of paths in the example web site is analyzed in details and the performance of the similarity measure is tested. Sec. 6 provides a conclusion and overview on the future works.

2. Structure of the Users Navigation Profile

The most detailed information we could gather from the Internet browsing of clients, is the list of links (s)he selected and the elapsed time between them. All other type of information, from the number of hits per page to the complete path profile and the time spent on a path, could be derived from the above data. In this section we formalize this structure and set the definitions. Moreover, the structure of a sample site is introduced. The sample site is used for the rest of this paper to illustrate the structure and efficiency of our approach.

The structure of an Internet server site could be abstracted as following. Let us denote the set of all hyper-text links exist in the WWW-pages of a site as $\mathcal{L} = \{l_1, \ldots l_N\}$. In the view of our applications, it is natural to consider a WWW-page as the set of all links in that page. Therefore, the set of all WWW-pages of a site, $\mathcal{P} = \{p_1, \ldots, p_n\}$, could be realized as a partition of $\mathcal{L}$ to the equivalent classes. Here links l_i and l_j are equivalent, *i.e.* $l_i \sim l_j$, if they are in the same page. Then $\mathcal{P}$ could be defined as

$$\mathcal{P} = \mathcal{L}/\sim . \tag{1}$$

On the other hand a graph structure could be recognized. Each link has a *starting* and an *ending* page. For some of the links starting points or the ending points could be on some page outside the site $\mathcal{P}$. Moreover it is possible to have links from a page to itself. A navigation path could be shown as a sequence of links. Formally, we are dealing with paths on a directed graph. The nodes of the graph are pages and the links are the WWW-hypertext links. We call this graph a site *connectivity graph*. Any page of a WWW-site could be potentially called from a page in some other site. Therefore the portion of navigation path which is inside the site could be started from any node. Similarly, any page could have links which points to the pages in other sites. In this paper, we are interested only in the part of clients navigation path inside the site. These paths are made only from the links in $\mathcal{L}$.

A sample site for a hypothetical entertainment center have been developed. The connectivity graph for the sample site is shown in Fig. 1. The names of the nodes are the title of the pages. The names of the links are the click-able hypertext, corresponding to those links. As it can be seen in Fig. 1, the connectivity graph could be quiet complicated. A subset of links in the sample site is shown in Fig. 2. If the site is well designed, navigation can be very informative. Only a few links to the outside sites are shown in Fig. 1.

Local caching at the client browser makes it possible for the client to jump back to some of the pages (s)he already visited. Each browser can have different caching strategy which gives ability to jump to all or part of the pages which are visited. Moreover, the possible jumps from each page dynamically depend on the history of the navigation of that specific client to reach to that page. Therefore the cache jumps are not shown in the connectivity graph. However, detection of the cache hits is important and a systematic method for this is presented in Sec. 3.

It is crucial to note that the sequence of pages in a path are not enough to accurately describe a client navigation path. This is due to the fact that two different links could have identical starting and ending pages. Knowing which one of these similar links is selected can be informative because of different context in which it is appeared. To illustrate, consider $News\overrightarrow{Evita}Evita$ and $News\overrightarrow{Argentina}Evita$ in our sample site (see Fig. 2). Choosing $\overrightarrow{Evita}$ can be due to the interest in Evita because of its box-office success. However, choosing $\overrightarrow{Argentina}$ can be due to the interest in the news about controversial screening of Evita in Argentina.

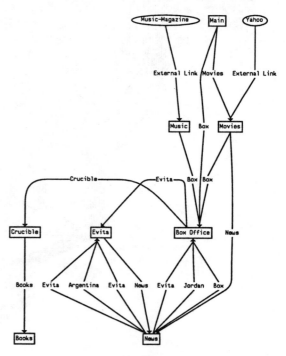

Figure 2. Simplified Graph

An important feature of the users navigation paths is the time they spend on different pages. We assign the time spent on each page by a user, to the link (s)he selected to leave that page. This should be the time that the user spent *viewing* the page and it should exclude the time spent on receiving and loading the page (see Sec. 3). We assign the viewing time of the last page to the last page itself. If a user remains on a page for a considerably long time before selecting the next link, we consider this as a sign that the client was not reading the page for the entire time. A time-out mechanism is explained in Sec. 3 that considers this page as the ending point of the client path. The next move of the client after the long pause is considered as the starting point of a new path.

We define the profile information of a user as the set of the links of his(er) navigation and the corresponding link times. We show the links sequence of the path traversed by the user u as $s_u = (l_{i_1}, \ldots, l_{i_n})$, the corresponding links time sequence as $T_u = (T_u(l_{i_1}), \ldots, T_u(l_{i_n}))$ and the user profile as pair of sequences, $(s_u; T_u)$.

Some examples of paths on the sample site (Fig. 2) are given in the following:

1. *Main $\overrightarrow{Movies}$: 20sec Movies $\overrightarrow{News}$: 15sec News $\overrightarrow{Box}$: 43sec Box Office $\overrightarrow{Evita}$: 52sec News $\overrightarrow{Argentina}$: 31sec Evita: 44 sec*

2. *Music $\overrightarrow{Box}$: 11sec Box Office $\overrightarrow{Crucible}$: 12sec Crucible $\overrightarrow{Books}$: 13sec Books:19 sec*

3. *Main $\overrightarrow{Movies}$: 33sec Movies $\overrightarrow{Box}$: 21sec Box Office $\overrightarrow{Evita}$: 44sec News $\overrightarrow{Box}$: 53sec Box Office $\overrightarrow{Evita}$: 61sec Evita :31 sec*

4. *Main $\overrightarrow{Movies}$: 19sec Movies $\overrightarrow{News}$: 21sec News $\overrightarrow{Box}$: 38sec Box Office $\overrightarrow{Evita}$: 61sec News $\overrightarrow{Evita}$: 24sec Evita $\overrightarrow{News}$: 31sec News $\overrightarrow{Argentina}$: 19sec Evita:39 sec*

5. *Movies $\overrightarrow{Box}$: 32sec Box Office $\overrightarrow{News}$: 17sec News $\overrightarrow{Jordan}$: 64sec Box Office $\overrightarrow{Evita}$: 19sec Evita:50*

6. *Main $\overrightarrow{Box}$: 17sec Box Office $\overrightarrow{Evita}$: 33sec News $\overrightarrow{Box}$: 41sec Box Office $\overrightarrow{Evita}$: 54sec Evita $\overrightarrow{News}$: 56sec News: 47*

These examples are used in the following sections to explain different aspects of our analysis.

3. Design and Implementation of a Profiler

For the purpose of recording users' path profile, we designed and implemented a profiler. A simple profiler can be a counter which counts the number of accesses to a web-page. A sample profiler can be found in[13] which is written in Perl script and provides a comprehensive view of daily accesses for the web-site. Due to the specific requirements of our analyzer (see Sec. 4), we require to capture more information than those captured by previous profilers (e.g., [23]).

Many research studies [13, 23, 5] and some commercial products [2, 1] have looked at capturing users' web access patterns and store them in log files for different purposes. Our profiler is distinguishable from all those studies due to its following main characteristics. Our profiler is executed at the client site instead of the server site. While this results in more accurate information gathered from the client (e.g., client cache hits, precise page viewing time), its implementation is very challenging. We achieved this by implementing a Java applet which its details are sketched in Sec. 3.1.2. Note that in [5], they also gathered accurate information about the client access. They achieved that by modifying the web-browser. Our profiler, however, requires no modification at the client site (including the browser), and it does not rely on user cooperation. In addition, no modification needs to be done in the current state of HTTP protocol and/or its packet structure. It is only required to modify the web-pages at the server site. This modification can be done automatically by some kind of a parser. That is, we define a new phase between the time that a web-page is constructed and the time it is made available through Internet. During this intermediate phase every page is parsed and modified automatically. First, a call to a Java applet is added to every page (see Sec. 3.1.2 for more details). Second, all the hypertext links are modified so that by clicking on them, more information will be transfered to the server site (see Sec. 3.3). A demo of our profiler is available on $http://www.usc.edu/dept/imsc/profiler.html$. For the rest of this section, we describe the design of our profiler.

For each user, our profiler should capture the ordered list of selected links and the viewing time of each page. The information content of our profile is a superset of statistical information such as frequency of access to a page and a link. To generate profile sequence accurately, the profiler needs to overcome three interesting challenges: 1) accurate recording of the time spent by client viewing a page, 2) detecting a page access at the server site, should the client observes a hit in its local cache, and 3) detecting the links traversed by the clients. For the rest of this section we describe these challenges and our proposed solutions.

3.1 Viewing Time

The time spent by a user viewing a page is a very important piece of information that can be employed to measure user's interest in the page. However, accurate recording of the viewing time is not trivial. To illustrate, consider Fig. 3. This figure demonstrates a client interactions with the server from the time the user requests a page (time t_0) until the time the server receives the user's subsequent request for another page (time t_5). We are interested in the duration $t_4 - t_3$ that is termed *viewing time*. Note that the difference between t_1

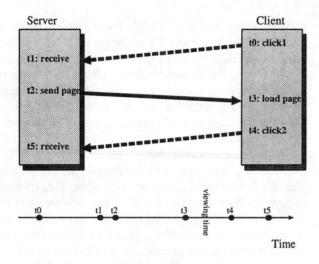

Figure 3. Client/Server Interactions

3.1.1 Server Site Profiler

If the profiler is running at the server site, it can trivially obtain t_1, t_2 and t_5. The server can then execute a *ping* command and measure its round-trip time (say δ). Subsequently, $(t_1 - t_0)$ (or $(t_5 - t_4)$) can be approximated as $\frac{\delta}{2}$. Using ping is appropriate because it incorporates the network congestion at the time of request. In other words δ is a function of network congestion. Finally, $(t_3 - t_2)$ can be approximated as $PageSize * \frac{\delta}{2}$, where $PageSize$ is the size of the page in number of TCP/IP packets. Having the above durations, the computation of $t_4 - t_3$ is straightforward.

Note that this method is relying heavily on approximation because some metrics such as the server load has not been considered. Consequently, the estimated viewing time might not be accurate. In the following section, we describe a more accurate method to capture the viewing time.

3.1.2 Remote Agent

If the profiler can be executed at the client site, then the measurement of viewing time can be done much more accurately. In this section we propose a method to run a *remote agent* at the client site without violating the security of the user. Our remote agent is implemented in Java [8] language. We developed a Java applet which is loaded into the client machine only once when the first page of our server has been accessed. Subsequently, every time a new HTML page (say page A) is loaded at the client display, the applet will send the system time as $(T_{load}(A))$ to the server. Similarly, once the page is unloaded, again the system time will be reported to the server as $(T_{exit}(A))$. Trivially, by deducting $T_{load}(A)$ from $T_{exit}(A)$, the server can compute the exact viewing time for page A.

The only disadvantage of this method is that the loading time of the applet is considered as part of the viewing time of the first page. After that, the applet becomes resident in the client's cache and no more loading time will be encountered. The loading time is unpredictable because it depends on various parameters such as connection speed, network congestion, number of classes being downloaded, speed of the just-in-time compiler etc. and varies from one platform/browser to the other. To resolve this problem, we investigated an alternative solution based on JavaScript [3] language which is a compact, object-based scripting language for developing client/server Internet applications. In comparison with Java applet, this implementation consumes very little or no time in interpretation as the JavaScript is a lightweight language. However, we abandoned the JavaScript implementation because the only time that the code can capture and report T_{exit}, was when the user clicks on a hypertext link. Instead, if the user clicks on hot-key buttons on the browser (e.g., *back*, *forward* or *go* buttons in Netscape) for navigation, the JavaScript code cannot capture and report T_{exit} to

and t_2 is in the order of a fraction of milli-second and can be ignored (i.e., $t_1 \approx t_2$). Currently, different web servers such as NCSA [12] and Apache [14] provide us with the flexibility to obtain t_1 and t_5 (actually t_2 and t_6) as the times the request was served. They store this information in Common [19] or Extended Log File [21] format. However, for the purpose of our analysis we need times t_0 and t_4. In addition, we need time t_3 to compute viewing time accurately.

Another argument to question the accuracy of viewing time information is that the user might load a page and then leave. Hence, even $t_4 - t_3$ is not the real time spent on viewing the page. One method to compensate is to compute a threshold based on the page size and reading speed of humans. If the viewing time exceeded the threshold, then the time information for that page must be invalidated and the threshold can be used as the viewing time. An alternative is to use smart cameras [18] to determine if the user is really viewing the page. This of course has privacy issues which might only be acceptable for certain applications (such as educational applications).

To illustrate the problem of using inaccurate viewing time, consider the following example. Suppose a clustering algorithm clusters users based on the time they spend viewing a page (as in [23]) and the profiler assumes $t_5 - t_1$ as the viewing time. The clustering algorithm will end up classify users based on the network traffic. For example, at 9:00am suddenly all the users show interest on page i while the reality is that the network was congested and it took longer to load the next page from page i for most of the users.

We propose two techniques to compute viewing time. The first one is based on a server-site profiler and has the disadvantage of using approximation. The second approach is a client-site profiler which is more accurate but it is possible for a user to disable it due to tight security considerations.

the server. Hence, we select the Java applet implementation and ignore the loading time of the applet for the first page.

To capture T_{load} and T_{exit} by the Java applet, each HTML page should be modified to incorporate a call to the applet. The following are sample statements that should be added (automatically) to the beginning of every HTML page ("index.html" page in this example):

```
<APPLET CODEBASE="/java"
 CODE="ViewTime" WIDTH=1 HEIGHT=1>
 <PARAM NAME="PAGE_NAME"
 VALUE="http://imsc.usc.edu/index.html">
</APPLET>
```

Incorporating the above statements at the beginning of the page results in invocation of the applet "ViewTime" immediately when the page is loaded. Subsequently, the applet stops execution when the page is unloaded.

T_{load} and T_{exit} are captured by the applet using the *currentTimeMillis()* method from *java.lang.System*. We implemented our own class to send T_{load} and T_{exit} to the server using *java.net.Socket* class. The submissions of T_{load} and T_{exit} to the server are incorporated into the *start* and *stop* methods of *java.applet.Applet* class, respectively. The *start* method is called each time the applet is revisited in the webpage. The *stop* method is called when the web-page that contains this applet has been replaced by another page and also just before the applet is to be destroyed. In addition to T_{load} and T_{exit}, the applet also sends the URL of the loaded page. This information is utilized later to detect client cache hits (see Sec. 3.2).

At the server site, a Perl script is running that will gather all the information sent by the client (e.g., T_{load}, T_{exit}) and record it as the user profile. This information will be analyzed by our path clustering techniques as described in Sec. 4. The major drawback of the remote agent is that some users might disable Java from their browser due to security concerns.

3.2   Client Cache

Typically, web browsers employ some techniques to cache the pages that has recently been accessed. If the user decides to return to an already accessed page, the server will not be notified and hence a server site profiler cannot record this information. There are many alternative methods to detect cache hits.

One method is to assign a short expiration time to HTML pages, enforcing the browser to retrieve every page from the server (and hence notifying the server). This can be done using *Expires* entity-header field in the HTTP protocol. This allows the web server to select a date after which the information may no longer be valid. One can set the date to value

of zero (0) or an invalid date format that results in immediate expiration of a page after its retrieval. Alternatively the user can also set the browser cache size to zero. However, this requires the user cooperation and cannot be enforced. The obvious disadvantage of both of the above methods is the performance degradation resulted from observing many cache misses.

An alternative method to capture references to cached pages is by doing some kind of detective work. This method is based on the fact that the links of a path should be consistent, i.e., the ending page of each link should be the same as the starting page of the next link. Violation of this rule in a user profile is the sign of local cache usage. This can be best shown by an example. Assume the following access pattern for a user: p_i, p_j, p_i, and p_k. However, due to some caching mechanism, the server is only notified of the following pattern: p_i, p_j, and p_k. This is because the second access to page p_i observed a hit at the client's cache. The server can analyze the access pattern and assuming there is no link from p_j to p_k (which is a likely true assumption; otherwise, the user could have directly used that link to load p_k) detect that the user has loaded p_i first and then p_k. We developed a heuristic to generate as accurately as possible the real access pattern from reported access patterns. In our heuristic method, we use the Referrer request-header field in HTTP protocol [15]. However, due to lack of space and since our alternative method to capture cache hits (described in the following paragraphs) is more reliable and accurate, we do not elaborate more on this heuristic method. Note that another serious shortcoming of our heuristic method is that it might not be able to detect the link sequences. To illustrate, in the previous example, if there are two different links from p_j to p_i, the server cannot find out which link was selected. This is because no report about this access was sent to the server. The situation becomes worse if the client uses hot-key buttons on the browser (e.g., *back* button in Netscape).

In contrast to all the above methods, our remote agent design can capture cache hits simply and accurately. Recall from Sec. 3.1.2, that for every HTML page, either loaded from cache or sent by the server, the "ViewTime" applet submit T_{load} and T_{exit} to the server. Hence, if the server receives T_{load} for a page that has not been requested (say page A), it can interpret it as a cache hit for page A. Note that this technique is independent of how the cached page was referenced, i.e., by using hot-key buttons or by directly clicking on hypertext links.

3.3   Traversed Links

One of the major differences between this approach (see Sec. 4) and previous studies is that we consider the order of page accesses. Our profiler has even made one more step forward and captures the links the client has selected to access pages. To illustrate, in Fig. 2, the user can select either $\overrightarrow{Argentina}$ or $\overrightarrow{Evita}$ hypertext links to navigate from the *News* web-page to the *Evita* web-page. In order for our path clustering algorithm to differentiate between these two users, our profiler should be able to capture the link information. This becomes even more challenging when the links have both identical names and target pages, but appear in different contexts. For example, in Fig. 2, there are two links with the identical name of $\overrightarrow{Evita}$, but in two different contexts (i.e. a "song" context and an "Oscar" context).

News.html

```
Oscar:
<A href="Evita.html"> Evita</A>

Screening in Argentina:
<A href="Evita.html"> Argentina</A>

Song:
<A href="Evita.html"> Evita</A>
```

Figure 4. The original *News* web-page

News.html

```
Oscar:
<A href="Evita1.html"> Evita</A>

Screening in Argantina:
<A href="Evita2.html"> Argentina</A>

Song:
<A href="Evita3.html"> Evita</A>
```

Sever-resident Table

id	name	number
1	*Evita*	1
2	*Argentina*	1
3	*Evita*	2

Figure 5. The modified *News* web-page

Currently, only the URL of the page requested by the client is passed to the server. This information is not sufficient to distinguish between links pointing to the same page (either with or without identical names). Briefly, our profiler extends the URL address of the pages with a *link identifier*. The link identifier is an index to a server resident table whose rows contain link names and numbers.

As mentioned before, we add a new phase between the time that a page is constructed and the time that it is made available through Internet. During this intermediate phase each page is parsed and modified automatically. For example, Fig. 4 shows the structure of the *News* web-page prior to applying the intermediate phase. Subsequently, Fig. 5 depicts the result of applying the intermediate phase on the *News* web-page. Hence, the three references to *Evita.html* are augmented with three different link identifiers. In addition, a table is generated that is indexed by link identifiers. Each row of the table contains a link identifier, its corresponding reference name and the number of occurance of the reference name in the page. Now the page is ready to become available on the Internet. That is, if a user clicks on

"Argentina", the target page, *Evita2.html*, will be passed to the server. The server decomposes *Evita2.html* into the target page address, *Evita.html*, and the link identifier 2. From the link identifier, the server retrieves the 2nd row of the index table and realizes that the link "Argentina" was selected. Subsequently, it sends the target page *Evita.html* to the client and record the following access pattern for the user: *News.html* $\overrightarrow{Argentina}$ *Evita.html*. Note that without the above steps, the server could have only recorded *News.html Evita.html* access pattern. Similarly, a user interested in Oscar nominations who selects the first occurance of "Evita" to access *Evita.html* can be distinguished from the other user interested in music who selects the second occurance of "Evita". The server will record *News.html* $\overrightarrow{Evita * 1}$ *Evita.html* as the access pattern of the first user and *News.html* $\overrightarrow{Evita * 2}$ *Evita.html* as the access pattern of the second one.

Since the above technique requires no modification at the client site, it can be employed by both server or client site profilers. We have incorporated this technique into our remote agent design (see Sec. 3.1.2).

4. Knowledge Discovery from Users Profile

The purpose of knowledge discovery from users profile, is to find clusters of similar interests among the users. If the site is well designed, there will be strong correlation among the similarity of the navigation paths and similarity among the users interest. Therefore, clustering of the former could be used to cluster the latter. In the following section we show this correlation using many examples from our sample site. We call WWW-sites with high correlation between users interests and their navigation path a *Server Informative WWW-site*. In [25] some design guidelines to construct Server Informative web-sites are explained.

The basic question is: what do we mean by calling two paths *similar*? Similarity among the navigation paths should be based on some of their features. The definition of the similarity is application dependent. Here we provide an overview on a powerful path clustering method called *path-mining*[24]. This approach is suitable for knowledge discovery in databases with partial ordering in their data. In this method, first a general *path feature space* is characterized. Then a *similarity* measure among the paths over the *feature space* is introduced. Finally this similarity measure is used in the clustering purposes. For more in-depth analysis of the path-mining approach and its other applications consult [24]. Here we cover different aspect of path-mining in the context of the WWW-site navigation analysis.

4.1 Path Feature Space

Defining a similarity measure among paths is not straightforward. This is due to the fact that we need to measure the distance between paths with different length and/or different starting pages. Moreover, paths are defined on a directed graph that can potentially have many cycles.

We consider a space of path features which is rich enough to capture important features of a path but yet has a simple underline structure. Consider a path s consisting of n links. We call s a n-hop path. Let's define $\mathcal{S}_m$ as the set of all possible m-hop sub-paths of s. Therefore, $\mathcal{S}_m(s)$ has $n-m+1$ elements. As a convention a page is considered as a 0-hop path. The set of m-hop sub-paths contains all possible orders of m connected links in the path. Note that a cyclic path includes some of its sub-paths more than once. The union of all $\mathcal{S}_m(s)$'s for all $0 \leq m \leq n$, which is shown by $\mathcal{S}(s)$, is called the *feature space* of path s. Note that path s itself belongs to $\mathcal{S}(s)$.

To illustrate, consider the first and the third path in the example of Sec. 2. The feature space which is embedding these two paths is the union set of all sub-paths of these two paths. This set of features is listed in the following (only up to : 2-hops)

- 0-hops: *Main, Movies, News, Box Office, Evita*

- 1-hops: *Main $\overrightarrow{Movies}$ Movies, Movies $\overrightarrow{News}$ News, News $\overrightarrow{Box}$ Box Office, Box Office $\overrightarrow{Evita}$ News, News $\overrightarrow{Argentina}$ Evita, Box Office $\overrightarrow{Evita}$ Evita*

- 2-hops: *Main $\overrightarrow{Movies}$ Movies $\overrightarrow{News}$ News, Movies $\overrightarrow{News}$ News $\overrightarrow{Box}$ Box Office, News $\overrightarrow{Box}$ Box Office $\overrightarrow{News}$ News, Box Office $\overrightarrow{News}$ News $\overrightarrow{Argentina}$ Evita, Main $\overrightarrow{Movies}$ Movies $\overrightarrow{Box}$ Box Office, Box Office $\overrightarrow{News}$ News $\overrightarrow{Box}$ Box Office, News $\overrightarrow{Box}$ Box office $\overrightarrow{Evita}$ Evita*

Considering all possible m-hops up to 5-hops, the feature space of these two paths includes 30 sub-paths.

The time spent over a sub-path is simply defined by the sum of the times spent on the links of that sub-path. As we mentioned in Sec. 2, the link time is defined by the viewing time on the end page of that link. The total viewing for the user u on the sub-path s is denoted as $T_u(s)$.

4.2 Path Angles and Path Clustering

A natural *angle* among the paths can be constructed by using an *inner product* over the feature space[24]. The angle among the navigation paths s_1 and s_2 over sub-paths with length m is given by

$$\cos(\theta_{m;s_1,s_2}) = \frac{<s_1,s_2>_m}{(<s_1,s_1>_m)^{\frac{1}{2}}(<s_2,s_2>_m)^{\frac{1}{2}}} \quad (2)$$

where the *inner product* over sub-paths with length m for the paths s_1 and s_2 is defined by

$$<(s_1;T_{u_1}),(s_2;T_{u_2})>_m = \sum_{k=0}^{m} \sum_{s \in \mathcal{S}_k(s_1) \cap \mathcal{S}_k(s_2)} T_{u_1}(s) \times T_{u_2}(s). \quad (3)$$

Based on the above definitions, the paths with no common page are *perpendicular*. Also each path has zero angle with itself. This angle can be employed as a natural *similarity* measure. Note that above definition works for any non-negative integers n_1, n_2 and m, where n_1 and n_2 are the lengths of s_1 and s_2, respectively. For $m \geq \min(n_1, n_2)$ all the inner-products are equal and we drop the m index.

Here we investigate the sample paths given in the Sec. 2 to check if the path angle measure predicts reasonable results. A simple calculation based on Eq. 3 produces the path angle among every pair of the six paths given in that example. The result is shown in the following path angle matrix.

$$\cos(\theta_{s_1,s_2}) = \begin{pmatrix} 1 & 0.10 & 0.250 & 0.319 & 0.031 & 0.190 \\ 0.010 & 1 & 0.019 & 0.010 & 0.010 & 0.004 \\ 0.250 & 0.019 & 1 & 0.010 & 0.120 & 0.306 \\ 0.319 & 0.010 & 0.010 & 1 & 0.072 & 0.105 \\ 0.031 & 0.010 & 0.120 & 0.072 & 1 & 0.107 \\ 0.190 & 0.004 & 0.306 & 0.105 & 0.107 & 1 \end{pmatrix} \quad (4)$$

Up to here we showed how to calculate the similarity between each pairs of the paths. Hereafter, using the path angle as a measure for similarity, we can apply a handful of algorithms in the classical theory of data mining[9, 6, 10]. In the next section we use K-means algorithm to classify a large number of paths on our sample site. For the purpose of illustration, henceforth a simple threshold method to classify our six example paths are employed.

Knowing the number of desired classes we could determine a threshold angle θ_{th} to split the classes. Paths with angels less than the threshold angle are considered in the same class. A membership matrix could be constructed by changing elements of the similarity matrix to ones or zeros depending if they are larger or smaller than the threshold. For a threshold angle in the following range

$$0.250 < \cos(\theta_{th}) < 0.306 \quad (5)$$

the membership matrix for our example is

$$M_{s_1,s_2} = \begin{pmatrix} 1 & 0 & 0 & 1 & 0 & 0 \\ 0 & 1 & 0 & 0 & 0 & 0 \\ 0 & 0 & 1 & 0 & 0 & 1 \\ 1 & 0 & 0 & 1 & 0 & 0 \\ 0 & 0 & 0 & 0 & 1 & 0 \\ 0 & 0 & 1 & 0 & 0 & 1 \end{pmatrix} \quad (6)$$

In this matrix, a 1 in row i and column j suggests similarity between paths i and j. We could transform this membership matrix to a block diagonal matrix with simple swapping of the rows and columns (see Tab.1). From Tab.1, we can clas-

Path ID	1	4	3	6	2	5
1	1	1	0	0	0	0
4	1	1	0	0	0	0
3	0	0	1	1	0	0
6	0	0	1	1	0	0
2	0	0	0	0	1	0
5	0	0	0	0	0	1

Table 1. Results after clustering

sify our sample paths to the following four classes: path 1 and 4 are in the first class, paths 3 and 6 are in the second class. Paths 2 and 5 each make an isolated class.

The power of path-mining algorithm is in probing the order of the links. For example, consider paths 1 and 3. Although, these two paths visit the same pages, path-mining did not cluster them in the same group. This is because they have visited different links and/or different links order. Other methods in which similarity function is only based on visiting similar pages[23], are not able to address this issue. Notice the distinction among path 1 and 3 is mapped to a distinction between the interests of the two users. User with path 1 may be interested in news about Evita while user with path 3 is interested in Evita because of the box office records.

Two paths are considered perpendicular if they have no link or page in common. For example the angle between path 2 and 6 is close to 90 since they have only one page in common. Examine paths 4 and 1 to see how path-mining algorithm handles path with cycles. These examples indicate that clustering based on the path angles follows an intuitive clustering. Fast algorithms in finding the path angles are important when the graph size is very large. For a detailed analysis consult[24].

5. Performance Evaluation

To evaluate the merit of our profiler and path-mining algorithm, we conducted a two step experiment on our sample web-site shown in Fig. 1. The parameters of this site are reported in Table 2. First we chose ten users to surf on the sample web-site. Using our profiler the links and their corresponding viewing time were captured. The profiler output was checked against a direct measurement of the users activities. The profiler recorded the viewing time and link access accurately.

Subsequently, we generated from 30 to 150 paths around the ten *nucleus* paths. The mean length of the generated

Number of pages	34
Number of links	136
Avg number of links per page	4
Avg similar target-different links per page	2
Avg similar target-identical links per page	2
Total number of links to outside web pages	11

Table 2. Sample web-site parameters

ID	# of paths in original cluster	Result BF=5%	Error %	Result BF=10%	Error %
1	100	113	13	131	31
2	115	87	24	92	20
3	43	48	11	57	32
4	56	54	3	44	21
5	93	86	8	86	14
6	140	151	7	119	15
7	30	35	17	15	50
8	84	96	14	123	46
9	129	139	7	110	15
10	150	131	7	163	9

Table 3. K-Means clustering Result

paths was 8 *links*. To generate a path s_k around the nucleus path s_n, we employed Markov Chain model as follows. Suppose i, j is a link in s_n and we want to generate the next link after i for s_k. Subsequently, we go to j with 95% probability as opposed to any other node in the graph. We call this a path with branching factor(BF) or noise level %5. Therefore, the probability of generating an 8-hops identical to the nucleus path is about 66%. The other 34% of generated paths are in a range of similar to entirely different from the nucleus path. The generated paths can be different in links, time, and length of a given path.

We report the result of the clustering on paths generated with branching factor (BF) 5% and 10%. A total of 940 paths were generated and fed into our path-mining algorithm. Subsequently, we applied K-Means clustering algorithm [6, 9] on the path angles computed from our path similarity algorithm. The result for K-Means algorithm with $K = 10$ (i.e., 10 clusters) is presented in Table 3. Our experiment shows that the average error margin in recovering the original clusters are %10 and %27 for the branching factors %5 and %10, respectively. Note that due to the impact of inserted noise, some of the generated paths might legitimately belong to some class different than which they have been originated.

6. Conclusions and Future Research Directions

Conventionally, web users access have been captured by profilers to the advantage of the user in order to achieve a smoother navigation or understand the user behavior [10, 17]. In this study, we propose to capture user navigation path to the advantage of web site owner. Capturing this information requires a more elaborated user profiler which has been designed and implemented as part of this study. Traditional profilers only count the frequency of access to a page as well as some data regarding the clients system[13]. Other studies in this area focussed on how to differentiate users who are logging in with the same IP address using *session identifier*[20, 16] in conjunction with identifier timeout mechanism (as mentioned in [23]), which has also been incorporated by our profiler. Some studies mentioned the importance of the page viewing time [23] while no feasible implementation to accurately collect this piece of information was proposed. Our profiler, in addition to the above, captures clients: 1) access page order, 2) link access, 3) cache reference, and 4) accurate page viewing time. We also proposed a design and implementation for a remote agent. The tradeoff between user privacy and servers' requirement to capture user information is currently under investigation by alternative standardization committees [20, 22]. In this study, we assumed the current status of HTTP standard and Java security system.

Next, we implemented the *path-mining* algorithm[24] to cluster the navigation paths detected by the our profiler. This algorithm finds a scalar number as the similarity among the paths. These similarity numbers could be fed to standard data-mining algorithms [7] to cluster the users interests. The advantage of this approach over previous attempts [23] is the utilization of the links orders in addition to the users page access viewing times.

There are many interesting applications that can benefit from the knowledge extracted by our method [11]. Dynamic link generation and pre-fetching the pages have already been mentioned in [23, 4]. Our clustering method provides a better knowledge base for these applications due to path order considerations. Another interesting application is to map the user navigation path data to the answers of a specific questionnaire. Having this done, the marketing division of a business could *implicitly* get the answers to some of its marketing questions just from users navigation on their web-site. We need a systematic web-site design methodology to create new web-pages, or modify existing web-pages, such that different users' navigation patterns could be better mapped to the answers to a set of specific questions. We have already developed some preliminary design rules and our experimental results have been promising and will appear in [25]. This direction involves the use and test of our package with more sophisticated knowledge discovery methods, like *associated rules*.

References

[1] Interse market focus 3 by interse corporation. http://www.interse.com.

[2] Netcount service from pricewaterhouse llp. http://www.netcount.com.

[3] See. http://home.netscape.com/eng/mozilla/Gold/handbook/javascript/index.html.

[4] A. Bestavros. Using speculation to reduce server load and service time on the www. In *Proceedings of CIKM'95: The 4th ACM International Conference on Information and Knowledge Management*, Baltimore, Maryland, November 1995.

[5] C. Cunha, A. Bestavros, and M. Crovella. Characteristics of www client-based traces. Technical Report TR-95-010, Boston University, CS Dept, Boston, MA 02215, April 1995.

[6] B. Everitt. *Cluster Analysis*. H-E-B Ltd., 1974.

[7] U. M. Fayyad, G. Piatetsky-Shapiro, G. Smyth, and P. Uthurusamy. *Advances in Knowledge discovery and Data Mining*. AAAI/MIT Press, 1996.

[8] M. A. Hamilton. Java and the shift to net-centric computing. *IEEE Computer*, 29(8):31–39, 1996.

[9] J. Hartigan. *Clustering Algorithms*. New York: John Wiley & Sons Inc., 1975.

[10] H. Lieberman. An agent that assist web browsing. In *Procedding of 14th Int. Joint Confernce on Artificial Intelligence*, pages 924–929, Mnotreal, Canada, 1995.

[11] G. Piatetsky-Shapiro, R. Braachman, T. Khabaza, W. Kloesgen, and E. Simoudis. An overview of issues in developing industrial data mining and knowledge discovery applications. In *Proceeding of The Second Int. Confernce on Knowledge Discovery and Data Mining*, pages 89–95, 1996.

[12] See. http://hoohoo.ncsa.uiuc.edu.

[13] See. http://netpressence.com/accesswatch/.

[14] See. http://www.apache.org.

[15] See. http://www.ics.uci.edu/pub/ietf/http/rfc1945. In *Request For Comments 1945*.

[16] See. http://www.pathfinder.com.

[17] See. http://www..public.iastate.edu/ cyberstacks/aristotle.html.

[18] See. http://www.usc.edu/dept/imsc/smcam.html.

[19] See. http://www.w3.org/pub/WWW/Daemon/User/Config/Logging.html#common_logfile_format.

[20] See. http://www.w3.org/pub/WWW/TR.

[21] See. http://www.w3.org/pub/WWW/TR/WD-logfile.html.

[22] See. http://www.ai.mit.edu/projects/iiip/conferences/survey96/cfp.html. In *Workshop on Internet Survey,Methodology and Web Demographics*, Cambridge, MA, January 29-30 1996.

[23] T. W.Yan, M. Jacobsen, H. Garcia-Molina, and U. Dayal. From user acess patterns to dynamic hypertext linking. In *Proceedings of the 5th International World-Wide Web Conference*, Paris, France, May 1996.

[24] A. Zarkesh and J. Adibi. Pathmining: Knowledge discovery in patialy ordered databases. Submmitted to KDD-97.

[25] A. Zarkesh, J. Adibi, C. Shahabi, and V. Shah. Discovery of the answers to hidden questionnaires based on users web-site navigation. In preparation.

SESSION :2

---◆---

DATA MINING AND WAREHOUSING

Tackling the Challenges of Materialized View Design in Data Warehousing Environment

Jian Yang
Dept of Computer Science
University College
University of New South Wales
Canberra ACT 2600
Australia
jian@cs.adfa.oz.au

Kamalakar Karlapalem   Qing Li*
Dept of Computer Science
Hong Kong University of Science & Technology
Clear Water Bay,
Kowloon,
Hong Kong
{kamal, qing}@cs.ust.hk

Abstract

How to design materialized views in a data warehousing environment is an important problem which has been largely overlooked in the past. If we regard data warehouse queries as integrated views over the base databases, then there exists a need of selecting a set of views to be materialized so that the best combination of good performance and low maintenance cost can be achieved. In this paper, we compare materialized view design (MVD) work with such related problems as common subexpressions and multiple query processing, discuss the unique requirements of MVD, and outline possible solutions of addressing some of the challenging issues of MVD.

1. Introduction

Providing integrated access to multiple, distributed, heterogeneous databases and other information sources has become one of the leading issues in database research and industry [2]. The traditional approach to this problem is based on a very general two-step process: (1) determine the appropriate set of information sources to answer the query, and generate subqueries for each of the sources; (2) gather results from the information sources, combine them, and return the final answer to the user. This approach is referred as a *lazy* or *on-demand* approach to data integration [18], and often uses *virtual view(s)* technique to simplify query specification.

The most recent approach on the other hand is to extract and integrate information of interest from each source in advance and store them in a centralized repository. When a query is posed, the query is evaluated directly at the repository, without accessing the original information sources. We refer to this approach as *data warehousing*, since the repository serves as a warehouse storing the data of interest. One of the techniques this approach uses to improve the efficiency of query processing is *materialized view(s)*.

The virtual view approach may be better if the information sources are changing frequently, whereas the materialized view approach may be better if the information sources change infrequently and very fast query response time is needed. The virtual and materialized view approaches represent two ends of vast spectrum of possibilities. In paper [11], the authors pointed out that the hybrid integrated views, i.e., the combination of fully materialized and virtual views is beneficial, and provided a framework for data integration using the materialized and virtual view approaches. However, they did not develop the guidelines for determining what should be materialized and what should be virtual views.

Further, the current research work [8] on materialized views is mainly focused on the techniques for processing and maintenance of materialized views. However, the methodologies for materialized view design, such as how to determine the set of materialized views based on applications, is merely discussed. We believe that only by providing a framework and techniques for materialized view design an efficient data warehouse can be built.

The work presented in this paper highlights some issues of materialized view design in a distributed data

---

*This author is currently affiliated with the Department of Computing, Hong Kong Polytechnic University, Hung Hom, Kowloon, Hong Kong.

32

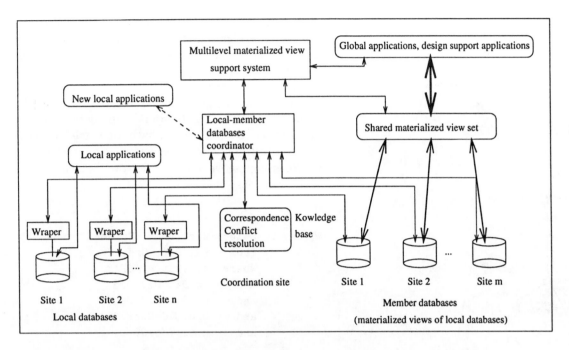

Figure 1. The Architecture of Data Warehousing Systems

warehouse environment. The framework of our research is as illustrated in Figure 1, which is a modified version of [13]. *Wrappers* [3, 6] convert data from each source into a common model and also provide a common query language. The knowledge base is used to store information such as correspondence between local database schemas and conflict resolution for any mismatched structures of local database schemas. These components are common in many integration projects [15, 3, 4, 14, 5]. However, the focus of our project is on the following two components:

- *Member databases:* these are derived databases through what we call "mirroring process" [13], the purpose of which is to convert the local heterogeneous databases into a set of homogeneous databases which can be efficiently managed by a single robust DBMS.

- *Shared materialized view set:* for supporting different global and local applications on a data warehouse. When the views required for local and global applications are related to each other, it may be more efficient not to materialize all the views, but rather to materialize certain commonly shared views, or portions of the base data, from which the warehouse views can be derived.

By using the specification of *Multiple View Processing Plan (MVPP)*, we discuss the problems to be solved, the possible solutions, and the analysis of the

existing research which is applicable to our problems. The discussion here is presented in terms of the relational model with select, project, and join operations, but we believe that our approach can be easily extended to include more complex operations in the relational model, such as query with aggregation functions, and nested queries.

The outline for our paper is as follows. Section 2 uses a simple example to illustrate the problem in materialized view design, while section 3 analyze the possible solutions and points out the issues arisen with the problem we defined. In section 4 we conclude the presentation of materialized view design methodology by summarizing our results and suggesting some ideas for future work.

2. A Motivating Example

This section presents an example to give a progressive overview of several key aspects of materialized view design problem.

Suppose that the member databases contains the following relations:
Product (<u>Pid</u>, name, Did)
Division (<u>Did</u>, name, city)
Order (<u>Pid, Cid</u>, quantity, date)
Customer (<u>Cid</u>, name, city)
Part (<u>Tid</u>, name, Pid, supplier)

33

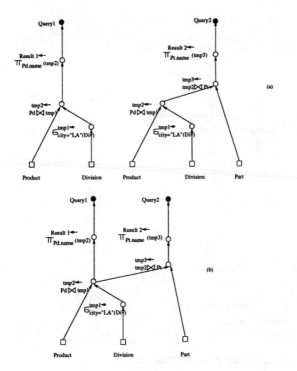

Figure 2. Individual Query Processing Graph

We use the shorthands **Pd, Div, Ord, Cust, Pt** to stand for the above relations respectively. For simplicity, we assume here that these relations are all at the same site, so the data communication cost is ignored in the following calculation.

Assume that we have the following two frequently asked data warehouse queries:

```
Query 1: Select Pd.name
         From   Pd, Div
         Where  Div.city=''LA''
         and    Pd.Did=Div.Did

Query 2: Select Pt.name
         From   Pd, Pt, Div
         where  Div.city=''LA''
         and    Pd.Did=Div.Did
         and    Pt.Pid=Pd.Pid
```

Figure 2 (a) gives one access plan for each of the above queries. In order to achieve fast response time, we can materialize some intermediate nodes of each access plan for individual queries. Then the materialized view maintenance costs should be taken into account when we calculate the total cost for processing the query with materialized views. We notice that **tmp2** of **query1** is equivalent to that of **query2** in Figure 2 (a), which is called *common subexpression* in [16].

Therefore, we can merge these two plans into one plan as shown in Figure 2 (b). If we choose node **tmp1** to be materialized, as it can be used for both **query1** and **query2**, then the query cost for these two queries will be less than accessing directly from the base relations **Product**, **Division** and **Part**, and the total maintenance cost will be less than maintaining two **tmp1**s in local plans. Overall we will have some gains in terms of total cost of global access and view maintenance.

Now suppose we have another two frequently asked data warehouse queries:

```
Query 3: Select Cust.name, Pd.name, quantity
         From   Pd, Div, Ord, Cust
         Where  Div.city=''SF''
         and    Pd.Did=Div.Did
         and    Pd.Pid=Ord.Pid
         and    Ord.Cid=Cust.Cid
         and    date>7/1/96

Query 4: Select Cust.city, date
         From   Ord, Cust
         Where  Quantity>100
         and    Ord.Cid=Cust.Cid
```

Figure 3 represents a global query access plan for the above four queries, in which the local access plan for individual queries are combined based on the shared operations on common data sets. We call it **Multiple View Processing Plan (MVPP)**. Now we have to decide which node(s) of MVPP have to be materialized so that the sum of query cost and view maintenance cost is minimal.

It is obvious from this graph that we have several alternatives for choosing the set of materialized views: e.g., (1) materialize all the application queries; (2) materialize some of the intermediate nodes (e.g., **tmp1**, **tmp2**, **tmp4** etc.); (3) leave all the non-leaf nodes virtual. The cost for each alternative shall be calculated in terms of query processing and view maintenance.

The assumed size of the relations and other related statistical data is listed in Table 1. Let s stand for the *selectivity* for the selection condition of above queries, and js stand for *join selectivity* for a relation involved in a join operation. Here we assume that methods for implementing select and join operation are linear search and nested loop approach respectively. The cost for each operation node in Figure 3 based on data in Table 1 is labeled at the right side of each node. Here the cost is calculated in terms of block access. For example, the cost for obtaining **tmp3** by using **tmp2** and **Part** is 50.06 million block access.

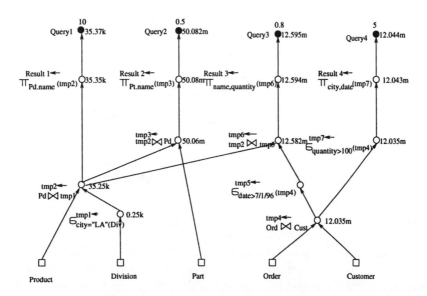

Figure 3. An MVPP for the Example

relation	size of relation	s or js	no. of blocks
Product	30k records	$js = 1/30k$	3k
Division	5k records	$s = 0.02$ $js = 1/5k$	0.5k
Order	50k records	$s = 0.5$	6k
Customer	20k records	$js = 1/20k$	2k
Part	80k records		10k
Product$Join$Division	30k records		5k
Product⋈Division⋈Part	80k records		20k
Order⋈Customer	25k records		5k
Product⋈Division⋈Order⋈Customer	25k records		5k

Table 1. Sizes of Relations and Statistical Data

For simplicity, we assume that all the member database relations **Product**, **Division**, **Part**, **Order**, and **Customer** are updated only once for a certain period of time; while within the same period of time, the number of access for each query is: 10 for query1, 0.5 for query2, 0.8 for query3, and 5 for query4, which is labeled on top of each query node in Figure 3.

Now we can calculate the costs of different view materialization strategies. Suppose there are some materialized intermediate nodes. For each query, the cost of query processing is query frequency multiplying the cost of query access from the materialized node(s). The maintenance cost for materialized view is cost used for constructing this view (here we assume the worst-case scenario of recomputation is used whenever a update of involved base relation occurs). For example, if **tmp2** is materialized, the query processing cost for query1 is $10 * 0.1k$. The view maintenance cost is $35.25k$. The

total cost for an MVPP is the sum of all query processing and view maintenance costs. Our goal is to find a set of nodes to be materialized, so that the total cost is minimal.

In Table 2, we list some materialized view design strategies based on the above example, as well as their costs. From this table, we have the following observations:

- materializing all the application views in the data warehouse can achieve the best performance at the highest cost of maintenance;

- leaving all the application views virtual will have the poorest performance but the lowest maintenance cost;

- if we have the intermediate results of some operations materialized, and some virtual, especially

Materialized views	Cost of query processing	Cost of maintenance	Total cost
Pd, Div, Pt, Ord, Cust	95.671m	0	95.671m
tmp2, tmp4, tmp6	85.237m	12.583m	97.82m
tmp2, tmp6	25.506m	12.382m	37.888m
tmp2, tmp4	25.512m	12.065m	37.577m
Q1, Q2, Q3, Q4	7.25k	62.653m	62.66m

Table 2. Costs for different view materialization strategies

when there are some shared operations on common data involved, then we can achieve an optimal result with both performance and maintenance taking into account (e.g., materializing as views **tmp2** and **tmp4** gives the lowest cost among all the listed strategies).

3. Problems and Issues in Materialized View Design

As illustrated by the previous example, materialized view design can be achieved with the help of a **Multiple View Processing Plan (MVPP)**, which has been formally defined in [19]. An MVPP specifies the views that the data warehouse will maintain (either materialized or virtual). We can conclude from the example of previous section that the steps towards materialized view design can be divided as follows:

1. finding all the common subexpressions and combining individual query access plans into one MVPP, such that all the common sub-expressions are merged;

2. finding a set of intermediate nodes in the MVPP, such that if the members of this set are materialized, the total cost of global query access and view maintenance is minimal.

The determination of the set of views to be materialized depends on four factors: (1) frequencies of global query access, (2) frequencies of member database relation update, (3) costs of query processing from materialized view(s), and (4) costs for materialized view maintenance. In the following subsections, we first analyze the related work done, then we discuss the possible solutions to the problem. We also address some further issues related to the materialized view design within the framework we have defined.

3.1. Analysis

The first issue listed above has been examined in the past in various contexts. [9, 10] used heuristics to identify common subexpressions, especially within a single query. They use operator trees to represent the queries and a bottom-up traversal procedure to identify common parts. [12] discussed the problem of common subexpression isolation. It presents several different formulations of the problem under various query language frameworks such as relational algebra, tuple calculus, and relational calculus. In the same paper, the author also described how common expressions can be detected and used according to their type (e.g., single relation restrictions, joins, etc).

A lot of research has been done in the area of multiple-query processing (MQP), which is related to the second issue discussed in the previous section. The focus in this area is to find an optimal execution plan for multiple queries executed at the same time, based on the idea that the temporary result sharing should be less expensive compared to a serial execution of queries. In [7], the authors described the optimization of sets of queries in the context of deductive databases and proposed a two-stage optimization procedure: during the first stage ("Preprocessor"), the system obtains at compile time information on the access structures that can be used in order to evaluate the queries; at the second stage, the "Optimizer" groups queries and executes them in a group instead of one at a time. In [1], the authors proposed an algorithm based on the construction of integrated query graphs. Using integrated query graphs, the authors suggested a generalization of the query decomposition algorithm. [16, 17] suggested a heuristic algorithm to solve the MQO problem. The algorithm performs a search over some state space defined over access plans.

What distinguishes our problem from common subexpression and MQP is the following:

- Although common subexpressions are good candidates considered for materialization, there are other cases that materializing non-shared intermediate nodes turns out to be a better choice. Moreover our problem framework is general enough to include the case where there is no common subexpression among individual query access plans;

- MQP is to find an optimal execution plan for multiple queries executed at the same time by sharing some temporary results which are common subexpressions, while our problem is to find a set of relations (which can be any intermediate result from query processing), to be materialized so that that the total cost (query accessing plus view maintenance) is optimal;

- In MQP, a global access plan derived from the idea of temporary result sharing should be less expensive compared to a serial execution of queries. However, this cannot be true for any database state. For example, sharing temporary result may prove to be a bad decision when indexes on base relations are defined. The cost of processing a selection through an index or through an existing temporary result clearly depends on the size of these two structures. While in our MVPP, if an intermediate result is materialized, we can establish a proper index on it afterwards if necessary. Therefore, it is guaranteed that there is a performance gain if an intermediate result is materialized. If the intermediate result happens to be a common subexpression which can be shared by more than one query, then the view maintenance cost gets amortized as well;

- In MQP, the ultimate goal is to achieve the best performance, while our problem has to optimize both query and view maintenance cost.

- In MQP, the input is a set of queries and the output is a global optimal plan; while in our problem, the inputs are: a set of global queries and their access frequencies, and a set of base relations and their update frequencies, and the output is a set of views to be materialized.

In summary, some of the techniques used in common subexpression and MQP can be applicable to MVPP, however, our problem is more general and thus more complicated than MQP; some new (perhaps combined) solutions are needed in order to deal with such a complicated problem satisfactorily.

3.2. Solutions to the problem

Normally for one query, there are several processing plans, among which there is one optimal plan. Therefore we will have multiple MVPPs based on different combinations of individual plans. At the current stage of this project, we have identified two possible algorithms to the problem: the first algorithm provides a feasible solution by dealing with optimal plan instead of all possible plans for each query; the second algorithm on the other hand, considers all possible plans for each query to generate a single optimal MVPP by applying 0-1 integer programming technique.

The basic idea of the first algorithm for generating an MVPP is as following: (1) for every individual optimal plan, if there is a join operation involved, push the select and project operations up along the tree; (2) for two such modified optimal query plans, find the common subexpressions for the join operations if they share the same source relations, and then merge them; (3) push down all the select and project operations as deep as possible; if there is more than one query sharing a join operation, and these queries have different select conditions on the attributes of two base relations of the join operation, then the select condition for a base relation attribute is the disjunction of all the select conditions on that attribute. Also, the attributes which should be projected for a base relation should be the union of the projection attributes of queries which shares the common join operation, plus the join attribute(s) (if required).

In order to reduce the search space, we proposed a heuristic algorithm (for detail see [19]). We start from individual optimal plans, and order them based on the query access frequencies and costs. Once the order of the query plans is fixed, we pick up the first optimal plan, and incorporate the second one with it based on the idea of incorporating the common subexpressions if there is any. After the first two are merged, the next one is picked up to incorporate with the merged plan. We keep doing it until all the plans are merged. Then we repeat this procedure by incorporating all other plans with the second expensive query execution plans, so on and so forth, until all the plans have been incorporated with. If there are k number of global plans, we will end up with having k MVPPs.

Figure 4 presents four optimal processing plans for four queries, denoted as op_1, op_2, op_3, op_4, respectively. We first transfer these plans into a form wherein all the select and project operations are pushed up, and the order of the leaf nodes is the same as the way they are joined. Based on the data in Figure 3, the values of *access frequency*∗*cost* for these queries are: $10 * 35.37k$,

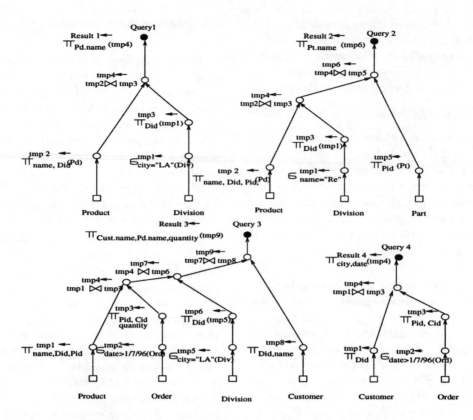

Figure 4. Individual Optimal Query Processing Plans

$0.5 * 50.082m$, $0.8 * 12.595m$, and $5 * 12.044m$ respectively. Therefore, list $l = <op_4, op_2, op_3, op_1>$, initially. Based on the order in l, we should keep op_4 as it is, and merge the rest of the plans with it in the order of the list l. The result $MVPP(1)$ is presented in Figure 5 (a). For simplicity, we ignore the select and project operations. We start with $MVPP(1) = op_4$. When op_2 is merged with $MVPP(1)$, we simply add these two plans together since there is no overlapping between the leaf nodes of these two plans. When op_3 is merged, we can divide the leaf nodes of op_3 into two sets: {Customer, Order} and {Product, Division}, which elements are already joined in $MVPP(1)$. So a new node, which will be the source node of Query 3, is introduced as a join operation between the results: Customer⋈Order and Product⋈Division in $MVPP(1)$. Then link this new nodes with Query 3 node and remove all other nodes and associated edges below the Query 3 node. When op_1 is merged, the leaf nodes of op_1 are already joined in $MVPP1$, so we link the node of Product⋈Division in $MVPP(1)$ to Query 1 node, remove all the join operation nodes in op_1.

After we generate the first $MVPP$, the first element of l is moved to the end of the list l, so the list l becomes $l = <op_2, op_3, op_1, op_4>$. The $MVPP$ for this list is presented in Figure 5 (b). We repeat this procedure

until all the ops have been the first element of l once.

After all the MVPPs are derived, we have to optimize each MVPP by pushing down the select and project operations as far as possible. What differentiates MVPP optimization with traditional heuristic query optimization is that in MVPP, several queries can share some intermediate nodes, therefore, there can be several irrelevant select conditions on base relations. Our approach to solve this problem is to take the union of select conditions for a base relation, which is shared by multiple queries. The way to push down the project operations is similar to traditional approach, i.e., take the union of project attributes of queries including the join attributes.

Figure 6 is one of the MVPPs we have constructed after merging the individual plans. To optimize it, we again push down all the select and project operations as far as possible. For **Division** relation, for example, all the selections it involves are $city = "LA"$, $name = "Re"$, and $city = "SF"$, which are from **Query 1**, **Query 2** and **Query 3** respectively. Therefore we can push the select condition $city = "LA" \lor city = "SF" \lor name = "Re"$ down to **Division** node. For **Product**, the projected attributes are $\{name\} \cup \{Did\} \cup \{Pid\}$. The final optimal MVPP is presented in Figure 7.

The limitation of this algorithm lies in the fact that

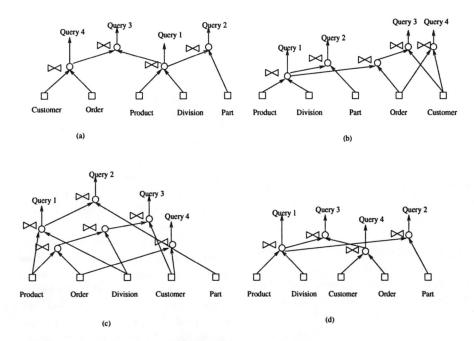

Figure 5. Multiple MVPPs

it may not guarantee that the optimal MVPP can always be obtained (and not missed), since only a subset of the possible MVPPs (for a given set of queries) has been considered, which contains at least one individual optimal plan in each MVPP generated. Nevertheless, we believe that it captures a reasonable subset of MVPPs, out of which a satisfactory (and balanced) solution can be found out with an acceptable efficiency.

In order to overcome the limitations of the first algorithm by looking into all possible combinations of individual query plans and then selecting the most beneficial MVPP(s), we analyse the join patterns for the queries, and successfully map the optimal MVPP generation problem as a 0-1 integer programming problem so that we are guaranteed to have an optimal solution in terms of query processing cost.

Given a selected MVPP, we then find a set of materialized views such that the total cost for query processing and view maintenance is minimal by comparing the cost of every possible combination of nodes. Suppose there are n nodes in MVPP excluding leaf nodes, then we have to try 2^n combinations of nodes to evaluate.

In [19] we employed a heuristic algorithm, which allows us to reduce the search space significantly. The idea is that: (1) all the nodes are ordered based on their weights (which are calculated as the saving the nodes can bring if they are materialized, subtracting their maintenance costs); (2) when a new node is considered for materialization, it will be checked whether it can bring any saving or not.

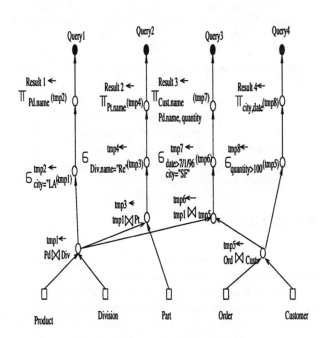

Figure 6. An MVPP Before Optimization

Every generated MVPP will be checked with this procedure and compared the against total cost of query access and view maintenance. A best MVPP together with its set of nodes to be materialized can then be chosen.

3.3. Further issues related to the problem

Determining the set of views to be materialized is the first step towards data warehouse design, and we believe that there are some related issues which should be addressed and resolved as well. In particular, the following enumerates some of these issues.

- How to analyze and handle more complicated queries such as a query with aggregation functions, query with parameters, and recursive queries which frequently occur in the data warehouse environment?

- How to build indexes on materialized views to obtain efficient query access? What kind of online index building facilities we should provide to the data warehouse developers? If an index is built on a materialized view, the cost for view maintenance should include the cost of building index and updating the index. Then this cost should be justified when we select the best MVPP and the nodes to be materialized.

- How to handle data warehouse application evolution since the framework of materialized view design is based on the applications? What kind of incremental materialized view update techniques should we adopt or develop within this framework? How to re-organize the member databases so that a more efficient materialized view maintenance can be obtained?

4. Conclusions

We believe that without a clear framework and efficient algorithms for materialized view design, there is no other way that a good data warehouse could be built. Facilities for analyzing data warehousing applications and determining a set of views to be materialized have to be provided to the data warehouse developers.

In this paper, the issues involved in the multiple materialized view design are discussed. Such issues include how to select a set of intermediate results to be materialized so that the overall cost (i.e., sum of the cost of processing all the queries and maintaining materialized views) is minimal. Some solutions are provided and analyzed. The main motivation for performing inter-global view analysis is due to the fact that the common intermediate results may be shared among multiple global queries. The cost model takes into consideration of query access frequencies, base relation update frequencies, query access costs, and view maintenance costs, which makes our problem even more complicated and challenging than related work such as Multiple Query Processing.

The work presented here is the outcome of the first stage of research in Materialize View Design project that we have been conducting. We are working on materialized view design for more complicated queries such as those with aggregation functions and recursive queries, which may occur frequently in the data warehousing environment. We are also working on the algorithm for choosing the best MVPP for materialized view design. Moreover we are looking into the possibility of utilizing the modeling power of object-orientation in materialized view design for reducing the cost for maintaining the materialized views by using procedures (methods). Finally, we will focus on developing an analytical model for a multiple view processing environment. Using a good analytical model will allow us to simulate various environments with different view mixes so as to validate the methodologies and algorithms proposed for materialized view design.

References

[1] U. Charkravarthy and J. Minker. Processing multiple queries in database systems. *Database Engineering*, 5(3):38–44, Sep 1982.

[2] I. Computer. *Special Issues on Heterogeneous Distributed Database Systems*, 24(12), December 1991.

[3] M. C. et al. Towards heterogeneous multimedia information systems: The garlic approach. *technical Report RJ 9911, IBM Almaden Research Center*, 1994.

[4] R. A. et al. The pegasus heterogeneous multidatabase system. *IEEE Computer*, 24:19–27, 1991.

[5] W. K. et al. On resolving schematic heterogeneity in multidatabase systems. *Distributed and Parallel Databases*, 1:251–279, 1993.

[6] J. Franchitti and R. King. Amalgame: a tool for creating interoperating persistent, heterogeneous components. *Advanced Database Systems*, pages 313–36, 1993.

[7] J. Grant and J. Minker. Optimization in deductive and conventional relational database systems. *Advances in Data Base Theory*, 1, 1981.

[8] A. Gupta and I. Mumick. Maintenance of materialized views: problem, techniques, and applications. *IEEE*

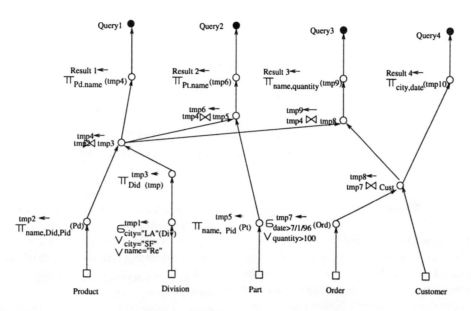

Figure 7. An MVPP After Optimization

Data Engineering Bulletin, Special Issue on Materialized Views and Data Warehousing, 18(2):3–18, June 1995.

[9] P. Hall. Common subexpression identification in general algebraic systems. *Tech. Rep. UKSC 0060, IBM United Kingdom Scientific Centre*, Nov. 1974.

[10] P. Hall. Optimization of a single relation expression in a relational data base system. *IBM J. Res. Dev. 20, 3*, pages 244–257, May 1976.

[11] R. Hull and G. Zhou. A framework for supporting data integration using the materialized and virtual approaches. *SIGMOD Record*, 25(2):481–92, June 1996.

[12] M. Jarke. Common subexpression isolation in multiple query optimization. *Query Processing in Database Systems*, pages 191–205, 1984.

[13] K. Karlapalem, Q. Li, and C. Shum. Hodfa: An architectural framework for homogenizing heterogeneous legacy databases. *SIGMOD RECORD*, 24(1), March 1995.

[14] W. Litwin, L. Mark, and N. Roussopoulos. Interoperability of multiple autonomous databases. *ACM Computing Surveys*, 22:267–293, 1990.

[15] Y. Papakonstantinou, H. Garcia-Molina, and J. Widom. Object exchange across heterogeneous information sources. *In Proc. ICDE Conf.*, pages 251–60, 1995.

[16] T. Sellis. Multiple-query optimization. *ACM Transactions on Database Systems*, 13(1):23–53, March 1988.

[17] K. Shim, T. Sellis, and D. Nau. Improvements on a heuristic algorithm for multiple-query optimization. *Data & Knowledge Engineering*, 12:197–222, 1994.

[18] J. Widom. Research problems in data warehousing. *Proc. of 4th Int'l Conference on Information and Knowledge Management (CIKM)*, Nov 1995.

[19] J. Yang, K. Karlapalem, and Q. Li. A framework for designing materialized views in data warehousing environment. *Technical Report HKUST-CS96-35, Department of Computer Science, Hong Kong University of Science and Technology*, 1996.

Evaluation of Sampling for Data Mining of Association Rules *

Mohammed Javeed Zaki, Srinivasan Parthasarathy, Wei Li, Mitsunori Ogihara
Computer Science Department, University of Rochester, Rochester NY 14627
{zaki,srini,wei,ogihara}@cs.rochester.edu

Abstract

Discovery of association rules is a prototypical problem in data mining. The current algorithms proposed for data mining of association rules make repeated passes over the database to determine the commonly occurring itemsets (or set of items). For large databases, the I/O overhead in scanning the database can be extremely high. In this paper we show that random sampling of transactions in the database is an effective method for finding association rules. Sampling can speed up the mining process by more than an order of magnitude by reducing I/O costs and drastically shrinking the number of transactions to be considered. We may also be able to make the sampled database resident in main-memory. Furthermore, we show that sampling can accurately represent the data patterns in the database with high confidence. We experimentally evaluate the effectiveness of sampling on different databases, and study the relationship between the performance, and the accuracy and confidence of the chosen sample.

1. Introduction

With large volumes of routine business data having been collected, business organizations are increasingly turning to the extraction of useful information from such databases. Such high-level inference process may provide information on customer buying patterns, shelving criterion in supermarkets, stock trends, etc. Data mining is an emerging research area, whose goal is to extract significant patterns or interesting rules from such large databases. It combines research in machine learning, statistics and databases. In this paper we will concentrate on the discovery of association rules.

The problem of mining association rules over *basket* data was introduced in [1]. Basket data usually consists of a record per customer with a transaction date, along with items bought by the customer. The main computation step consists of finding the frequently occurring item sets via an iterative process. In the k-th scan of the database all frequent items sets of length k are obtained. For disk resident databases, the I/O overhead in scanning the database during each iteration can be extremely high for large databases.

Random sampling from databases has been successfully used in query size estimation. Such information can be used for statistical analyses of databases, where approximate answers would suffice. It may also be used to estimate selectivities or intermediate result sizes for query optimization [11]. In the context of association rules, sampling can be utilized to gather quick preliminary rules. This may help the user to direct the data mining process by refining the criterion for "interesting" rules.

In this paper we show that random sampling of transactions in the database is an effective way for finding association rules. We empirically compare theory and experimentation, present results on the percentage of errors and correct rules derived at different sampling values, the performance gains, and also the relationship between performance, accuracy and confidence of the sample size. More specifically, we make the following contributions:

- Sampling can reduce I/O costs by drastically shrinking the number of transaction to be considered. We show that sampling can speed up the mining process by more than an order of magnitude.

- Sampling can provide great accuracy with respect to the association rules. We show that the theoretical results (using Chernoff bounds) are extremely conservative, and that experimentally we can obtain much better *accuracy* for a given *confidence*, or we can do with a smaller sample size for a given *accuracy*.

We begin by formally presenting the problem of finding association rules in section 2. Section 3 presents an analysis of random sampling from databases. The effectiveness of sampling is experimentally analyzed in section 4, and section 6 presents our conclusions.

*This work was supported in part by an NSF Research Initiation Award (CCR-9409120) and ARPA contract F19628-94-C-0057.

2. Data mining for association rules

We now present the formal statement of the problem of mining association rules over basket data. The discussion below closely follows that in [1, 3].

Let $\mathcal{I} = \{i_1, i_2, \cdots, i_m\}$ be a set of m distinct attributes, also called *items*. A set of items is called an *itemset*, and an itemset with k items is called a *k-itemset*. Each transaction T in the database $\mathcal{D}$ of transactions, has a unique identifier TID, and *contains* a set of items, such that $T \subseteq \mathcal{I}$. An *association rule* is an expression $A \Rightarrow B$, where itemsets $A, B \subset \mathcal{I}$, and $A \cap B = \emptyset$. Each itemset is said to have a *support* s if $s\%$ of the transactions in $\mathcal{D}$ contain the itemset. The association rule is said to have *confidence* c if $c\%$ of the transactions that contain A also contain B, i.e., $c = support(A \cup B)/support(A)$, i.e., the conditional probability that transactions contain the itemset B, given that they contain itemset A.

The data mining task for association rules can be broken into two steps. The first step consists of finding all *large* itemsets, i.e., itemsets that occur in the database with a certain user-specified frequency, called *minimum support*. The second step consists of forming implication rules among the large itemsets [3]. In this paper we only deal with the computationally intensive first step.

Many algorithms for finding large itemsets have been proposed in the literature [1, 7, 3, 10, 12, 6, 13, 2]. In this paper we will use the *Apriori* algorithm [2] to evaluate the effectiveness of sampling for data mining. We chose *Apriori* since it fast and has excellent scale-up properties. We would like to observe that our results are about sampling, and as such independent of the mining algorithm used.

2.1. The *Apriori* algorithm

The naive method of finding large itemsets would be to generate all the 2^m subsets of the universe of m items, count their support by scanning the database, and output those meeting minimum support criterion. It is not hard to see that the naive method exhibits complexity exponential in m, and is quite impractical. *Apriori* follows the basic iterative structure discussed earlier. However the key observation used is that any subset of a large itemset must also be large. In the initial pass over the database the support for all single items (1-itemsets) is counted. During each iteration of the algorithm only candidates found to be large in the previous iteration are used to generate a new candidate set to be counted during the current iteration. A pruning step eliminates any candidate which has a small subset. *Apriori* also uses specialized data structures to speed up the counting and pruning (hash trees and hash tables, respectively.) The algorithm terminates at step t, if there are no large t-itemsets. Let L_k denote the set of Large k-itemsets and

$C_k = L_{k-1} \times L_{k-1}$, the set of candidate k-itemsets. The general structure of the algorithm is given in figure 1. We refer the reader to [2] for more detail on *Apriori*, and its performance characteristics.

$$
\begin{array}{l}
L_1 = \{\text{large 1-itemsets}\}; \\
\textbf{for } (k = 2; L_{k-1} \neq \emptyset; k++) \\
\quad C_k = \text{Set of New Candidates}; \\
\quad \textbf{for } \text{all transactions } t \in \mathcal{D} \\
\quad\quad \textbf{for } \text{all } k\text{-subsets } s \text{ of } t \\
\quad\quad\quad \textbf{if } (s \in C_k) \ s.count++; \\
\quad L_k = \{c \in C_k | c.count \geq \text{minimum support}\}; \\
\text{Set of all large itemsets} = \bigcup_k L_k;
\end{array}
$$

Figure 1. The *Apriori* algorithm

We now present a simple example of how *Apriori* works. Let the database, $\mathcal{D} = \{T_1 = (1, 4, 5), T_2 = (1, 2), T_3 = (3, 4, 5), T_4 = (1, 2, 4, 5)\}$. Let the minimum support value $MS = 2$. Running through the iterations, we get

$$
\begin{array}{rcl}
L_1 &=& \{\{1\}, \{2\}, \{4\}, \{5\}\} \\
C_2 &=& \{\{1,2\}, \{1,4\}, \{1,5\}, \{2,4\}, \{2,5\}, \{4,5\}\} \\
L_2 &=& \{\{1,2\}, \{1,4\}, \{1,5\}, \{4,5\}\} \\
C_3 &=& \{\{1,4,5\}\} \\
L_3 &=& \{\{1,4,5\}\}
\end{array}
$$

Note that while forming C_3 by joining L_2 with itself, we get three potential candidates, $\{1,2,4\}, \{1,2,5\}$, and $\{1,4,5\}$. However only $\{1,4,5\}$ is a true candidate, and the first two are eliminated in the pruning step, since they have a 2-subset which is not large (the 2-subset $\{2,4\}$, and $\{2,5\}$ respectively).

3. Random sampling for data mining

Random sampling is a method of selecting n units out of a total N, such that every one of the $\mathcal{C}_n^N$ distinct samples has an equal chance of being selected. In this paper we consider *sequential* random sampling *without replacement*, i.e., the records are selected in the same order as they appear in the database, and a drawn record is removed from further consideration.

3.1. Sampling algorithm

For generating samples of the database, we use the **Method A** algorithm presented in [15], which is simple and very efficient for large sample size, n. A simple algorithm for sampling generates an independent uniform random variate for each record to determine whether that record should be chosen for the sample. If m records have been chosen from the first t records, then the next record will be chosen with the probability $(n - m)/(N - t)$. This algorithm, called **Method S** [9], generates $\mathcal{O}(N)$ random variates, and also runs in $\mathcal{O}(N)$ time. **Method A** significantly speeds up the sampling process by efficiently determining the number of records to be skipped over before the next one is chosen for the sample. While the running time is still $\mathcal{O}(N)$, only n random variates are generated (see [15] for more details).

3.2. Chernoff bounds

Let τ denote the support of an itemset I. We want to select n transactions out of the total N in the Database $\mathcal{D}$. Let the random variable $X_i = 1$ if the i-th transaction contains the itemset I ($X_i = 0$, otherwise). Clearly, $P(X_i = 1) = \tau$ for $i = 1, 2, \cdots n$. We further assume that all $X_1, X_2, \cdots, X_n$ are independent 0-1 random variables. The random variable $\mathbf{X}$ giving the number of transactions in the sample containing the itemset I, has a binomial distribution of n trials, with the probability of success τ (note: the correct distribution for finite populations is the *Hypergeometric distribution*, although the Binomial distribution is a satisfactory approximation [4]). Moreover, $\mathbf{X} = \sum_i^n X_i$, and the expected value of $\mathbf{X}$ is given as $\mu = E[\mathbf{X}] = E[\sum_{i=1}^n X_i] = \sum_{i=1}^n E[X_i] = n\tau$, since $E[X_i] = 0 \cdot P(X = 0) + 1 \cdot P(X = 1) = \tau$.

For any positive constant, $0 \leq \epsilon \leq 1$, the Chernoff bounds [5] state that

$$P(\mathbf{X} \leq (1 - \epsilon)n\tau) \leq e^{-\epsilon^2 n\tau/2} \qquad (1)$$
$$P(\mathbf{X} \geq (1 + \epsilon)n\tau) \leq e^{-\epsilon^2 n\tau/3} \qquad (2)$$

Chernoff bounds provide information on how close is the actual occurrence of an itemset in the sample, as compared to the expected count in the sample. This aspect, which we call as the *accuracy* of a sample, is given by $1 - \epsilon$. The bounds also tell us the probability that a sample of size n will have a given accuracy. We call this aspect the *confidence* of the sample (defined as 1 minus the expression on the right hand size of the equations). Chernoff bounds give us two set of confidence values. Equation 1 gives us the lower bound – the probability that the itemset occurs less often than expected (by the amount $n\tau\epsilon$), while equation 2 gives us the upper bound – the probability that the itemset occurs more often than expected, for a desired accuracy. A low probability corresponds to high confidence, and a low ϵ corresponds to high accuracy. It is not hard to see that there is a trade-off between accuracy and confidence for a given sample size. This can been seen immediately, since $\epsilon = 0$ maximizes the right hand side of equations 1,2, while $\epsilon = 1$ minimizes it.

3.3. Sample size selection

Given that we are willing to accommodate a certain accuracy, $\mathcal{A} = 1 - \epsilon$, and confidence $\mathcal{C} = 1 - c$ of the sample, the Chernoff bounds can be used to obtain a sample size. We'll show this for equation 1, by plugging in $c = e^{-\epsilon^2 n\tau/2}$, to obtain

$$n = -2\ln(c)/(\tau\epsilon^2) \qquad (3)$$

If we know the support for each itemset we could come up with a sample size n_I for each itemset I. We would still have the problem of selecting a single sample size from among the n_I. One simple heuristic is to use the user specified minimum support threshold for τ. The rationale is that by using this we guarantee that the sample size contains all the large itemsets contained in the original database. For example, let the total transactions in the original database $N = 3,000,000$. Let's say we desire a confidence $\mathcal{C} = 0.9(c = 0.1)$, and an accuracy $\mathcal{A} = 0.99(\epsilon = 0.01)$. Let the user specified support threshold be 1%. Using these values in equation 3, we obtain a sample size of $n = 4,605,170$. This is even greater than the original database! The problem is that the sample size expression is independent of the original database size. Moreover the user specified threshold is also independent of the actual itemset support in the original database. Hence, using this value may be too conservative, as shown above. In the next section we will compare experimental results obtained versus the theoretical predictions using Chernoff bounds.

4. Experimental evaluation

In this section we describe the experiments conducted in order to determine the effectiveness of sampling. We demonstrate that it is a reasonably accurate technique in terms of the associations generated by the sample, as compared to the associations generated by the original database. At the same time sampling can help reduce the execution time by more than an order of magnitude.

4.1. Experimental framework

All experiments were conducted on a 233MHz DEC Alphaserver 2100 processor, with 256MB of main memory. The databases are stored on an attached 2GB disk, and data is obtained from the disk via an NFS file server. We used four different databases to evaluate the effectiveness of sampling. These are:
• **SYNTH800, SYNTH250:** These are synthetic databases which mimic the transactions in a retailing environment. They have been used as benchmark databases for many association rules algorithms [3, 6, 12, 13, 2]. Each transaction

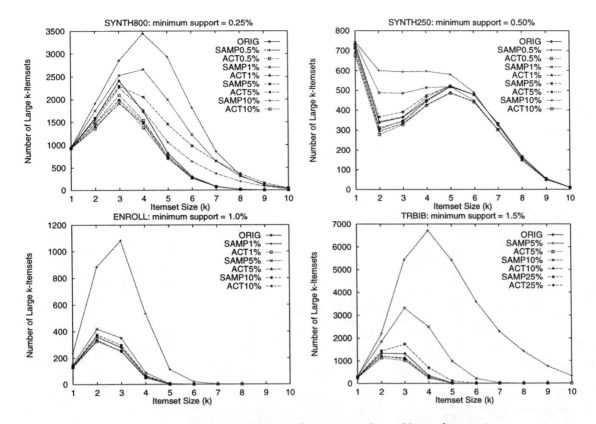

Figure 2. Itemset size vs. number of large itemsets

has a unique ID followed by a list of items bought in that transaction. We obtained the database $T10.I6.D800K$, by setting the number of transactions $|\mathcal{D}| = 800,000$, average transaction size $|T| = 10$, average maximal potentially large itemset size $|I| = 6$. For $T10.I4.D250K$, $|\mathcal{D}| = 250000$, $|T| = 10$, $|I| = 4$. For both databases the number of maximal potentially large itemsets $|L| = 2000$, and the number of items $N = 1000$. We refer the reader to [3] for more detail on the database generation.

• **ENROLL:** This is a database of student enrollments for a particular graduating class. Each transaction consists of a student ID followed by information on the college, major, department, semester, and a list of courses taken during that semester. There are 39624 transactions, 3581 items and the average transaction size is 9.

• **TRBIB:** This is a database of the locally available technical report bibliographies in computer science. Each item is a key-word which appears in a paper title, and each transaction has a unique author ID followed by a set of such key-words (items). There are 13793 transactions, 10363 items, and the average transaction size is 22.

4.2. Accuracy measurements

We report experimental results for the databases described above. Figure 2 shows the number of large itemsets found during the different iterations of the *Apriori* algorithm, for the different databases, and sample size. In the graphs, ORIG indicates the actual number of large itemsets generated when the algorithm operates on the entire database. SAMPx refers to the large itemsets generated when using a sample of size $x\%$ of the entire database. ACTx refers to the number of itemsets generated by SAMPx that are *true* large itemsets in the original database. The number of *false* large itemsets is given as (SAMPx − ACTx). From figure 2 we can observe that the general trends of sampled databases resemble actual results. Smaller sample sizes tend to over-estimate the number of large itemsets, i.e., they find more false large itemsets. On the other hand, larger sample sizes tend to give better results in terms of fidelity or the number of true large itemsets. This is indicated by the way ACT.x comes closer to ORIG as x (the sample percentage) is increased.

More detailed results are shown in figure 3, which shows the percentage of true and false itemsets generated for different values of sampling and minimum support. The values of minimum support were chosen so that there were enough large k-itemsets, for $k >= 2$. For example, for SYNTH800 and SYNTH250, only large 1-itemsets were found at support more than 1%. Therefore, only support values less than those were considered. Furthermore, support values were

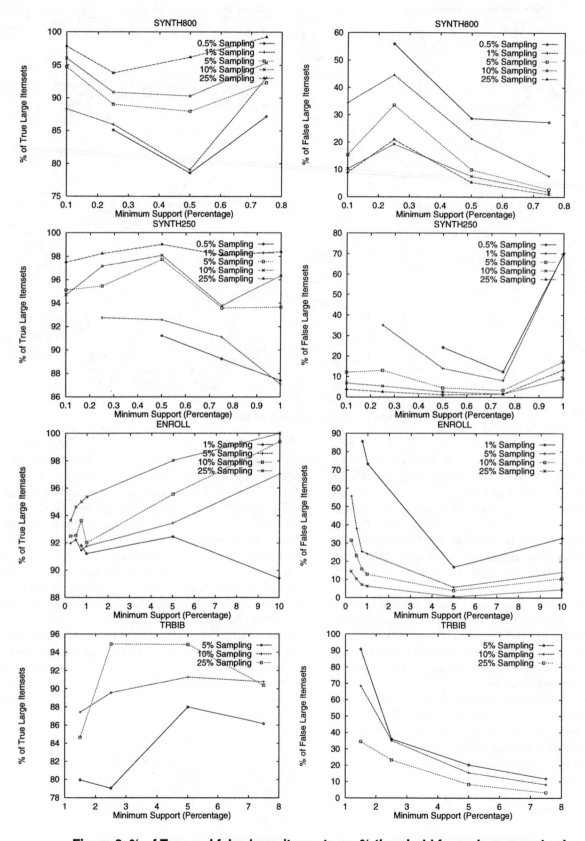

Figure 3. % of True and false large itemsets vs. % threshold for various sample sizes

chosen so that we don't generate too many large itemsets. For example, for ENROLL at 1% sampling size, we get a sample of 396 transactions. For support of 0.5%, we must find all itemsets which occur at least 2 times, in effect finding all possible large itemsets. Thus only support values greater than 0.5% were used.

The figure shows that at higher sampling size we generate a higher percentage of true large itemsets, and a smaller number of false large itemsets. It is interesting to note that in all cases we found more than 80% of all the large itemsets. We further observe that for other than very small sampling size, we can keep the false large itemsets under 20%.

4.3. Performance

Figure 4 shows the speedup obtained for the databases on different minimum support and different sampling size values. The speedup is relative to the algorithm execution time on the entire database. For SYNTH800 we obtain a speedup of more than 20 at small sample size and high support. For SYNTH250 we get more than 10 speedup in the same range. The performance at lower support is poor due to the large number of false large itemsets found. At higher sampling we get lower performance, since the reduction in database I/O is not that significant, and due to the introduction of more inaccuracies. For the smaller databases (ENROLL and TRBIB), at small sample size, we get no speedup, due to the large number of false large itemsets generated. We can observe that there is a trade-off between sampling size, minimum support and the performance. The performance gains are negated due to either a large number of false large itemsets at very low support or due to decreased gains in I/O vs. computation. We can conclude that in general sampling is a very effective technique in terms of performance, and we can expect it to work very well with large databases, as they have higher computation and I/O overhead.

4.4. Confidence: comparison with chernoff bounds

In this section we compare the Chernoff bound with experimentally observed results. We show that for the databases we have considered the Chernoff bound is very conservative.

Consider equations 1 and 2. For different values of accuracy, and for a given sampling size, for each itemset I, we can obtain the theoretical confidence value by simply evaluating the right hand side of the equations. For example, for the upper bound the confidence $C = 1 - e^{-\epsilon^2 n\tau/3}$. Recall that confidence provides information about an item's actual support in the sample being away from the expected support by a certain amount ($n\tau\epsilon$). We can also obtain experimental confidence values as follows. We take s samples of size n, and for each item we compute the confidence by evaluating

the left hand side of the two equations, as follows. Let ι denote the sample number, $1 \leq \iota \leq s$. Let

$$l_I(\iota) = \begin{cases} 1 & \text{if}(n\tau - \mathbf{X}) \geq n\tau\epsilon \quad \text{in sample } \iota \\ 0 & \text{otherwise} \end{cases}$$

$$h_I(\iota) = \begin{cases} 1 & \text{if}(\mathbf{X} - n\tau) \geq n\tau\epsilon \quad \text{in sample } \iota \\ 0 & \text{otherwise} \end{cases}$$

The confidence can then be calculated as $1 - \sum_{\iota=1}^{m} h_I(\iota)/s$, for the upper bound, and $1 - \sum_{\iota=1}^{m} l_I(\iota)/s$, for the lower bound.

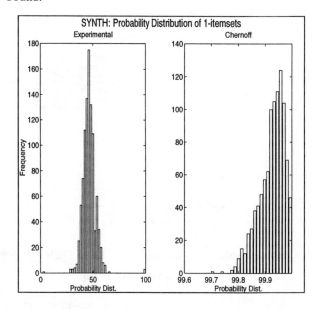

Figure 5. Probability distribution: experiment vs. chernoff

Figure 5 compares the distribution of experimental confidence to the one obtained by Chernoff upper bounds, for all m 1-itemsets or single items. It is possible (though impractical) to do this analysis for all the 2^m itemsets, however we present results for only single items. This should give us an indication whether the sample faithfully represents the original database. The results shown are for the SYNTH250 database with $\epsilon = 0.01$, $n = 2500$ (1% of total database size), and the number of samples taken, $s = 100$. We can see that the probability distribution across all items varies from 0.30 to 0.60 for the experimental case, with a mean probability close to 0.43. The Chernoff bounds produce a distribution clustered between 0.998 and 1.0, with an average probability of 0.9992. Chernoff bounds indicate that it is very likely that the sample doesn't have the given accuracy, i.e., with high probability, the items will be overestimated by a factor of 1.01. However, in reality, the probability of being over-estimated is only 0.43. The obvious difference in confidence depicts the limitation of Chernoff bounds in

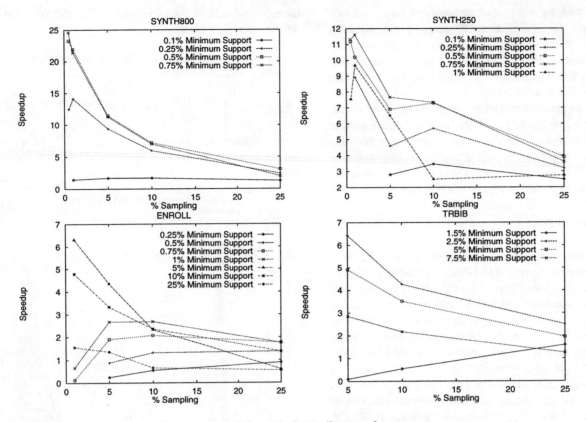

Figure 4. Sampling performance

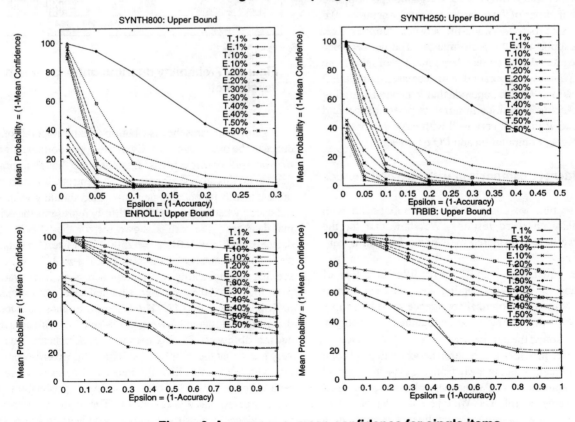

Figure 6. Accuracy vs. mean confidence for single items

this setting. This was observed in all of the databases we looked at.

Figure 6 gives a broader picture of the large gap between Chernoff bounds and experimentally obtained effectiveness of sampling. For all four databases we plot the mean of the confidence or the probability distribution for different accuracies $(1 - \epsilon)$. The mean confidence obtained from Chernoff bounds is marked as T.x, and that obtained experimentally is marked as E.x. Different values of the sample size x are plotted (from 1% to 50%), and results for only the upper bound are shown. For all the databases the upper and lower bounds give similar results. There is a small difference in the Chernoff bound values due to the asymmetry in equations 1 and 2. This is also true for the experimental results. For both cases the lower bounds give a slightly higher confidence for the same value of accuracy, as expected from the Chernoff bounds.

For SYNTH800 and SYNTH250 we observe that as the accuracy is compromised (as ϵ increases) the mean confidence across all items increases exponentially (therefore, only ϵ values upto 0.5 are shown). Furthermore, as the sample size increases, the curve falls more rapidly, so that we have higher confidence even at relatively higher accuracies. For SYNTH800 we get higher confidence for higher accuracy, when compared to SYNTH250. For both ENROLL and TRBIB we get the same general trends, however the increase in confidence for lower accuracies is not as rapid. This is precisely what we expect. For example, consider the right hand side of Chernoff upper bounds (equation 2), $e^{-\epsilon^2 n \tau / 3} = C$. For a given ϵ and τ (the support for an item), a higher value of n gives us high confidence, as it results in a lower value for C. For a given sampling percentage, since SYNTH800 and SYNTH250 are large, we expect a higher confidence than that for ENROLL or TRBIB (for example, with sampling = 10%, $\epsilon = 0.1$, and $\tau = 0.01$, we get $n = 80000$, $C = 0.07$ for SYNTH800; $n = 25000$, $C = 0.43$ for SYNTH250; $n = 3962$, $C = 0.88$ for EN-ROLL; and $n = 1379$, $C = 0.96$ for TRBIB). We get the same effect for the experimental results.

We can observe that for all the databases, the experimental results predict a much higher confidence, than that using Chernoff bounds. Furthermore, from the above analysis we would expect sampling to work well for larger databases. The distribution of the support of the itemsets in the original database also influences the sampling quality.

5. Related Work

Many algorithms for finding large itemsets have been proposed in the literature since the introduction of this problem in [1] (AIS algorithm). The *Apriori* algorithm [2] reduces the search space effectively, by using the property that any subset of a large itemset must itself be large. The DHP algorithm [12] uses a hash table in pass k to do efficient pruning of $(k + 1)$-itemsets to further reduce the candidate set. The *Partition* algorithm [13] minimizes I/O by scanning the database only twice. In the first pass it generates the set of all potentially large itemsets, and in the second pass their support is obtained. Algorithms using only general-purpose DBMS systems and relational algebra operations have also been proposed [6, 7].

A theoretical analysis of sampling (using Chernoff bounds) for association rules was presented in [2, 10]. We look at this problem in more detail empirically, and compare theory and experimentation. In [8] the authors compare sample selection schemes for data mining. They make a claim for collecting the sample dynamically in the context of the subsequent mining algorithm to be applied. A recent paper [14] presents an association rule mining algorithm using sampling. A sample of the database is obtained and all association rules in the sample are found. These results are then verified against the entire database. The results are thus exact and not approximations based on the sample. They also use Chernoff bounds to get sample sizes, and lowered minimum support values for minimizing errors. Our work is complementary to their approach, and can help in determining a better support value or sample size. We also show results on the percentage of errors and correct rules derived at different sampling values, the performance gains, and also the relationship between performance, accuracy and confidence of the sample size.

6. Conclusions

We have presented experimental evaluation of sampling for four separate databases to show that it can be an effective tool for data mining. The experimental results indicate that sampling can result in not only performance savings (such as reduced I/O cost and total computation), but also good accuracy (with high confidence) in practice, in contrast to the confidence obtained by applying Chernoff bounds. However, we note that there is a trade-off between the performance of the algorithm and the desired accuracy or confidence of the sample. A very small sample size may generate many false rules, and thus degrade the performance. With that caveat, we claim that for practical purposes we can use sampling with confidence for data mining.

References

[1] R. Agrawal, T. Imielinski, and A. Swami. Mining association rules between sets of items in large databases. In *ACM SIGMOD Intl. Conf. Management of Data*, May 1993.

[2] R. Agrawal, H. Mannila, R. Srikant, H. Toivonen, and A. I. Verkamo. Fast discovery of association rules. In *Advances in Knowledge Discovery and Data Mining, U. Fayyad, G.*

Piatetsky-Shapiro, P. Smyth, R. Uthurusamy (Eds.). AAAI Press, Melo Park, CA, 1996.

[3] R. Agrawal and R. Srikant. Fast algorithms for mining association rules. In *20th VLDB Conference*, Sept. 1994.

[4] W. G. Cochran. *Sampling Techniques.* John Wiley & Sons, 1977.

[5] T. Hagerup and C. Rüb. A guided tour of chernoff bounds. In *Information Processing Letters*, pages 305–308. North-Holland, 1989/90.

[6] M. Holsheimer, M. Kersten, H. Mannila, and H. Toivonen. A perspective on databases and data mining. In *1st Intl. Conf. Knowledge Discovery and Data Mining*, Aug. 1995.

[7] M. Houtsma and A. Swami. Set-oriented mining of association rules. In *RJ 9567*. IBM Almaden, Oct. 1993.

[8] G. John and P. Langley. Static versus dynamic sampling for data mining. In *2nd Intl. Conf. Knowledge Discovery and Data Mining*, Aug. 1996.

[9] D. E. Knuth. *The Art of Computer Programming. Volume 2. Seminumerical Algorithms.* Addison-Wesley, 1981.

[10] H. Mannila, H. Toivonen, and I. Verkamo. Efficient algorithms for discovering association rules. In *AAAI Wkshp. Knowledge Discovery in Databases*, July 1994.

[11] F. Olken and D. Rotem. Random sampling from database files - a survey. In *5th Intl. Conf. Statistical and Scientific Database Management*, Apr. 1990.

[12] J. S. Park, M. Chen, and P. S. Yu. An effective hash based algorithm for mining association rules. In *ACM SIGMOD Intl. Conf. Management of Data*, May 1995.

[13] A. Savasere, E. Omiecinski, and S. Navathe. An efficient algorithm for mining association rules in large databases. In *21st VLDB Conference*, 1995.

[14] H. Toivonen. Sampling large databases for association rules. In *22nd VLDB Conference*, 1996.

[15] J. S. Vitter. An efficient algorithm for sequential random sampling. In *ACM Trans. Mathematical Software*, volume 13(1), pages 58–67, Mar. 87.

Mediator Join Indices

Ling Ling Yan   M. Tamer Özsu   Ling Liu
Laboratory for Database Systems Research
Department of Computing Science
University of Alberta, Edmonton, Alberta, T6G 2H1
{ling, ozsu, lingliu} @cs.ualberta.ca

Abstract

A mediator join index (MJI) is proposed to speed up N-way inter-database joins by reducing the amount of data transfer during evaluation. A family of algorithms, the Query Scrubbing Algorithms (QSA), are developed to maintain MJI and to evaluate queries using MJI. QSA algorithms use query scrubbing to cope with update and query anomalies related to materialized views in the mediator context. Compared with existing algorithms, QSA algorithms incur less overhead in handling the anomalies and makes MJI a promising technique for efficient mediator query processing.

1. Introduction

In recent years, the need to access data in multiple data sources increased dramatically. This type of access is complicated by heterogeneities and autonomy of the data sources. The mediator architecture can be used to manage this complexity [7]. Mediators are used in many contexts. When using mediators to provide integrated views over multiple information sources and entertain mediator queries posed against these views, a major research issue is the performance of mediator query processing, that is, mediator query optimization. There are many established techniques for query optimization in distributed and centralized database systems. One important technique in this category is indexing. It has long been established that the proper use of indices can greatly speed up the processing of certain queries. In the mediator context, indexing would offer the same benefit but is rarely discussed. Indeed, indices in mediator context can not be maintained and used in the same way as in centralized systems; they pose new problems. In this paper, we investigate using *Mediator Join Index (MJI)* to speed up N-way inter-database joins in the mediator context.

1.1. What is MJI?

We start with a motivating example. Consider a mediator view relation

$$R_V = R_1 \bowtie_{f_1} R_2 \bowtie_{f_2} R_3$$

where R_1, R_2 and R_3 reside in different databases. Let K_1, K_2 and K_3 be the respective keys of the 3 relations. To process a query against R_V, the mediator must evaluate a 3-way inter-database join. If we materialize relation

$$IDX_{R_V} = \pi_{K_1,K_2,K_3}(R_V)$$

in the mediator, then at query evaluation time, the mediator *knows* which tuples contribute to the final join result and only retrieves these "useful" tuples from the respective sources. Hence the amount of data transferred is minimized. This idea is similar to join index [6] except that we use relational keys instead of surrogates.

Generally, a mediator join index (MJI) is a structure defined over an N-way join view

$$V = R_1 \bowtie_{f_1} R_2 \bowtie_{f_2} ... \bowtie_{f_{N-1}} R_N$$

where relations $R_1, ..., R_N$ reside in different data sources. Let $K_1, ..., K_N$ be the respective keys of these N relations. The MJI over V is defined as

$$MJI_V = \pi_{K_1,...,K_N}(V)$$

The maintenance of MJI and its usage in query evaluation are two important issues that pose new problems in the mediator context (Section 1.2). Our goal is to solve these problems and establish MJI as an indexing technique that supports fast N-way inter-database joins.

1.2. Maintaining and Using MJI

Given an N-way join view, its MJI will be maintained and used by the mediator. Both maintenance and usage of

51

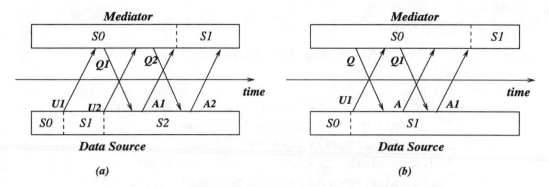

Figure 1. View Update Anomaly and Query Anomaly

MJI poses new problems. We review these problems in this subsection.

MJI is a materialized view in the mediator. Materialized views are not a new idea; they have long been used as a means for improving the performance of certain queries. Traditionally, materialized views are maintained incrementally [1]. To propagate an update U_1 on R_1 into a materialized view $V = v(R_1, ..., R_N)$, a *view maintenance query (VMQ)* due to U_1, $VMQ(U_1)$, is performed, such that

$$v(R_1 + U_1, R_2, ..., R_N) = v(R_1, ..., R_N) + VMQ(U_1)$$

The source updates (e.g. U_1), the VMQ of these updates (e.g. $VMQ(U_1)$), and the view updates are performed atomically in a single transaction. In mediator context, incremental maintenance of materialized views involves a new problem as illustrated in Figure 1(a). VMQ $Q1$ is evaluated in state $S2$, while it *should be* evaluated in $S1$. The interleaving of source updates and VMQs causes *view update anomalies* [8]. Using the traditional view maintenance algorithm in the mediator context may result in invalid view states. Algorithms have been developed to cope with these anomalies in data warehousing environment [8, 9]. The relationship between these algorithms and our algorithms will become clear in Section 1.3.

When processing a view query using MJI, we decompose the query based on the current content of MJI, send the subqueries to relevant sources, and assemble the query answer using the subquery results. This simplistic strategy works incorrectly in the scenario shown in Figure 1(b). The query is decomposed based on MJI state corresponding to source state $S0$. However, subquery Q sent to the source is evaluated in state $S1$ while it *should be* evaluated in state $S0$. When such a case occurs, we say there are *query anomalies*. Analysis and example of query anomalies are given in Section 4.

1.3. Scope and Contributions

Algorithms for maintaining and evaluating queries with MJI must cope with both update anomalies and query anomalies. In this paper, we present such algorithms. These algorithms use *query scrubbing* and are hence called the *Query Scrubbing Algorithms*, or the QSA family. The general idea of query scrubbing is the following. We notice that anomalies happen only when we query a source, either for the purpose of view maintenance, or for processing view queries. We further observe that ultimately, the anomalies arise when these queries are processed in a source state that is "newer" than the "old" source state based on which the materialized information held at the mediator is derived. Assume the mediator is aware of all the difference between the new state and the old source state. To eliminate anomalies, all the mediator has to do is to make modifications to the query results to *pretend* that the query is evaluated based on the "old" source state. This is what we refer to as query scrubbing.

We further illustrate the idea of query scrubbing using Figure 1. In Figure 1(a), a QSA algorithm for view maintenance will do the following: upon receiving answer $A1$ and knowing that $A1$ is affected by $U2$ (since $U2$ notification arrived before $A1$), it "scrubs" $A1$ with $U2$, that is, it modifies $A1$ so that it appears as if $U2$ did not happen before $Q1$ was evaluated. This means that we design a procedure $VMQscrub(A1, U2)$, which "scrubs" $A1$ and returns the scrubbed $A1$ as the result. This scrubbing must satisfy the following condition:

$$V^{U1} = V + VMQscrub(A1, U2)$$

where V^{U1} is the updated state of V with $U1$ being the only source update. The "scrubbed" $A1$ is merged with the view content.

In Figure 1(b), a QSA algorithm for view query processing will do the following: upon receiving answer A and knowing that A is affected by $U1$, it scrubs A using $U1$ before returning it as the answer to Q. That is, we design a

52

procedure $queryScrub(A, U1)$, which "scrubs" A and returns the scrubbed A as the result. This scrubbing must satisfy the following condition:

$$Q(S0) = queryScrub(A, U1)$$

where $Q(S0)$ is the result of Q evaluated in state $S0$.

A Strobe family algorithm for maintaining materialized mediator views, the C-Strobe [9], uses query scrubbing. While QSA algorithms perform scrubbing entirely in the mediator, without further querying the data sources, C-Strobe does so by issuing source queries. These source queries may need to be scrubbed too, incurring more source queries. C-Strobe does not terminate until all such queries are cleared. QSA algorithms incur less overhead in query scrubbing and they keep the view content "fresher", as shown in Section 3. A MJI-indexed view is indeed a *hybrid view*, or a partially materialized view. A reversed Eager Compensation Algorithm (ECA) [8] is briefly suggested in [4] to overcome query anomalies but no algorithmic details are provided. The query processing algorithm we give solves this problem in the special case of MJI.

The rest of this paper is organized as follows. Section 2 contains definitions, notions and assumptions. Section 3 presents MJI maintenance algorithms. Section 4 discusses query processing using MJI. Section 5 discusses the limitations of using MJI and gives a performance perspective. Section 6 contains conclusions and future work.

2. Mediator Join Index

2.1. Join Indices and Mediator Join Indices

Join indices were studied in [6]. Assume that each tuple of a relation is identified by a unique *surrogate* that never changes. Denote the surrogate of tuple i in R as r_i and the surrogate of tuple j in S as s_j. Denote the tuple identified by a surrogate c as $tuple(c)$. The join index for join $R \bowtie_f S$ is defined as

$$JI = \{[r_i, s_j] \mid f(tuple(r_i), tuple(s_j)) = true\}$$

To adapt this definition into the mediator context, we use the relational keys instead of surrogates.

DEFINITION 2.1 [Mediator Join Index (MJI)]
Let $R_1, ..., R_N$ be relations that reside on (possibly) different databases. Let $K_1, ..., K_N$ be the keys of relations $R_1, ..., R_N$, respectively. Let V be a mediator view defined as

$$V = R_1 \bowtie_{f_1} R_2 \bowtie_{f_2} ... \bowtie_{f_{N-1}} R_N$$

The mediator join index (MJI) for V is a relation $MJI(K_1, ..., K_N)$ defined by the following:

$$MJI = \pi_{K_1, ..., K_N}(R_1 \bowtie_{f_1} R_2 \bowtie_{f_2} ... \bowtie_{f_{N-1}} R_N)$$

□

2.2. Consistency, Freshness and Correct Query Processing with MJI

We adopt the definitions of consistency and freshness in [4]. Let

$$MJI = \pi_{K_1, ..., K_N}(R_1 \bowtie_{f_1} R_2 \bowtie_{f_2} ... \bowtie_{f_{N-1}} R_N)$$

MJI is *consistent* with $R_1, ..., R_N$ if (1) At any time t, MJI is based on states of $R_1, .., R_N$ at times $t_1, ..., t_N$, respectively, where t_i's are in the past of t. That is, MJI is *valid* and does not forecast the future; and (2) The more recent MJI state corresponds to more recent states of $R_1, ..., R_N$. That is, MJI does not "flash back". The *guaranteed freshness*, $< T_1, ..., T_N >$, is such that, at any time t, if MJI corresponds to R_i state at time t_i $(1 \leq i \leq N)$, then $t - t_i \leq T_i$. Given a query Q against a MJI-indexed view relation, the processing of Q is *correct* if the MJI state based on which query decomposition is performed is consistent with the source states based on which subqueries are evaluated.

2.3. Notions and Assumptions

We assume that update notifications issued by data sources are in the form of

$$insert(DB_i, R_i, t)$$

or

$$delete(DB_i, R_i, t)$$

where $1 \leq i \leq N$. For MJI maintenance, deletions are propagated without querying the sources since MJI includes keys of all source relations. For insertions, *View Maintenance Queries (VMQs)* are generated as:

$$\begin{aligned} VMQ(insert(DB_i, R_i, t)) = \\ \pi_{K_1, ..., K_N}(R_1 \bowtie_{f_1} ... \bowtie_{f_{i-1}} \{t\} \bowtie_{f_i} \\ R_{i+1} \bowtie ... \bowtie_{f_{N-1}} R_N) \end{aligned} \quad (1)$$

We make the following assumptions about data sources:

1. Each DB_i $(1 \leq i \leq N)$ provides *immediate notifications* to the mediator. That is, DB_i sends a notification to the mediator immediately after an update is successfully committed.

2. Mediator receives messages from $DB_i (1 \leq i \leq N)$ in the same order as they are sent.

In Section 5, problems related to these assumptions are discussed. In what follows, we use

$$DEL_{cond}(S, p)$$

to denote an operation that deletes all S tuples that satisfy predicate p.

3. Mediator Join Index Maintenance

Once created, a MJI is maintained by propagating changes in the source relations into the index content incrementally. In this section, we present the MJI maintenance algorithm, QSA-MJI. This algorithm uses query scrubbing, introduced in Section 1.3. We maintain a *Pending Update Queue*, PUQ, that contains all source updates to be propagated into the index. Updates in PUQ are propagated into the index in a FIFO order. For any $U \in PUQ$, if U is a deletion, it is propagated without querying the sources; if U is an insertion, a VMQ is generated as in formula (1). This VMQ is evaluated by function $VMQevaluate$. The answer returned by $VMQevaluate$ is merged into the materialized view immediately unless some updates in *front* of U in PUQ are still waiting for answers to their VMQs to be computed. Given VMQ $Q = \pi_{K_1,...,K_N}(R_1 \bowtie_{f_1} ... \bowtie_{f_{i-1}} \{t\} \bowtie_{f_i} R_i \bowtie ... \bowtie_{f_{N-1}} R_N)$, $VMQevaluate$ identifies a permutation of $\{1,...,N\}$, $Z = \{i, j_1, ..., j_{N-1}\}$ and a set of predicates $\{f'_1, ..., f'_{N-1}\}$, such that $R_1 \bowtie_{f_1} ... \bowtie_{f_{i-1}} \{t\} \bowtie_{f_i} R_i \bowtie ... \bowtie_{f_{N-1}} R_N = \{t\} \bowtie_{f'_1} R_{j_1} \bowtie_{f'_2} ... \bowtie_{f'_{N-1}} R_{j_{N-1}}$. The right hand side of his equation is computed in $N-1$ loops. In the first loop, R_{j_1} is joined with $\{t\}$. Subsequent loops join the result of the previous loop with the next relation in sequence Z, identified by function $next\_source$ which returns the next relation to be joined as well as the join predicate to be used. $next\_source$ returns nil when Z is exhausted. Each join is computed by issuing a query to the source where the next relation resides. As shown in Figure 1(a), the result of this query is potentially "dirty" and must be scrubbed. Query scrubbing is performed by function $VMQscrub$, which eliminates the effect of further updates in the data source from the query result.

Algorithm-1 QSA-MJI

At $DB_i(1 = 1...N)$:

- Upon committing update U: notify the mediator of U.

- Upon receiving query Q: evaluate Q based on the current state and return answer to mediator.

At Mediator:

- Upon receiving an update U_i:

  1. Add U_i to the end of PUQ.

  2. If U_i is an insertion, let $Q = VMQ(U_i)$. Call $A = VMQevaluate(V, U, Q)$.

  3. If U_i is the first element in PUQ, call $ViewUpdate$; otherwise do nothing. ∎

Function $VMQevaluate(V, U, Q)$
Input:

V: the view being indexed.
$V = R_1 \bowtie_{f_1} ... \bowtie_{f_{i-1}} \{t\} \bowtie_{f_i} R_i \bowtie ... \bowtie_{f_{N-1}} R_N$.

U: an insert notification from DB_i,
$U = insert(DB_i, R_i, t)$.

Q: $Q = VMQ(U) = \pi_{K_1,...,K_N}(R_1 \bowtie_{f_1} ... \bowtie_{f_{i-1}} \{t\} \bowtie_{f_i} R_{i+1} \bowtie ... \bowtie_{f_{N-1}} R_N)$.

Output: A: a correct answer to Q.

1. $A = \{t\}$. $EVAL = \{R_i\}$. $< source, pred > = next\_source(V, EVAL)$.

2. **WHILE** ($source \neq nil$) **DO**

   (a) $Q_s = A \bowtie_{pred} R_{source}$.
   Send Q_s to DB_{source} and wait for the answer.

   (b) When answer to Q_s, A_s, arrives at the mediator, do the following:

      i. Set $UUQ = \{$all DB_{source} updates that are behind U in $PUQ\}$.

      ii. $A = VMQscrub(DB_{source}, Q_s, A_s, UUQ)$.

   (c) $EVAL = EVAL \cup \{R_{source}\}$.
   $< source, pred > = next\_source(V, EVAL)$.

3. **RETURN** $\pi_{K_1,...,K_N}(A)$. ∎

Function $VMQscrub(DB_i, Q_s, A_s, UUQ)$
Input:

DB_i: the relevant data source.

Q_s: $Q_s = A \bowtie_f R_i$, where A is some intermediate result as in $VMQevaluate$ 2 (a).

A_s: a "dirty" answer to Q_s.

UUQ: $UUQ = U_1, ..., U_M$, $U_k(k = 1, M)$ is $insert(DB_i, R_i, t)$ or $delete(DB_i, R_i, t)$.

Output: A "clean" (correct) answer to Q, that is, the effect of updates in UUQ removed from A_s.

1. **FOR** $k = M, 1$ **DO**

   If $U_k = insert(DB_i, R_i, t_x)$, then $DEL_{cond}(A_s, A_s[K_i] = t_x[K_i])$.
   If $U_k = delete(DB_i, R_i, t_d)$, then $A_s = A_s \cup (A \bowtie_f \{t_d\})$.

2. **RETURN** A_s. ∎

Procedure *ViewUpdate*

WHILE (true) **DO**

1. If PUQ is empty, **RETURN**; otherwise, let U be the first element in PUQ.

2. If $U = delete(DB_i, R_i, t_d)$, then $DEL_{cond}(MJI, MJI[K_i] = t_d[K_i])$.

3. If $U = insert(DB_i, R_i, t_i)$ and the answer to $VMQ(U)$, A, has been received and scrubbed by the mediator, $MJI = MJI \cup A$.

4. If the mediator is still computing the answer for $VMQ(U)$, **RETURN**.

5. Remove U from PUQ. ∎

Remarks. QSA-MJI can be adapted to work in a "batch" mode, where updates that cancel each other are not propagated or used for query scrubbing. This adaptation does not raise new issues. In QSA-MJI, the number of source queries needed to propagate an insertion into a N-way MJI is at most $N - 1$. Scrubbing does not incur any source queries. C-Strobe [9] uses a larger number of queries because it issues source queries to scrub (compensate) these $N - 1$ queries. These compensation queries must be compensated for if the source is further updated, and so on. C-Strobe does not terminate until all the compensation queries are cleared. Besides incurring less scrubbing/compensation overhead, QSA-MJI always terminates faster than C-Strobe and hence keeps the MJI fresher.

Theorem-1. *Assume that a MJI is consistent with the relations involved in it at time t_0. Then algorithm QSA-MJI ensures the same consistency at any time $t > t_0$.* ∎

Proof: Obviously, based on the immediate update notification assumption, $ViewUpdate$ mandates a correct sequence (FIFO) in propagating updates into the index. What left to be shown is that each update is propagated into the index without violating consistency. Given a consistent state of MJI at time t_0, corresponding to source states at times $< t_0^1, ..., t_0^N >$, consider the first update received at the mediator after t_0, U_j from DB_j, at time t_1. Since DB_j provides immediate notification, we know that the time at which U_j occurred, t_1^j, satisfies $t_0^j < t_1^j$. Now we prove that after propagating U_j using QSA-MJI, MJI is consistent with the states of the sources at times $< t_0^1, ..., t_0^{j-1}, t_1^j, t_0^{j+1}, ..., t_0^N >$. If $U_j = delete(DB_j, R_j, t_d)$, then we need to remove all tuples in MJI with $MJI[K_j] = t_d[K_j]$. Obviously QSA-MJI does this. If $U_j = insert(DB_j, R_j, t_x)$, a VMQ $Q = \pi_{K_1, ..., K_N}(R_1 \bowtie_{f_1} ... \bowtie_{f_{j-1}} \{t_x\} \bowtie_{f_j} R_{j+1} \bowtie ... \bowtie_{f_{N-1}} R_N)$ must be evaluated. $VMQevaluate$ evaluate this query

by sending queries to each data source(except DB_j). Consider data source $DB_i(i \neq j)$. R_i might have been changed since time t_0^i but these changes are unwanted since we want to make sure that the query is evaluated based on the R_i state at time t_0^i. To eliminate the effect of these changes on the subquery sent to DB_i, we perform $VMQscrub$. So now the proof boils down to establishing the following:

Given $Q_s = A \bowtie_f R_i$, and $UUQ = U_1, ..., U_M$, a queue of updates to R_i that are behind U in PUQ, where U is the update such that Q_s is a subquery of $VMQ(U)$. Let $Answer(Q, R, r)$ denote the query result of query Q with the state of relation R be r. Let r_i' be the state of R_i before the sequence of updates $U_1, ..., U_M$ happened. Let r_i be the state of R_i based on which Q_s is evaluated, that is, $A_s = Answer(Q_s, R_i, r_i)$. $VMQscrub(DB_i, Q_s, A_s, UUQ)$ satisfies the following:

$$Answer(Q_s, R_i, r_i') = VMQscrub(DB_i, Q_s, Answer(Q_s, R_i, r_i), UUQ)$$

That is, after A_s is scrubbed, it is as if updates in UUQ did not happen before Q_s is evaluated.

$VMQscrub$ "reverse" the effect of $U_1, ..., U_M$ on A_s. It does so by removing the effect of U_M, then of U_{M-1}, ..., and so on. We construct the proof by induction on M:

<u>$M = 1$.</u> If $U_1 = delete(DB_i, R_i, t_d)$, when Q_s is evaluated, the state of relation R_i, $r_i = r_i' - \{t_d\}$, where r_i' is the state of relation R_i before U_1 happened. Considering that U_1 is a successful deletion, we have: $r_i' = r_i \cup \{t_d\}$. For $Q_s = A \bowtie_f R_i$, $Answer(DB_i, Q_s, R_i, r_i') = Answer(Q_s, R_i, r_i) \cup (A \bowtie_f \{t_d\})$. $VMQscrub$ does this and is correct. If $U_1 = insert(DB_i, R_i, t_y)$, Q_s is evaluated in the state of relation R_i, $r_i = r_i' \cup \{t_y\}$, where r_i' is the state of relation R_i before U_1 happened. Considering that U_1 is a successful insertion, we have: $r_i' = r_i - \{t_y\}$. For $Q_s = A \bowtie_f R_i$, $Answer(Q_s, R_i, r_i') = DEL_{cond}(A_s, A_s[K_i] = t_y[K_i])$. $VMQscrub$ does this and is correct.

<u>$M = k + 1$.</u> Assume that $VMQscrub$ is correct for $M = k$ and consider $M = k + 1$. Let the state of relation R_i based on which Q_s is evaluated be r_i. Let the state of R_i before $U_1, ..., U_{k+1}$ happened be r_i'. Let the state of R_i *before* U_{k+1} happened be r_i''. Using the same process as in the case of $M = 1$, we can prove that after the first round of the **FOR** statement, we obtain $A_s = Answer(Q_s, R_i, r_i'')$, that is, the effect of update U_{k+1} is eliminated from A_s. The rest of $VMQscrub$ achieves

$$VMQscrub(DB_i, Q_s, Answer(Q_s, R_i, r_i''), \{U_1, ..., U_k\})$$

Applying the induction assumption to the above expression, we have:

$$Answer(Q_s, R_i, r_i') = VMQscrub(DB_i, Q_s,$$
$$Answer(Q_s, R_i, r_i''), \{U_1, ..., U_k\})$$

Hence:

$$Answer(Q_s, R_i, r_i') = VMQscrub(DB_i, Q_s,$$
$$Answer(Q_s, R_i, r_i), \{U_1, ..., U_{k+1}\}). \blacksquare$$

Example 3.1 [QSA-MJI case study] Let

$$V = R_1 \bowtie_{R_1.W=R_2.W} (R_2) \bowtie_{R_2.Y=R_3.Y} (R_3)$$

be a join view. The 3 relations and the MJI on V are shown in Table 1. We omit the join conditions when they are obvious. At time t_0, the MJI is consistent with R_1, R_2 and R_3 (Table 1). Consider the following scenario:

t_1: Mediator receives notification

$$U_1 = insert(DB_3, R_3, [32, 102])$$

from DB_3. We have $PUQ = \{U_1\}$ and

$$Q_1 = VMQ(U_1) = R_1 \bowtie R_2 \bowtie \{[32, 102]\}$$

Mediator calls $VMQevaluate(V, U_1, Q_1)$. First, query

$$Q_2 = R_2 \bowtie \{[32, 102]\}$$

is sent to DB_2.

t_2: DB_1 makes two updates

$$U_2 = insert(DB_1, R_1, [11, 1])$$

$$U_3 = (insert(DB_2, R_2, [12, 2])$$

and notifies the mediator of both updates. Processing of these updates are omitted from this example. $PUQ = \{U_1, U_2, U_3\}$.

t_3: Q_2 is returned by DB_2 as

$$A_2 = \{[22, 2, 32, 102]\}$$

At the mediator, since there is no DB_2 update in PUQ, no scrubbing. $VMQ((V, U_1, Q_1)$ continues to send query

$$Q_3 = A_2 \bowtie R_1 = \{[22, 2, 32, 102]\} \bowtie R_1$$

to DB_1.

t_4: Answer to Q_3 is returned by DB_1 as

$$A_3 = \{[12, 2, 22, 32, 102]\}$$

At the mediator, this answer must be scrubbed with updates U_2 and U_3 from DB_1, result being ϕ. If we use the traditional view maintenance algorithm, A_3 would be merged into MJI as it is, resulting in a MJI state $\{[12, 22, 32]\}$. This state is invalid because the state of R_1 that contains key 12 must also contain key 11, and the state of R_3 that contains key 32 must also contain key 31. Hence, a valid MJI state that contains [12,22,32] must also contain [11,21,31].

$\square$

4. Query Processing Using MJI

Similar to join index, MJI is designed to speed up specific types of queries. Without loss of generality, we consider the following query in the rest of this section:

$$Q = \sigma_{p_1}(R_1) \bowtie_{f_1} ... \bowtie_{f_{N-1}} \sigma_{p_N}(R_N)$$

A simple strategy to evaluating this query using MJI consists of two steps. First, *query decomposition*. Let

$$Q_i = \sigma_{p_i}(R_i) \bowtie \pi_{K_i}(MJI)(1 \leq i \leq N)$$

Send Q_i to DB_i. Second, *answer assembly*. Let the answer to Q_i be A_i $(1 \leq i \leq N)$, compute the answer to query Q as

$$A = A_1 \bowtie_{f_1} ... \bowtie_{f_{N-1}} A_N$$

This strategy is not correct as demonstrated by the following example.

Example 4.1 Let

$$V = R_1 \bowtie_{R_1.W=R_2.W} R_2$$

be a join view. The 2 relations and the MJI on V are shown in Table 2. We omit the join conditions when they are obvious. We also omit the propagation of source updates U_1 and U_2. Assume that at time t_0, we have the states shown in Table 2, and process the query

$$Q = R_1 \bowtie R_2$$

Consider the following sequence of events:

t_0: Send query

$$Q_1 = R_1 \bowtie \pi_{K_1}(MJI)$$

to DB_1. $\pi_{K_1}(MJI) = \{[11], [12]\}$. Send query

$$Q_2 = R_2 \bowtie \pi_{K_2}(MJI)$$

to DB_2. $\pi_{K_2}(MJI) = \{[21], [22]\}$.

	$R_1(K_1, W)$	$R_2(K_2, W, Y)$	$R_3(K_3, Y)$	$MJI(K_1, K_2, K_3)$
t_0	ϕ	$[21, 1, 101], [22, 2, 102]$	$[31, 101]$	ϕ
t_1	ϕ	$[21, 1, 101], [22, 2, 102]$	$[31, 101], [32, 102]$	ϕ
t_2	$[11, 1], [12, 2]$	$[21, 1, 101], [22, 2, 102]$	$[31, 101], [32, 102]$	ϕ

Table 1. Example 3.1

	$R_1(K_1, X_1, W)$	$R_2(K_2, X_2, W)$	$MJI(K_1, K_2)$
t_0	$[11, x_{11}, 1], [12, x_{12}, 2]$	$[21, x_{21}, 1], [22, x_{22}, 2], [23, x_{23}, 3]$	$[11, 21], [12, 22]$
t_1	$[11, x_{11}, 1], [12, x_{12}, 2], [13, x_{13}, 3],$	$[21, x_{21}, 1], [22, x_{22}, 2], [23, x_{23}, 3]$	$[11, 21], [12, 22]$
t_2	$[11, x_{11}, 1], [13, x_{13}, 3],$	$[21, x_{21}, 1], [22, x_{22}, 2], [23, x_{23}, 3],$	$[11, 21], [12, 22]$

Table 2. Example 4.1

t_1: DB_1 performs

$$U_1 = insert(DB_1, R_1, [13, x_{13}, 3])$$

and notifies the mediator.

t_2: DB_1 performs

$$U_2 = delete(DB_1, R_1, [12, x_{12}, 2])$$

and notifies the mediator.

t_3: Q_1 arrives at DB_1 and is evaluated to

$$A_1 = \{[11, x_{11}, 1]\}$$

A_1 is sent to the the mediator.

t_4: Q_2 arrives at DB_2 and is evaluated to

$$A_2 = \{[21, x21, 1], [22, x_{22}, 2]\}$$

A_2 is sent to the mediator.

t_5: A_1 is received at the mediator.

t_6: A_2 is received at the mediator and the query answer to Q is computed as

$$A_1 \bowtie_W A_2 = \{[11, x_{11}, 1, 21, x_{21}]\}$$

This answer is incorrect. While the state of R_2 has never been changed, a valid state of R_1 that includes tuple $[11, x_{11}, 1]$ must contain either tuple $[12, x_{12}, 2]$ or $[13, x_{13}, 3]$. Hence a valid query answer that includes tuple $[11, x_{11}, 1, 21, x_{21}]$ must include either $[12, x_{12}, 2, 22, x_{22}]$ or $[13, x_{13}, 3, 23, x_{23}]$.

□

The above anomaly is due to the inconsistency between the data retrieved from the data sources by subqueries and the content of the MJI based on which query decomposition is done. We use a QSA algorithm to solve this problem. When processing query

$$Q = \sigma_{p_1}(R_1) \bowtie_{f_1} \ldots \bowtie_{f_{N-1}} \sigma_{p_N}(R_N)$$

we decompose it into sub-queries

$$Q_i = \sigma_{p_i}(R_i) \bowtie \pi_{K_i}(MJI) \quad (1 \le i \le N)$$

and send them to DB_i's. When answer to Q_i, A_i, arrives from DB_i, we scrub A_i to eliminate the effect of all the updates made by DB_i since Q_i was sent.

Algorithm-2 QUERY-MJI-QSA(V, MJI, Q)

Input:

V: a view. $V = R_1 \bowtie_{f_1} R_2 \bowtie_{f_2} \ldots \bowtie_{f_{N-1}} R_N$.

MJI: the MJI on V.

Q: $Q = \sigma_{p_1}(R_1) \bowtie_{f_1} \ldots \bowtie_{f_{N-1}} \sigma_{p_N}(R_N)$.

Output: A: A valid answer to Q.

- Lock MJI for read until query Q is completed.

- **FOR** $i = 1, N$ **DO**

    Let $Q_i = \sigma_{p_i}(R_i) \bowtie \pi_{K_i}(MJI)$.
    Send Q_i to DB_i.

- Upon receiving answer A_i to Q_i $(1 \le i \le N)$, let UUQ_i be the queue of all DB_i updates received by the mediator after Q_i is sent. Call $queryScrub(DB_i, Q_i, A_i, UUQ_i)$.

- Once all A_i's $(i = 1, N)$ are received and scrubbed by the mediator, assemble the answer to Q, A, as $A = A_1 \bowtie_{f_1} A_2 .... \bowtie_{f_{N-1}} A_N$. ∎

Function $queryScrub(DB_i, Q_i, A_i, UUQ_i)$
Input:

A_i: answer to Q_i, returned by DB_i.

DB_i: data source involved in Q_i.

Q_i: the subquery sent to DB_i, $Q_i = \sigma_{p_i}(R_i \bowtie MJI[K_i])$.

UUQ_i: the unwanted update queue for Q_i, $UUQ_i = U_1, ..., U_M$.

Output: Scrubbed A_i with effect of updates in UUQ_i eliminated.

1. **FOR** $k = M$ to 1 **DO:**

   (a) If $U_k = insert(DB_i, R_i, t_x)$,
   $DEL_{cond}(A_i, A_i[K_i] = t_x[K_i])$.

   (b) If $U_k = delete(DB_i, R_i, t_d)$ and $t_d[K_i] \in \pi_{K_i}(MJI)$, apply predicate p_i to tuple t_d. If it is true, $A_i = A_i \cup \{t_d\}$.

2. **RETURN** A_i. ∎

Theorem-2. Algorithm QUERY-MJI-QSA processes queries correctly (ref. Section 2.2). ∎

This theorem can be established in similar fashion as Theorem-1.

Example 4.2 We apply the new algorithms to handle the scenario in Example 4.1. At t_5, when Q_1 arrives, the mediator knows that since Q_1 was sent, there has been two updates in DB_1, U_1 and U_2. Scrub A_1 with these two updates, we get $A_1 = \{[11, x_{11}, 1], [12, x_{12}, 2]\}$. At t_6, A_2 arrives but there has been no updates from DB_2, hence A_2 is not scrubbed. Assemble the query result as usual we get $A = A_1 \bowtie_W A_2 = \{[11, x_{11}, 1, 21, x_{21}], [12, x_{12}, 2, 22, x_{22}]\}$. This answer is valid. □

5. Limitations and Performance

5.1. Limitations of MJI

In general, the use of MJI is limited by the capabilities of the data sources involved in providing update notifications with certain qualities. So far, we have assumed that (1) data sources provide immediate update notification; and (2) messages from a given source are delivered to the mediator in the same order as they are sent. Queries sent to sources that do not satisfy (1) and (2) can not be scrubbed, as discussed in this paper, or compensated for, as in [8, 9], hence their validity can not be guaranteed. If a source provides unordered update notification, we can attach a sequence number to the messages from this source to the mediator. This way, the mediator can trace the source state changes. We say a source is *inactive* if it only provides periodical update notifications or no update notifications. When a mediator view involves such a data source, a simple solution is to hold it virtual; any degree of materialization must be *self-maintainable* [2]. For hybrid views involving inactive sources, one must be careful when querying these sources to bring the virtual and materialized portion together; the consistency between the two portions is difficult to guarantee.

5.2. Performance Perspectives

To establish the performance of MJI, we must emphasize that MJI is a technique in the mediator context, which is a significantly different environment from centralized or distributed databases. In this context, data sources are highly autonomous. Many of the traditional query optimization techniques do not apply directly. This is essentially due to the fact that the mediator query processor may not even have a working cost model. For instance, an important technique for optimizing distributed joins is to use semi-joins. In the mediator context, we don't always know the values for various parameters that are necessary for deciding whether a semi-join is beneficial. The general model of mediator query optimization is an open research problem [5]. Until such a model is clearly defined, comparing MJI with traditional query processing techniques may not make much sense.

Given a N-way join view, V, we compare the operational and space cost of three strategies for holding V in the mediator: (1) virtual; (2) fully materialize; and (3) MJI-indexed. For space, virtual view is the most cost-effective, MJI the second and fully materialized views are the worst. For view maintenance, virtual views require no maintenance. The operational cost of maintaining a fully materialized view and that of maintaining MJIs of views are comparable. For query processing, fully materialized view performs the best since the query is processed entirely at the mediator. If V is virtual, unless a cost model is available in the mediator for multi-source queries, there is no promise for the performance of queries. If V is MJI-indexed, the number of "useless" tuples retrieved from the data sources is minimized with the overhead of shipping the keys of useful tuples ($\pi_{K_i}(MJI)$'s) to respective sources and that of query scrubbing. However, this overhead may be less than that of shipping data among sites for performing a N-way inter-database join without brutal-force or using semi-join based

58

techniques.

As shown above, we expect MJI to outperform the virtual view approach in terms of query processing speed and to outperform the fully materialized view approach in terms of space consumption.

6. Conclusions and Future Work

In this paper, we describe the mediator join index (MJI) that support fast N-way inter-database joins. A new family of algorithms, the Query Scrubbing Algorithms (QSA), are given for maintaining and evaluating queries with MJI. The QSA algorithm for index maintenance improves over previous algorithms given in [9] on termination performance. The QSA algorithm for query processing handles query processing in partially materialized views at the algorithm level.

As future research, we plan to do a comprehensive performance study of MJI. To establish MJI as an effective means for speeding up inter-database joins, it must be compared with other strategies for performing such joins. Currently, the parameters that affect the performance of inter-database join methods are not yet clear. Identifying these parameters will also be a useful step towards establishing a mediator query cost model.

References

[1] J. A. Blakeley, P. A. Larson, and F. W. Tompa. Efficiently Updating Materialized Views. In *Proc. ACM SIGMOD Int'l. Conf. on Management of Data*, pages 61–71, Washington,D.C., June 1986.

[2] A. Gupta, H. Jagadish, and I. Mumick. Data Integration Using Self-Maintainable Views. In *The Fifth International Conference on Extending Database Technology*, pages 140–144, Avignon, France, Mar. 1996.

[3] E. N. Hanson. A Performance Analysis of View Materialization Strategies. In *Proc. ACM SIGMOD Int'l. Conf. on Management of Data*, pages 440–453, 1987.

[4] R. Hull and G. Zhou. A Framework for Supporting Data Integration Using the Materialized and Virtual Approaches. In *Proc. ACM SIGMOD Int'l. Conf. on Management of Data*, pages 481–492, Montreal, May 1996.

[5] H. J. Lu, B. C. Ooi, and C. H. Goh. On Global Multidatabase Query Optimization. *ACM SIGMOD Record*, 21(4):6–11, Dec. 1992.

[6] P. Valduriez. Join Indices. *ACM Transactions on Database Systems*, 12(2):219–246, June 1987.

[7] G. Wiederhold. Mediators in the Architecture of Future Information Systems. *IEEE Computer*, pages 38–49, Mar. 1992.

[8] Y. Zhuge, H. Garcia-Molina, J. Hammer, and J. Widom. View Maintenance in a Warehousing Environment. In *Proc. ACM SIGMOD Int'l. Conf. on Management of Data*, pages 316–327, San Jose, California, May 1995.

[9] Y. Zhuge, H. Garcia-Molina, and J. Wiener. The Strobe Algorithms for Multi-Source Warehouse Consistency. In *The Proceedings of the Fourth International Conference on Parallel and Distributed Information Systems (PDIS)*, Dec. 1996.

SESSION :3

---◆---

WORK IN PROGRESS: PROJECTS FUNDED BY THE EC

DAFS: Data Mining File Server

Iain McLaren Ed Babb
Parsys Ltd, Boundary House
Boston Road, London, W7 2QE, UK
{iain,edbabb}@parsys.co.uk

Jorge Bocca
Integral Decision Systems, Belfortstr 6+8
D-817667 Munich, Germany
jorge@ids.de

Abstract

This report gives an overview of the DAFS Esprit project (no. 20169). The objective of the DAFS project is to build a parallel data mining file server. Current data mining tools often suffer from limited functionality and poor cost performance on data sets greater than 1 GByte. The DAFS project aims to overcome these problems through the close integration of data mining and database technologies on a scaleable parallel platform.

1. Introduction

Interest in data mining is growing rapidly as more market sectors realise the potential it offers to them. However, as more companies build data warehouses expecting to gain real business knowledge from their data, they are finding that current data mining solutions offer poor cost performance and limited functionality on databases greater than 1 GByte [6]. Sampling is often used to overcome these limitations, but this can cause a number of further problems. Firstly, it is possible that many meaningful relationships are overlooked because they are not apparent in the sample taken [3]. Secondly, building samples from large databases is not straightforward as the iterative nature of data mining demands a high degree of interaction between the database and data mining technology [12]. And finally, even if an adequate model is produced, most existing data mining tools do not produce models which can be deployed efficiently against the rest of the database (e.g., as SQL queries).

The limitations of conventional data mining systems has led to an increased interest in solutions which exploit parallel technology. Such systems include DecisionHouse from QuadStone [11], Darwin from Thinking Machines [8], the Data Mining Option from Red Brick [7] and Data Surveyor from Data Distilleries [4].

Generally, these systems have explored the parallelisation of their artificial intelligence components in isolation from the database component. However, we believe that this conflicts with the well established fact that at least 80% of the data mining effort is spent preparing the data to be mined. Taking this into consideration in the context of the iterative nature of the knowledge discovery process indicates that there are enormous benefits to be gained from closely integrating the artificial intelligence and database technologies within a parallel data mining environment. It is this integration which is driving the DAFS Esprit project (no. 20169) [1, 10].

2. Project overview

DAFS takes an existing data mining product called Clementine [9] and re-engineers it using a client server approach, where the client is based on Clementine's visual language interface and the server exploits parallel database and machine learning technology. This architecture is illustrated in figure 1. The Clementine data mining system allows users to create data mining streams which integrate the operation of data access, manipulation, transformation, machine learning (such as neural networks and rule induction) and visualisation techniques through an advanced visual programming language [13].

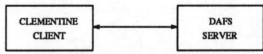

Figure 1. Client-server architecture.

The technical development of the DAFS project is driven by four supplier partners. Parsys Ltd (UK), who are the project co-ordinators, are parallelising the database and machine learning functionality of the server. Integral Solutions Ltd (UK), the developers of the Clementine system, are developing the client user interface. Integral Decision Systems GmbH (Germany) are improving the database functionality of the system. And finally, the University of Stuttgart (Germany) are extending the artificial intelligence functionality of the system. These partners are working together to produce the key deliverable of the project, the DAFS data mining file server. The architecture and principles behind the design of the DAFS server are discussed in the next section.

Although the basic functionality which must be supported by the DAFS server is defined by the current functionality of Clementine, additions to this functionality will be made to keep pace with the fast moving data mining market. The requirements for additional functionality are driven by the DAFS user partners: Royal and Sun Alliance PLC (UK), Equifax PLC (UK) and IDS GmbH (Germany). As such, the functionality of the DAFS server is focused on the three industries represented by these companies: insurance, finance and communications.

3. The DAFS server

The architecture of the DAFS server is based on a generic master-slave approach to parallelism, as shown in figure 2. In operation, the master process receives a data mining query from the client and compiles it into a form understood by the slave processes. This slave language is optimised to run on the distributed data set held in the different slave processors. Each slave then executes the query which it has received, and returns the results obtained to the master process. The master then combines the answers into a form appropriate to be returned to the client.

The DAFS server architecture was designed to adhere to the principles of scaleability, flexibility and portability, in addition to the overall objective of achieving high performance. These each had different effects on the server design.

- *Scaleability*: The DAFS server runs on a variety of different configurations, ranging from a single processor server up to a server with many processors. This means that as the size of a users data increases extra processors can be added to support the new workload. This scaleability is ensured by basing the design of the server on the generic master-slave configuration using a shared nothing processor architecture. The shared nothing approach has been shown to be scaleable to hundreds of processors [14], although at this stage

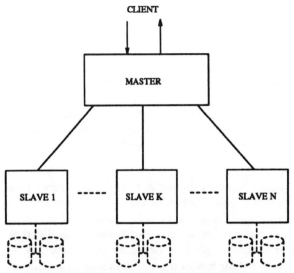

Figure 2. Master-slave server architecture.

the DAFS server aims to run on more modest processor configurations (of the order of 4 or 5 processors).

- *Flexibility*: The DAFS database technology follows on the principles and techniques explored by the MegaLog family of systems [2]. It implements a full database engine which supports an advanced logic programming interface. This language allows the range of data mining operations supported by DAFS to be easily extended. This may involve the development of procedures to support particular applications. These extensions can either be written in the DAFS database language or as new builtins in an external language such as C. In fact, most of the new data mining functions supported by the DAFS server are implemented in this way. There was no need to make any fundamental changes to the underlying database architecture.

- *Portability* The DAFS database is implemented using a virtual machine approach. The DAFS virtual machine is very close to the actual instruction sets and data management of modern processors, and is used as the execution engine in the master and slave processes. This ensures portability of the software across different hardware platforms. To carry out a port simply requires an implementation of the virtual machine on each new platform. Although the virtual machine is normally written in C, it can also be written in assembler for very fast emulation. This is considered as the last stage in projects which require very high performance.

To achieve high performance, the master process supports a range of parallel algorithms to maximise workload distribution among the slaves at each stage of the knowledge discovery process. In turn, the slave processes maximise I/O bandwidth through the use of an advanced multi-dimensional indexing mechanism. This allows the parallel algorithms to have very fast access to the data they require from each slave node.

- *Maximising workload distribution*: The data to be mined is evenly spread across the slave processors using a hashing based scheme. To ensure efficiency, the algorithms used attempt to minimise the communication required between the different processors. This is achieved by using data driven, rather than model driven, database and artificial intelligence algorithms [15]. That is, the algorithms which run on each slave process run similar algorithms to standard sequential algorithms, but only on their subset of data. The master process then receives results from the slaves which are either combined and returned to the user, or the master requests more information from the slaves. This contrasts with model based solutions which develop specialised algorithms to exploit the parallelism. As only small scale parallelism is used in the DAFS server, there is little value in taking this approach.

- *Maximising I/O bandwidth*: The DAFS server uses a derivative of the BANG multi-dimensional file system to hold and organise the data to be mined [5]. One of the main conflicts between conventional database systems and data mining tools is that the design of conventional databases is based on knowledge of what queries are going to be asked. This knowledge is then built into the indices of the database. However, the queries to be asked of a data mining system can not be predicted as there is no knowledge of which parts of the data are going to produce interesting results. In the quest for good average and guaranteed worst case performance across all and any arbitrary combination of attributes in a table, file systems such as BANG are ideal. The BANG multi-dimensional file system makes no assumptions about the search criteria, using a combination of all attributes to generate the index.

These techniques ensure a scaleable data mining environment which is able to support the functionality of Clementine at good cost-performance for data sets over 1 GByte in size.

4. Conclusions

This paper has presented an overview of the DAFS Esprit project which aims to develop a parallel data mining file server. The design of the DAFS server has been driven by the principles of scaleability, flexibility and portability in the quest for high performance on data sets greater than 1 GByte. This goal is achieved in DAFS through the close integration of artificial intelligence and database technology on a scaleable parallel platform.

A prototype of the DAFS system has been produced, and early performance figures on a single processor based system have demonstrated the benefits of the integrated architecture employed by DAFS against conventional data mining systems. Furthermore, simulations of the proposed data driven machine learning algorithms have been run, and have established the validity of the approach, exhibiting near linear speed up characteristics. Their integration with the main body of the data mining software is now taking place.

Acknowledgements

The authors would like to thank all colleagues involved in the DAFS project from Parsys Ltd, Integral Solutions Ltd, Integral Decision Systems, the University of Stuttgart, Royal and Sun Alliance, and Equifax(UK).

References

[1] E. Babb (editor). DAFS ESPRIT project no. 20169, Technical annex. European Commission, September 1995.

[2] J. Bocca. Megalog: a platform for developing knowledge base management systems. In *Proceedings of the International Symposium on Database Systems for Advanced Applications*, pages 374–380, Tokyo, Japan, Apr. 1991.

[3] J. Catlett. *Megainduction*. PhD thesis, Basser Department of Computer Science, University of Sydney, Australia, 1991.

[4] Data Distilleries. Data surveyor, http://www.ddi.nl/, 1996.

[5] M. Freeston. The BANG file: a new kind of grid file. In *Proceedings of the ACM SIGMOD International Conference on the Management of Data*, pages 260–269, San Francisco, USA, June 1987.

[6] S. Hedberg. Parallelism speeds data mining. *IEEE Transactions on Parallel and Distributed Technology*, 3(4):3–6, Winter 1995.

[7] Red Brick Inc. Red Brick: Data mining option, http://www.redbrick.com/, 1996.

[8] Thinking Machines Inc. Darwin data mining system, http://www.think.com/, 1996.

[9] Integral Solutions Limited. *Clementine User Guide: Version 2.0.* 1995.

[10] Parsys Limited. DAFS project information page, http://www.parsys.com/dafs.htm, 1996.

[11] Quadstone Limited. DecisionHouse scaleable data mining system , http://www.quadstone.co.uk/, 1996.

[12] N. Radcliffe and I. Flockhart. Scaleable data mining systems. Technical report, Quadstone Ltd., Edinburgh, UK, 1996.

[13] C. Shearer and T. Khabaza. Data mining for data owners. In *Proceedings of Data Mining 96*, pages 235–259, London, UK, Apr. 1996.

[14] M. Stonebraker. The case for shared nothing. *Database Engineering*, 9(1):4–9, 1986.

[15] E. Tyree. Parallel implementation strategies for Clementine machine learning algorithms. Technical report, Parsys Ltd, London, UK, 1996.

High Performance Banking[*]

J.A. Keane [†]
Department of Computation
UMIST
PO Box 88, Manchester, M60 1QD
UK

EMAIL: jak@co.umist.ac.uk

Abstract

The aim of the High Performance Banking (HYPERBANK) project is to provide the banking sector with the requisite toolset for increased understanding of existing and prospective customers, and better tailoring of products and services for those customers. The approach integrates three areas: business knowledge modelling, data warehousing and data mining, and parallel computing.

Keywords: Customer Profiling; Business Knowledge Modelling; Data Warehousing; Data Mining; Parallel Systems.

1 Introduction

The ever-increasing importance of IT to the banking and financial sector in terms of profitability, service provision, globalisation, and responsiveness to market change, increasing competition and customer needs is well illustrated in a series of recent papers [1, 2, 3, 4, 5].

In the past, given the cost of computing power and the paucity of data, only a rough analysis of statistically aggregate data was possible [6]. Recently, with improvements in data capture and network capacities, and the reduction in storage and processor costs, companies are able to build very large datastores. The problem is no longer the capture or storage of information, but its efficient exploitation.

Financial information systems contain vast quantities of data, including, for each customer, potentially, all transactions over the lifetime of a bank ac-

count. This source provides a phenomenal amount of data that can be used to lever competitive advantage. There is a perceived necessity that to compete in today's market, banks need to more precisely and completely *profile* their customers.

However, customer data is often in diverse sources spread across a number of databases, for example, a current account, a deposit account, a mortgage, a car loan etc. This is particularly an issue when different financial institutions merge and (attempt to) integrate their IT systems. Further, the sheer volume mitigates against current technologies being able to bring together and utilise this data.

More fundamentally, it is difficult to provide a precise answer to the question *"what is a customer?"*. For example, *"does the owner of an account constitute a customer?"*, what if a customer holds multiple accounts? A way to address this issue is to consider domain knowledge, for example, the knowledge that financial experts use to decide whether customers are good or bad risks.

What is required is a consistent user-based view of all the information concerning a customer, accessible in a timely and consistent manner. This accessibility, ultimately will enable a market segmentation at the level of an individual customer.

2 The *HYPERBANK* Approach

Given this situation, the aim of *HYPERBANK* is to provide the banking sector with the requisite toolset for increased understanding of existing and prospective customers, and better tailoring of products and services for those customers.

---

[*]This work is part of ESPRIT HPCN Project No 22693.
[†]The author wishes to thank all partners in the project.

This has two major aspects:

- the business goals and rules that express the objectives of the banks in which context the information can be utilised;

- the pragmatic issues of accessing and manipulating this data in a timely fashion, this involves both bringing disparate data sources together (data warehousing) and analysing this data to determine implicit relations (data mining).

The planned approach to exploiting banking customer information therefore, is an holistic integration of business knowledge modelling and data warehousing and mining, along with the enabling technology of parallel computing. In the following we consider each of these areas in more detail.

2.1 Business Knowledge Modelling

Business knowledge modelling (BKM) is about describing, in a formal way, an enterprise with its agents, work roles, goals, responsibilities and business rules together with the technological infrastructure that supports the enterprise.

The task of developing models for the three banking applications will be carried out through the use of enhanced versions of existing methods and tools of the *EKRD* approach [7, 8].

The enhancements to the EKRD approach, in order to form the BKM framework of *HYPERBANK*, concerns the ability to express data extraction and data mining requirements.

More precisely, the BKM framework will provide the ability to define business objectives and business concepts (the "things" dealt with in the enterprise), as well as data mining and data extraction requirements derived from those objectives and expressed in terms of the business concepts.

An important issue here that since we want to study the behaviour of customers and changes in this behaviour, information has to be collected over periods of time.

2.2 Data Warehousing and Data Mining

A *data warehouse* is defined as a single integrated data store which provides the infrastructural basis for information in an enterprise. Data warehousing is the application of replication and other technologies to bring data from a variety of sources into one or more collections that are designed to improve information access.

The average data warehouse query ranges dynamically over wide extremes of processing and assembles large volumes of separate data elements into small answer sets to be delivered to users.

The bringing together of many disparate sources of data with different schema definitions into a coherent whole for manipulation, as in *HYPERBANK*, represents an interesting data warehousing problem. Companion work using an object-oriented framework may be applicable here [9].

Currently, no industry standard exists for the interoperability of data warehousing tools, specifically for the exchange of meta-data. The translation and movement of such meta-data with regard to implementing a domain-specific tool has not been addressed by any vendors.

Data Mining is the process of extracting implicit information from a data warehouse, by the combination of various techniques, including data analysis, machine learning, knowledge based systems, and neural networks.

Current data mining tools do not embody the domain knowledge which could suggest appropriate derived attributes e.g. risk, profitability etc. Indeed it is unlikely that one approach to data mining would suffice for the diversity of banking concerns: Decision Support Systems may be projected in at least four distinct spaces: *Data, Aggregation, Influence* and *Variation*, and it is application-specific which is appropriate [11].

Elsewhere we have discussed the types of area in which data mining of banking data could be applicable, such as customer retention, product marketing and pricing, and credit card fraud [12].

Banks have already used both data warehousing and mining. For example, a UK bank, has used rule induction technology to profile characteristics of accounts to assess the risk of customers encountering problems. They conclude many advantages, but they also point out that:

- data warehousing is complex, and for large volumes of data requires parallel computing;

- extensive banking domain knowledge is required to steer the data mining;

- with large data sets, and in particular with large numbers of attributes, data mining becomes data and compute intensive.

2.3 Parallel Computing

It is estimated that above 5 gigabytes, parallel systems are necessary for effective results in data warehousing [10].

The upgrade path for mainframes is 20:1, for parallel systems the upgrade path is 1000:1 in terms of processor power, memory size, and disk capacity [13].Therefore, parallel systems addresses both the data and compute intensive nature of data warehousing and data mining:

- parallel systems offers both increased main memory space and the capability to use larger numbers of disks thus providing higher input-output capacity;

- parallel systems also offer higher processing capabilities: the performance of mainframes increases at the rate of 15% per year, whereas commodity processor power doubles every 18 months.

2.4 Summary of Approach

The approach in *HYPERBANK* is to use *EKRD* for the business knowledge modelling, and to integrate this with Carleton Europe's *PASSPORT* tool. Further we will extend this framework by adding data mining tools to analyse the data warehouse.

In data mining, a number of commercial tools exist, however, none feature both a domain-specific approach and an optimised version for the parallel environments considered necessary to analyse large volumes of data. At the time of writing (January 1997) a number of data mining tools are being considered for use in the project; it is probable that due to its commercial significance IBM's *INTELLIGENT MINER* will be one of those used.

At the same time, we intend to develop the integrated toolkit using the enabling technology of parallel systems. Again because of its commercial significance, we will target the *IBM SP2* system as a distributed memory MPP. We will also address implementation issues for SMP technology, perhaps by using the 4 processor SMP nodes now available for the SP2. The approaches taken to parallel data mining described in [14, 15] are of much interest, as is the ESPRIT-funded *DAFS* project.

However sophisticated the parallel platform, it is the application of domain knowledge that is crucial to the success of data mining in customer profiling in the financial domain.

3 Conclusions

A brief description of the rationale for, and approach to, the *HYPERBANK* project has been given. In exploiting the described technologies, the project intends to deliver the following major results:

1. a generic business knowledge model of 'customer profiling' within the banking sector, that can be instantiated for different banking methods and strategies;

2. an enhanced data extraction tool incorporating the business model;

3. a high performance data mining tool interfacing to both the data extraction and the business knowledge model.

Progress in any of the individual areas will benefit the banking partners. However, it is as a coherent, integrated whole that we expect the *HYPERBANK* products to provide the most significant benefit.

References

[1] K. Sandbiller et al., IT-Enabled Incentive Schemes in Telephone Banking, *Proc. HICSS-30 Vol.III*, IEEE Press, 1997.

[2] C. Marshall and R. Nolan, IT-Enabled Transformation: Lessons from the Financial Services, *Proc. HICSS-30 Vol.III*, IEEE Press, 1997.

[3] J. Kulijis and C. Scoble, Problems of Management and Decision Making in Multinational Banking, *Proc. HICSS-30 Vol.III*, IEEE Press, 1997.

[4] D.F. Channon, The Strategic Impact of IT on the Retail Financial Services Industry, *Proc. HICSS-30 Vol.III*, IEEE Press, 1997.

[5] C.P. Holland, A.G. Lockett and I.D. Blackman, The Impact of Globalisation and Information Technology on the Strategy and Profitability of the Banking Industry, *Proc. HICSS-30 Vol.III*, IEEE Press, 1997.

[6] K.M. Decker and S. Focardi, Technology Overview: A Report on Data Mining, CSCS-TR-95-02, CSCS-ETH, Swiss Scientific Computing Center, Switzerland, 1995.

[7] J. Bubenko, Experiences from Testing Enterprise Modelling- A Requirements Acquisition Method, Dagstuhl Seminar *System Requirements: Analysis, Management, and Exploitation*, Dagstuhl, Germany, 1994.

[8] P. Loucopoulos and E. Kavakli, Enterprise Modelling and the Teleological Approach to Requirements Engineering, *International Journal of Intelligent and Cooperative Information Systems*, 1995.

[9] M. Roantree, J.A. Keane and J. Murphy, A Three-Layer Model for Schema Management in Federated Databases, *Proc. of HICCS-30 Vol. I*, IEEE Press, 1997.

[10] Butler Group, Data Warehousing Management Guide: Strategies and Technologies, UK, 1995.

[11] K. Parsaye, Surveying Decision Support, *Database Programming and Design*, pp. 27-33, 1996.

[12] J.A. Keane, Parallel Systems in Financial Information Processing, *Concurrency: Practice and Experience*, 8(10), pp. 757-768, 1996.

[13] F.N. Teskey, Parallel Processing in a Commercial Open Systems Market, in *Parallel Information Processing*, J.A. Keane (Ed.), Stanley Thornes Publ., pp. 31-38, 1996.

[14] M. Holsheimer *et al.*, A Perspective on Databases and Data Mining, *Proc. of First International Conference on Knowledge Discovery and Data Mining*, 1995.

[15] M. Holsheimer, M. Kerten and A.P.J.M. Siebes, Data Surveyor: Searching the Nuggets in Parallel, in *Advances in Knowledge Discovery and Data Mining*, U.M. Fayyad *et al.* (Eds.), MIT Press, 1996.

CRITIKAL: Client-server Rule Induction Technology for Industrial Knowledge Acquisition from Large Databases

Akeel Al-Attar PhD MIEE CEng
Managing Director
Attar Software Ltd
Email : aalattar@attar.co.uk

Abstract

This paper describes a European Commission funded project to develop and demonstrate an advanced client-server induction system capable of supporting efficient, effective data mining of very large databases in business environments. The project combines the induction technology of Attar Software, the HPC application enabling expertise of the Universities of Southampton and Stuttgart, and the user-pull of two very different large database users; GEHE, the German pharmaceutical wholesaler, and Lloyds-TSB the British banking group.

1 Introduction

CRITIKAL is a European Commission funded project and is part of the ESPRIT programme. The project started in January 97 and is planned be completed in December 98. The basic premise for the project is the real business need for tools to enable in situ data mining against large databases in a client-server environment. The technological basis for the work of the project is Attar Software's mature, widely proven XpertRule induction technology and its newly released XpertRule Profiler client-server induction technology which is aimed specifically at the scaleable data mining marketplace.

The CRITIKAL project combines the technology and commercial exploitation capabilities of Attar Software, the HPC application enabling skills of the University of Southampton, the HPC research and the management decision support expertise of the University of Stuttgart, and the user-pull of two very different large database users; GEHE, the German pharmaceutical wholesaler, and Lloyds-TSB the British banking group.

2 Project Objectives

The objectives of the CRITIKAL project are to:

- demonstrate the potential for adding value to the information assets of organisations in different sectors through effective client-server induction from large corporate data warehouses;
- develop and demonstrate an advanced client-server induction system capable of supporting efficient, effective data mining of large databases in business environments;
- generate prototypes of a series of enhancements to Attar Software's XpertRule Profiler product which are enabled by HPC (High Performance Computing) technology and which are commercially exploitable during the lifetime of the project;
- generate a body of large-scale data mining experiences, from both the financial and pharmaceutical wholesale sectors, which will form the basis for generic dissemination and specific marketing activities.

3 Background to existing Rule Induction Technologies

Data mining is the process of discovering patterns (knowledge) in data. There are a number of knowledge discovery technologies; induction of classification trees, clustering and association rules discovery. Rule induction is a technique for discovering classification trees from data. It is one of the most mature and widely used knowledge discovery technologies. Given a data table, rule induction can generates tree patterns revealing how one data field is dependent on the other data fields. Such patterns or profiles can give a significant insight into the business process from which the data came. In practice, rule induction has been used successfully to generate profiles (patterns) of high risk loans, respondents to mailshots, lapsed insurance policies, insurance claimants, applications. A simple example of rule induction is shown in figures 1 and 2. In this example, data is available on the details of applicants for a bank loan and the decisions made by the risk underwriters at the bank. Applying rule induction to the data results in a tree of profiles revealing the risk assessment strategy of the underwriters.

S e x	A g e	Time Addr	ResStat	occup	Time Emp	Time Bank	House Exp	Decision
M	50	0.5	owner	unemploye	0	0	00145	reject
M	19	10	rent	labourer	0.8	0	00140	reject
F	52	15	owner	creative_	5.5	14	00000	accept
M	22	2.5	rent	creative_	2.6	0	00000	accept
M	29	13	owner	driver	0.5	0	00228	reject
F	16	0.3	owner	unemploye	0	01	00160	reject
M	23	11	owner	professio	0.5	01	00100	accept
F	27	3	owner	manager	2.8	01	00280	reject
F	19	5.4	owner	guard_etc	0.3	0	00080	reject
F	27	0.3	owner	manager	0.1	01	00272	reject
M	34	4	rent	guard_etc	8.5	07	00195	accept
M	20	1.3	rent	labourer	0.1	0	00140	reject
M	34	1.3	owner	guard_etc	0.1	0	00440	reject

Figure 1 : Data table of processed loan applications

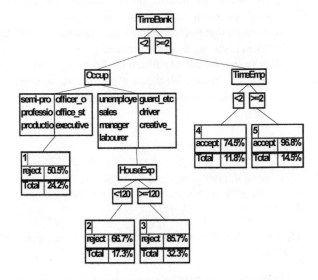

Figure 2 : A classification tree induced from the loans table

Over the last 17 years, the rule induction technology has evolved almost independently within the AI (artificial intelligence) and the Statistics research communities. The AI inspired rule induction algorithms, such as ID3 [2], use entropy as the criteria for selecting the data fields for tree branching and the grouping of field values between branches. The Statistics inspired algorithms, such as CHAID [1], use the Chi Squared test for branching. Both

energy consumption, hardware faults and many other AI and Statistical algorithms use Chi Squared tests as a stopping criteria when constructing a tree [3][1]. The rule induction algorithm in XpertRule Profiler uses a hybrid between ID3 and CHAID in addition to extensions developed by Attar Software over its eleven years experience in developing rule induction software [4][5].

The majority of commercial rule induction software generally runs on PC and workstation clients connected to database servers. Data is downloaded from the server to the client, using industry standard middle-ware such as ODBC, where the rule induction algorithm runs. The discovered patterns are then displayed to the user through the client's graphical user interface. Such an architecture is not scaleable since it only lends itself to data tables of tens of thousands of records and not enterprise-sized problems of millions of data records. In order to address this scaleability limitation, a number of vendors has developed rule induction engines that can run on database servers. Such server based induction engines use 'thin' clients to invoke the engine and to display the resulting patterns. This approach suffers from two disadvantages; the induction engine would have to be ported to various server platforms, and the processing burden of executing the data mining algorithms is added to servers whose performance is typically optimised for serving queries.

4 The Client-Server Rule Induction Algorithm of XpertRule Profiler

The induction algorithm within XpertRule Profiler differs from other commercially available algorithms in that it supports a two tier client-server architecture. The entropies and Chi Squared tests required by the tree induction algorithm are calculated from the results of intelligent queries submitted by Profiler to the database server. Profiler is a Windows (3.1, 95 and NT) based client which uses ODBC to connect to database servers. The advantages of this approach are:

- Portability : Any database server can be mined provided an appropriate ODBC driver is available
- Scaleability : Since the algorithm relies on database queries and not on loading the data table into the client, there is no practical limit on the size of the database table, on the server, that can be mined using rule induction.
- Performance : The calculations of entropies and Chi Squared tests are carried out by the clients and represent an insignificant percentage of the total induction time. The performance of the algorithm is

determined mainly by the speed of the database server. Thus the algorithm can effectively exploits the advantages offered by Massive Parallel Processing and parallel database architectures.

5 CRITIKAL : Advancing the Client-Server Rule Induction Technology

Whilst Attar Software's 2-tier client-server induction technology has many advantages over client based and server based induction technologies, its applicability in large corporate data warehousing environments has the following limitations :

- The 2-tier architecture provides only limited scope for the optimisation of the intelligent queries generated by the client tree builder because the client has no way of acquiring performance information from query execution and therefore cannot exploit specific database features.
- The present ODBC-based implementation of the client-server connectivity provides no support for multiple concurrent query streams, and therefore is unable to exploit the benefits offered by parallel query streams.
- The 2-tier architecture can not exploit the performance improvements resulting from the effective management of multiple concurrent users (clients) in a corporate data mining environment.

The CRITIKAL project will address the technological issues described above using a 3-tier implementation of Attar's Profiler rule-induction system capable of flexibly addressing the data mining needs of large corporate users (figure 3).

CRITIKAL will also involve the development of additional end-user inspired functionalities into XpertRule Profiler. The technological results of the CRITIKAL project will be proven prototypes of:

- The 3-tier architecture which will flexibly support a variety of client-server processing models to enable user organisations to implement the technology in a way which best suits their specific user load profiles and IT infrastructure. The Tree-node Evaluation server DLL translates query requirements from the tree induction algorithms relating to a tree node into SQL statements to submit to the database server.
- Query optimisation methodologies and software to improve the response times of queries issued against parallel RDBMSs by the client tree builder.
- Prototypes of tree-node evaluation servers for Teradata and Oracle enabling the generated SQL to exploit the specific performance features of these RDBMSs.
- a software framework enabling the specification of virtual (composite) fields and their use in the induction of decision trees.
- a software framework for the application of rule induction to time series transactional data.
- a software framework for the application of association rules discovery to transactional data.
- software modules enabling the generation of the profiles resulting from rule-induction as SQL to enable their re-use for further filtering of the database, and as OLE2 objects and Windows meta files to enable their re-use by other client desktop packages.

6 References

[1] Kass, G. V. (1980), An Exploratory Technique for Investigating Large Quantities of Categorical Data. Applied Statistics, 29, No. 2 pp 199-127.

[2] Quinlan, J. R. (1986) Induction of Decision Trees, Machine Learning 1.

[3] Quinlan, J. R. (1987) Simplifying Decision Trees, International Journal of Machine Studies, 27.

[4] Attar Software Ltd (1996) XpertRule Profiler User & Reference Manual

[5] Michie, D. , Al-Attar, A. (1991) Use of Sequential Bayes with Class Probability Trees, Machine Intelligence 12, Clarendon Press Oxford 1991.

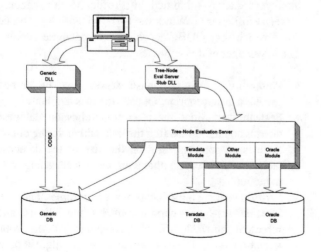

Figure 3 : The 3-tier rule induction architecture of CRITIKAL

The DBInspector Project

Paolo Stofella
Artificial Intelligence Software S.p.A.
Via Esterle, 9 - 20132 Milano, Italy
E-mail: paolos@ais.it

Abstract

This paper provides an overview of the DBInspector Esprit project, part of the HPCN PCI/Capri initiative. The project focused on the employment of High Performance Database and 3D Data Visualisation technologies for the construction of a data mining environment to be employed in the anti money laundering activities performed by the Ufficio Italiano dei Cambi (UIC). UIC, part of the Italian central bank, is in charge of the analysis of the Financial Flows Archive, a centralised database holding information on the transactions of the entire Italian financial system.

1. Introduction

The advent of scaleable open systems running merchant Relational Database Management Systems (RDBMS) has made enormous data processing power available at a fraction of the cost of conventional technology. However, the transfer of existing databases and applications from conventional systems to parallel ones, and the performance evaluation and tuning of these new high performance database systems are non-trivial.

The DBInspector project centres on the use of High Performance Computing (HPC) technology in the implementation of an advanced software environment (DBInspector) for the interrogation and analysis of large-scale databases. This involves the transfer of two significant databases from conventional systems to parallel ones, an investigation into performance optimisation and tuning techniques on the new systems, and implementation of the DBInspector environment as the first step in work that will provide a basis for the introduction of High Performance Computing and Networking (HPCN) into the government, financial, and industrial organisations that maintain and manage large databases.

DBInspector is an open environment for the analysis and inspection of large databases on HPC systems. The example application chosen for this project is to use DBInspector as the basic operational tool in research into, and detection of, money laundering related anomalies in the Ufficio Italiano dei Cambi (UIC) Financial Flows database. This Analysis and Inspection Environment provides a basic infrastructure for the integration of existing tools, as well as new development.

Application specific activities concentrated on the following: investigation into techniques for transfer of data to HPC database systems; evaluating and optimising the performance of HPC database systems; the production of a set of queries implementing known money laundering detection criteria applied to the UIC Financial Flows database; and the application of neural pattern recognition technology to the automatic detection of anomalies on the UIC Financial Flows database.

The consortium is lead by UIC, the central Italian organisation in charge of the management of the Financial Flows database for money laundering detection. The Catholic University of Milan is associated to UIC. Artificial Intelligence Software (AIS) a leading Italian company in the introduction of advanced IT technologies in the financial market, lead the technological development, in association with the Parallel Applications Centre, Southampton UK (Parallel Databases) and the University of Trento (Object Orientated Embedding).

AIS derived from the project work a commercial Visual Data Mining and Knowledge Discovery tool named VisualMine.

2. Project Achievements

Until recently hardware technology has not been capable of delivering the performance required to support the mixed transaction processing loads required to allow real-time analysis and inspection of large and complex databases.

HPC, specifically database servers based on parallel technology, has allowed the possibility of real time inspection and analysis of large scale relational data stores. This has not been possible in the past because of the lack of performance of available technology.

This project centred on the use of parallel technology in the implementation of an advanced software environment for the interrogation and analysis of large-scale databases. This involved the transfer of two significant databases (billions of records) from conventional systems to parallel ones, an investigation into performance optimisation and tuning techniques on the new systems, and the implementation of the DBInspector environment as the first step in work that will provide a basis for the introduction of High Performance Computing and Networking (HPCN) into the government, financial, and industrial organisations that maintain and manage large databases.

The DBInspector environment is a modular system based on the use of HPC Database systems and two key software technologies: Object Orientated Embedding, and Data Visualisation. An operating environment has been constructed, independently of any specific information processing technique, to assist the user in building and using specific agents operating on the database. The construction of this independent software layer provides fundamental support for the analysis and inspection of the UIC archives.

A data transformation tool, named TCF (Transformation Control Format), has been constructed in order to perform data preparation, extracting raw data from the database and aggregating them into matrix structures. This tool automatically generates SQL code to perform the transformations, on the basis of specifications defined interactively by the user. The generated code is optimised for the underlying parallel database architecture.

The Visualisation Environment allows the user to interactively and dynamically map large amounts of data on a set of 3D viewers. More than 15 different viewers have been constructed, ranging from simple 2-3D charts, to geographical mappings, to advanced 3D scattered data visualisation. This environment, currently in routine use

at the UIC Anti-money laundering Department, allows the user to interactively manipulate and visualise data, understanding the relationship between variables and graphically emphasising anomalies.

The combination of High Performance Databases, Agent based data extraction and transformation, and advanced 3D visualisation results in an efficient and effective approach to Data Mining and Knowledge Discovery. After a few months of routinely use at UIC, this High Performance interactive approach has confirmed its ability to emphasise anomalies, providing confirmation of existing suspect situations, as well as discovery of new cases. With respect to the classical statistical multivariate analysis employed for the detection of anomalies, this method provides a significant advantage in terms of the required time and resources. The software environment developed in the project became a commercial product, VisualMine, commercialised by Artificial Intelligence Software.

3. The DBInspector Architecture

The DBInspector software environment is an integrated and open set of tools for the analysis and inspection of large databases. The following figure outlines the main software modules and their internal and external interactions.

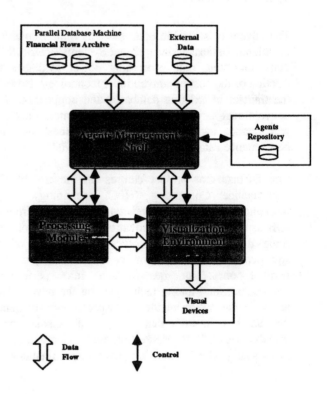

The environment allow users to interact with different data sources (relational databases, as well as formatted files), to load, to process and to visualise data flows.

3.1 Agents Management Shell

The Agents Management Shell (AMS) is responsible for the management of data extraction Agents. The AMS module enables the integration of different agent types, allowing the system to expand in the future. Support for the interactive building and execution of SQL queries and for file based I/O will be developed within the DBInspector project.

The AMS organises also an Agents Repository, where the data extraction agents are being archived for subsequent retrieval. Data flows loaded by means of the AMS tools are then exported to the processing and visualisation modules included in the Visualisation Environment. The AMS is integrated with the Visualisation Environment also by means of Control information, in order to support flexible interactions.

3.2 Processing Module

The Processing Module provides a set of mathematical and statistical functions for data preparation and pre-processing.

Statistical functions are primarily supporting time series analysis and multivariate analysis. They contribute to build graphical emphasis on information patterns (in particular, anomalous patterns) and multiple variables correlations.

Simple and joined frequency distributions are computed in order to segment and classify data, as well as to understand variable dependencies. Various *filters (such as smoothing, thresholding, data aggregations)* are provided to obtain significant visual representations, eliminating data inhomogeneities.

Interpolation functions are employed to emphasise data clusters. Visual clustering is also obtained by applying isolines, isosurfaces, isovolumes and orthogonal cutting planes.

3.3 Visualisation Module

Composed by a set of specific three dimensional viewers, the Visualisation Module allows to interactively build visual data representations. A simple interaction provides a flexible way to obtain different representations, by interactively mapping data columns onto graphical entities, such as axes, colours or geographic areas.

Three main viewers sets are available within the Visualisation Module:

- traditional 2D Business Charts
- 3D business viewers
- geographic 3D viewers

A full set of traditional charts is available for the analysis of limited amounts of information. Usually these charts are employed when drilling down to a detailed level, after having analysed large datasets using more advanced 3D representations.

The VisualMine charts library includes 2D scatter, lines, bars, pies and areas graphs.

3D visualisations in VisualMine have been developed to support multivariate analysis, cluster analysis, pattern identification and, through the animation available on any variable, dynamic analysis.

As an example, the 3D scattered representation enables the contemporary visualisation of up to twenty variables. Through the employment of colour, object dimensions and other graphical artefacts, it emphasises relationships between variables, clusters, and anomalies. The animations support the dynamic analysis related to time variables, as well as the visualisation of what-if simulations.

Cutting planes, isolines and isosurfaces allow to enrich the visualisation with new detailed or structured information.

When a geographic reference exist in the data, a visual analysis of them can be useful in order to understand the underlying phenomena. VisualMine supports the traditional thematic mapping technology, as well as specialised visualisations, such as those employed to represent financial flows. As usual, animations are supported for all the representations, on any variable.

4. Acknowledgements

The author would like to thank all the colleagues involved in the DBInspector Project from UIC, AIS, the Parallel Applications Centre, the Trento University and the Catholic University of Milan.

WIDE - A Distributed Architecture for Workflow Management

Stefano Ceri
Politecnico di Milano
Italy

ceri@elet.polimi.it

Paul Grefen
University of Twente
The Netherlands

grefen@cs.utwente.nl

Gabriel Sánchez
Sema Group sae
Spain

gsg@sema.es

Abstract

This paper presents the distributed architecture of the WIDE workflow management system. We show how distribution and scalability are obtained by the use of a distributed object model, a client/server architecture, and a distributed workflow server architecture. Specific attention is paid to the extended transaction support and active rule support subarchitectures.

1. Introduction to WIDE

Workflow management is currently considered a major application domain for information technology. To provide reliable data processing in workflow applications, database systems have become important as the basis for workflow management systems.

In the WIDE project, extended database technology is developed to serve as the basis for a commercial next-generation workflow management system. In WIDE, extending database technology focuses on extended transaction management and active rule support. Extended transaction management provides flexible and reliable workflow process semantics, active rule support provides reactive behavior to cope with workflow events. These advanced features are reflected in a rich workflow model [CG96] and specification language [CV96]. Design support is developed in WIDE to enable workflow application designers to effectively use these features.

WIDE (Workflow on Intelligent Distributed database Environment) is an ESPRIT project, the main contractor and industrial partner of which is Sema Group, a major European software firm. Politecnico di Milano and University of Twente are the academic partners. ING Bank, a major Dutch bank, and Hospital General de Manresa, a mid-sized Spanish hospital, are the end-user partners in the consortium.

For reasons of brevity, this paper concentrates on database technology aspects of WIDE. The organization of this short paper is as follows. Section 2 presents the overall WIDE architecture. Section 3 shows how distribution is handled in this architecture. Sections 4 and 5 discuss extended transaction management and active rule processing in the WIDE architecture. We end the paper with conclusions and a few words on future work.

2. The WIDE architecture

The WIDE architecture is designed to support next-generation workflow management functionality in a distributed environment. The architecture is based on a commercial database management system as implementation platform and extends this system with extended transaction management and active rule support. The design of the architecture is ruled by three major design decisions:

- the database management functionality should be orthogonal to the workflow management functionality,

- the transaction support functionality should be orthogonal to the rule support functionality,

- both extended database functionality and workflow management functionality should be independent from the underlying database management system.

The resulting architecture of the WIDE workflow management system is shown in Figure 1. The lowest layer of the architecture is formed by the commercial database management system (DBMS). In the project context, Oracle has been chosen as database platform. The DBMS layer is shielded from the upper layers by means of the basic access layer (BAL). The BAL provides an object-oriented database access interface to its clients and maps this to the relational interface of the DBMS to obtain data persistence. The mapping logic is generated by a translator that translates object-oriented data specifications into relational database manipulation operations.

Above the BAL, the server layer is located. In this layer, the database functionality of the DBMS is extended by a transaction support module and an active rule sup-

76

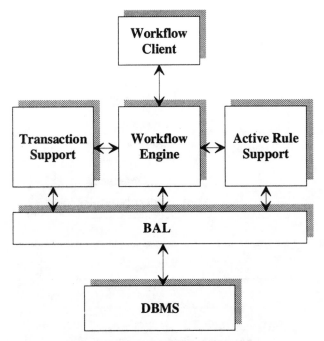

Figure 1: Global WIDE architecture

port module. These two modules are fully orthogonal and are discussed in more detail in Sections 4 and 5. Also located in the server layer, the workflow engine provides the 'heart' of the workflow management system. It uses the BAL for database access, the transaction support module to provide advanced transactional contexts for its operation, and the active rule support module to handle reactive workflow behavior.

Finally, in the client layer of the architecture, the workflow client module provides the interactive interface to the end-users of the workflow system. It communicates only with the workflow engine.

3. Distribution in WIDE

A major aspect of the WIDE architecture is distribution. Distribution is a main issue because of two reasons: workflow management is a distributed application by nature, and distribution opens the way to scalability of the architecture. Distribution is obtained in three different ways: a distributed object model, a client/server database architecture, and a distributed server architecture.

The distributed object model in WIDE is used to create workflow server modules and data objects that can transparently be accessed by multiple processes. These processes may be running on the same machine or on different machines in a network. The object model used conforms to the CORBA standard [OM95, Sie96]. The CORBA interface definition language (IDL) is used to describe the interfaces of the distributed objects. To obtain

the mapping logic of the BAL (as discussed in Section 2), an IDL-to-SQL translator has been constructed.

The distributed object model allows for flexible clustering of functionality into processes and flexible allocation of processes to machines. An example is the management of case objects, the objects that contain the data of workflow cases (work items). These case objects can all be managed by one process, or they can be distributed among several processes to distribute the work load. Clearly, the object model provides a powerful means to achieve scalability in the architecture.

In the WIDE architecture, a client/server interface is used between the BAL and the DBMS (see Figure 1). This client/server architecture allows flexible allocation of the low-level database processes and the client processes that use these (located in the workflow engine, the transaction support module, and the active rule support module). In the configuration with Oracle as database platform, the Oracle Call Interface (OCI) has been chosen to realize the interface (see e.g. [Mc96]).

A WIDE workflow management infrastructure can consist of a hierarchy of workflow engines. In such a hierarchy, each engine is associated with a workflow domain. The hierarchy of workflow domains can be derived from the organizational structure in which the workflow is implemented, or from the 'geographical' structure of the organization. The decomposition of a workflow system into a hierarchy of workflow engines provides a means to obtain scalability of workflow applications for large organizations.

4. Transactions in WIDE

Workflow processes usually can be hierarchically decomposed into subprocesses down to the level of individual tasks. In the higher levels of the process hierarchy, process semantics are usually different from those in the lower levels of the hierarchy. For this reason, we have adopted a two-layer transaction model in WIDE [GV96]. The upper layer provides global transactions with 'loose' semantics and is based on concepts from the saga transaction model [GS87]. The lower layer provides local transactions with more 'strict' transactional semantics and is based on the nested transaction model (see e.g. [DH91]). The overall model is constructed such, that the two layers are completely orthogonal.

Given the orthogonal two-layer model, the extended transaction support module in the WIDE architecture consists of two orthogonal submodules supporting global transactions respectively local transactions (see Figure 2).

Global transaction support is provided by the global transaction manager (GTM) process. The GTM manipulates global transaction (GT) objects. Both GTM and GT are CORBA objects, such that they can be accessed trans-

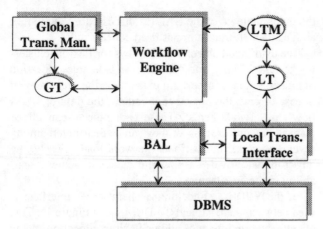

Figure 2: Transaction management architecture

parently from other processes. From a functional point of view, this means that one GTM process can serve multiple workflow engine processes. Global transaction support is completely independent from the underlying database platform.

Local transaction support is provided in two layers. The upper layer consists of the local transaction manager (LTM), which manipulates local transaction (LT) objects. The LTM can be seen as a transaction adapter [BP95]. The upper layer is independent from the underlying database management system, as it only assumes support for a standard 'flat' transaction model and uses logical transaction identifiers and operations. The lower layer of local transaction support consists of the local transaction interface (LTI), which maps logical transaction operations to physical transaction operations and logical transaction identifiers to physical transaction channels. With Oracle as database platform, the Oracle Call Interface (OCI) is used to realize the LTI-DBMS interface. OCI allows multiple concurrent transactions from one client using logon and cursor data areas [Mc96]. As the LTI addresses the DBMS directly, it can be considered part of the BAL layer in the layered architecture shown in Figure 1.

Further details on transaction management in WIDE can be found in [GV96].

5. Active rules in WIDE

Support of reactive behavior is of great importance in workflow management applications, e.g. to support exception handling. A convenient way to model reactive behavior is the use of active rules, i.e. event-condition-action (ECA) rules as they can be found in active database systems [WC96].

In the WIDE conceptual model, we distinguish four event classes: data events, external events, workflow events, and time events [CC96]. Data events are modifications to the workflow data, and can thus be considered

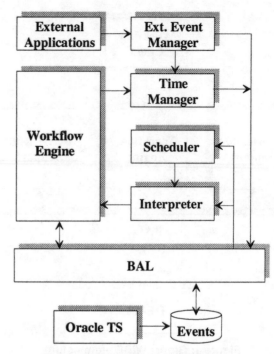

Figure 3: Rule support architecture

workflow process events. External events are raised by external applications used in the workflow context. Workflow events describe the workflow evolution, e.g., starts and ends of workflow tasks. Time events are related to absolute or relative time points in the execution of a workflow.

A decoupled rule execution model has been chosen in WIDE that is orthogonal to the transaction model. Detection of events and execution of rules are performed in a decoupled fashion, i.e. in the context of different local transactions provided by the LTI. This allows for flexible rule handling without too strict execution dependencies, as required in a workflow context.

A slightly simplified architecture of the active rule support module is shown in Figure 3. Event detection is performed by three different modules that record events in the events database (shown as Events in the figure). Data events are captured by low-level triggers that are installed in the database management system (Oracle TS). These triggers react on modifications to the workflow data relations and insert events into the events database. External events are captured by the external event manager. Time events are captured by the time manager, which is also used to generate timestamps for external and workflow events. Both external event manager and time manager insert event records into the events database using the BAL.

Rule execution is divided into scheduling and interpretation of rules. The scheduler inspects the events database (using the BAL) and matches the recorded events to rules. Selected rules are recorded in a to-execute list. This list is next emptied by invoking, for each rule, the rule interpreter. The interpreter is responsible for the evaluation of the condition of a rule and the execution of its action.

To enable distributed access, some submodules of the rule support subsystem are realized as CORBA objects. Further information on the WIDE rule system can be found in [CC96].

6. Conclusions

In this short paper, we have given an overview of the WIDE architecture. The aim has been to show how workflow management, extended transaction support, and active rule support have been combined in an orthogonal fashion that provides ample opportunities for distribution and scalability.

In the future course of the WIDE project, we will test the architecture at the end-user sites in the context of insurance and health care workflow applications. Also, we will further elaborate the transaction and rule model to provide fine-tuned support for diverse application contexts.

Acknowledgments

All members of the WIDE project are acknowledged for their contributions to the architecture described in this paper.

References

[BP95]   R. Barga, C. Pu; *A Practical and Modular Method to Implement Extended Transaction Models*; Procs. 21st Int. Conf. on Very Large Data Bases; Zurich, Switzerland, 1995.

[CC96]   F. Casati, S. Ceri, B. Pernici, G. Pozzi; *Deriving Active Rules for Workflow Enactment*; Int. Conf. on Database and Expert System Applications; Zürich, Switzerland, 1996.

[CG96]   F. Casati, P. Grefen, B. Pernici, G. Pozzi, G. Sánchez; *WIDE: Workflow Model and Architecture*; CTIT Technical Report 96-19; University of Twente, 1996.

[CV96]   D. Chan, J. Vonk, G. Sánchez, P. Grefen, P. Apers; *A Conceptual Workflow Specification Language*; CTIT Technical Report 96-47; Submitted for Publication; University of Twente, 1996.

[DH91]   U. Dayal, M. Hsu, R. Ladin; *A Transactional Model for Long-Running Activities*; Procs. 17th Int. Conf. on Very Large Databases; Barcelona, Spain, 1991.

[GS87]   H. Garcia-Molina, K. Salem; *Sagas*; Procs. 1987 ACM SIGMOD Int. Conf. on Management of Data; USA, 1987.

[GV96]   P. Grefen, J. Vonk, E. Boertjes, P. Apers; *Two-Layer Transaction Management for Workflow Management Applications*; In Preparation; University of Twente, 1997.

[Mc96]   D. McClanahan; *Oracle Developer's Guide*; Osborne McGraw-Hill; Berkely, USA, 1996.

[OM95]   Object Management Group; *The Common Object Request Broker: Architecture and Specification, Version 2.0*; Object Management Group, 1995.

[Sie96]   J. Siegel; *CORBA Fundamentals and Programming*; Wiley & Sons; New York, USA, 1996.

[WC96]   J. Widom, S. Ceri; *Active Database Systems: Triggers and Rules for Advanced Data Processing*; Morgan Kaufmann; San Mateo, USA, 1996.

SESSION :4

---◆---

ELECTRONIC COMMERCE AND WORKFLOW MANAGEMENT

Distributed Data Management in Workflow Environments

Gustavo Alonso
Institute of Information Systems
ETH Zentrum (IFW C 47.2)
CH-8092 Zürich, Switzerland
alonso@inf.ethz.ch

Berthold Reinwald
IBM Almaden Research Center
650 Harry Road (K55/B1)
San Jose, CA 95120-6099, USA
reinwald@almaden.ibm.com

C. Mohan
IBM Almaden Research Center
650 Harry Road (K55/B1)
San Jose, CA 95120-6099, USA
mohan@almaden.ibm.com

Abstract

Most existing workflow management systems (WFMSs) are based on a client/server architecture. This architecture simplifies the overall design but it does not match the distributed nature of workflow applications and imposes severe limitations in terms of scalability and reliability. Moreover, workflow engines are not very sophisticated in terms of data management, forgetting the fact that workflow is, to a great extent, data flow. In this paper, we propose a novel architecture to address the issue of data management in a WFMS. This architecture is based on a fully distributed workflow engine for control flow, plus a set of loosely synchronized replicated databases for data flow. The resulting system offers greater robustness and reliability as well as much better data handling capabilities than existing approaches. To better illustrate this novel architecture and its implications, two commercial systems are employed in this paper: Flow-Mark, as the workflow engine, and the replication capabilities of Lotus Notes, as the support system for distributed data management.

1 Introduction

Workflow Management Systems, WFMSs, are the first viable proposal to effectively coordinate multiple, heterogeneous information resources and monitor the overall progress in the execution of a business process. Precisely because of the emphasis on monitoring, most existing WFMSs tend to be based on a client/server architecture with a centralized repository. In practice, however, this

approach is inefficient and introduces severe limitations in terms of robustness, reliability, and scalability. Similarly, since the execution of a business process is usually based on a process model describing the control flow between workflow participants, many workflow engines have concentrated only on implementing the control flow, neglecting the data flow aspects. FlowMark [14], for instance, is one of the few workflow products that provides some built-in capabilities for passing data among activities. However, the *data repository* is intended only for storing control data, i.e., application data employed to evaluate the transition conditions governing the control flow. Users, however, lacking a good underlying data management system, opt for storing all the application data in those repositories, which often results in serious performance and scalability problems.

To address both issues, centralization and the lack of suitable data management capabilities, a different architecture is required. Preliminary steps in this direction were taken by the proposals in INCAS [2] and Exotica/FMQM [1] but without regard for the data management problem. In this paper, we address this limitation by extending the architecture of Exotica/FMQM to incorporate data management capabilities. The approach taken is to base the data handling mechanisms on a set of loosely synchronized replicated databases. These replicated databases are used as the common distributed repository for all the sites participating in the execution of a business process. The advantage of this approach is that the burden of data handling is no longer on the workflow engine, thereby augmenting its capacity as a coordination tool, and that the data manager can support additional functionality that would be very difficult to incorporate into a workflow engine.

In terms of a practical implementation, we have resorted

to existing commercial systems. The functionality these systems provide is fairly common and found in a variety of products, thereby guaranteeing that the results proposed can be also achieved on designs based on different components. The distributed environment is provided by Exotica/FMQM (FlowMark on Message Queue Manager) which offers FlowMark functionality modified to work in a set of autonomous servers that cooperate to complete the execution of a process. Persistent messaging is implemented using MQSeries [3, 21]. The data management functionality is based on Lotus Notes Release 4, a document store which supports replication [12, 15, 16]. Lotus Notes has been chosen as the data manager because it provides a sophisticated document management architecture as well as a powerful replication mechanism. Technical details aside, the contribution of the paper is twofold. First, the problem addressed, although very common in distributed workflow environments, has been largely ignored in the research literature. To our knowledge this is the first attempt to formalize the coupling of a workflow management system and corresponding data handling capabilities. Second, and to the extent allowed by the space provided, the paper provides an overview of how issues such as scalability and performance are being addressed in practice in large corporations.

The paper is organized as follows: in the next section, an example application is discussed to motivate the rest of the paper. Section 3 briefly describes Exotica/FMQM. Section 4 describes in more detail the role of the data manager in a workflow system and its functionality in terms of document replication. Section 5 presents the overall architecture incorporating the distributed WFMS and the data manager. Section 6 points out some limitations and open problems in the approach presented. Section 7 discusses related work and Section 8 concludes the paper.

2 Motivation and Example

As an example of the problems addressed in the paper, consider the following business process. The process is a rough approximation of the procedures followed during the processing of an application for an international patent. A patent application is a complex document encompassing a great deal of legal and technical information. Upon submission, the first step is to ensure that all the necessary documentation has been provided. Once the application has been found to be complete, it is assigned to a particular area (software, mechanical engineering, chemistry, electronics, and so forth). Then the claim is forwarded to special department in which the patent is examined and any relevant literature (books, articles, journal or conference papers, technical reports) as well as existing related patents are added to the application as part of the overall case. Once this search is completed, the application plus the added documentation

are sent for evaluation. The evaluation often involves a team of experts that analyzes the application and existing patents (evaluators do not search for relevant documentation, they work with what is provided). Frequently, the applicants are asked for clarifications and rewriting of the application to avoid conflicts with existing patents and laws. This might require several rounds until finally the evaluation team gives a recommendation.

The importance of this example is in its data handling requirements. Each patent application involves a significant number of documents referencing other information sources as well as other patents. Each existing patent is in itself a large collection of documents. Additional information such as articles and scientific papers are smaller in size but can be quite numerous. Besides the application itself, related patents and relevant articles are also part of the necessary documentation. Hence, transferring the "case" from the initial stages to the evaluation stages involves moving a great deal of information around (often from country to country as it is the case with the European Patent Office).

As this examples shows, any attempts to use a workflow system in such an environment will be only as successful as the data management capabilities it provides. In practice, and as proven by many workflow installations, it is the ability to pass data among the participants the main factor determining the applicability of a given WFMS. Most existing commercial workflow engines do not provide any support to deal with data management, although it is obvious that the transferring of the information is an integral part of the workflow process. The best solutions combine an imaging system with the workflow engine but the integration is often poor and the workflow engine has no real control over the flow of data, which complicates the task of adjusting it to the flow of control. In what follows, a distributed architecture is proposed as a first step to integrate the flow of control and data taking advantage of systems that have been optimized for only one of the two tasks. We believe that the result is more flexible and efficient than what has been so far proposed in the literature or implemented in practice.

3 Exotica/FMQM: Distributed Workflow

This section briefly summarizes the distributed architecture of *Exotica/FMQM* - FlowMark on Message Queue Manager. For a more detailed description see [1]. First, the FlowMark model is reviewed, and then we extend the centralized FlowMark design to a distributed architecture. The choice of FlowMark as the base architecture does not result in a loss of generality as FlowMark closely follows the WfMC reference model (Workflow Management Coalition, WfMC [9]).

3.1 Workflow Model

A business process is, in general, an acyclic directed graph in which nodes represent steps of execution and edges represent the flow of control and data. In Flow-Mark [14, 10, 11], the main components of the *workflow model* are: *processes*, *activities*, *control connectors*, *data connectors*, and *conditions*. Activities are the nodes in the process graph and they represent the steps to be completed. Control connectors are used to specify the order of execution between activities and are represented as directed edges in the process graph. Data connectors specify the flow of information from one activity to another in the form of mappings between the data containers of the activities and are also expressed as directed edges in the process graph. Each activity has one *input data container* and one *output data container*. Finally, conditions specify when certain events can happen. There are three types of conditions: *transition conditions* associated with control connectors determine whether the connector evaluates to true or false; *start conditions*, which specify when an activity will be started; and *exit conditions*, which are used to specify when an activity is considered to have terminated.

3.2 A distributed architecture

Exotica/FMQM is a distributed version of FlowMark based on a generic queuing system with recoverable queues. The main idea behind its design is that workflow models are partitioned into execution scripts that are distributed to the nodes where the actual execution of these parts will take place. Note that in workflow systems it is possible to predict much of the execution by analyzing the model and assigning the activities and tasks in advance, so the actual partition of the model is not a complex algorithm. Communication between the different nodes takes place through persistent queues, thereby guaranteeing the atomicity of operations, enhancing the overall reliability, and allowing asynchronous communication between the different components. The overall architecture of Exotica/FMQM is geared towards control flow and there is no significant support for data management, as was pointed out above. This architecture, however, solves many of the problems being encountered by existing workflow products. In particular, it offers better resilience to failures and better scalability than existing configurations. To take advantage of these features, Exotica/FMQM is used as the basic architecture for the system. In what follows, a brief description is provided regarding the most relevant details of its implementation.

Persistent queues guarantee that once a message is placed on a queue and the corresponding transaction is committed, the message becomes persistent until it is retrieved. Messages are added and retrieved from a queue using *PUT* and *GET* calls, which can be issued both on local and remote queues. Using these generic primitives, Exotica/FMQM implements a distributed architecture in which process execution is handled as follows [1]. When a user creates a process, the process is first compiled and then divided into several parts, which are distributed to the appropriate node(s). A node corresponds to a physical machine. It is possible to see this node as a "server" to other nodes in a multilayer architecture, but this is irrelevant for our purposes here. In what follows we will use the term node to refer to a remote location where workflow navigation takes place. Upon receiving its part of the process, a node creates a *process table* to store this information and starts a process thread which handles the execution of instances of that process. The process table must be saved in persistent storage as it describes which actions the node must take at each step in the execution of a process. This table is, in general, an "append only" structure. For efficiency reasons a copy can be kept in main memory. After creating this table, the process thread creates a queue for communicating with other nodes all information relevant to instances of the process. There will be a queue per process type. During execution, the information regarding the process instances will be stored in an *instance table* handled by activity threads. These threads are responsible for the execution of individual activities within an instance and are created when an activity instance becomes ready for execution. All PUT and GET calls to the queue are executed in a transactional manner, i.e., their effects are not permanent until the transaction commits.

When a process instance is started, messages are sent to the nodes where the starting activities are located. This is done by PUTting the messages in the appropriate queues. At each node, the arrival of a message triggers the process thread which will analyze the message, check in the process table for the steps that must be taken and start the appropriate activity threads. Messages are not "retrieved" but "browsed", which is important in case of failures. Browsing leaves the message in the queue, preserving its persistent. Once started by the process thread, the activity thread first checks the process table to find the data pertaining to that activity. With this data, it creates an entry for that activity in the instance table where it will record the progress of the activity. It then checks the start condition of the activity. If it cannot be evaluated, because not all incoming control connectors have been evaluated, it makes a note in the instance table about what control connector has been evaluated and goes to sleep until the process thread awakens it again with new messages. If the start condition is false, then the activity is considered terminated. Dead path elimination messages are sent along the outgoing control connectors using PUT calls to the corresponding queues; upon receiving such messages, the corresponding entries are removed from the instance table and any related messages retrieved from the queue are discarded. All the operations performed upon termination of the activity are one atomic action. This can be accomplished by using the transactional properties of the GET and PUT calls.

If the start condition evaluates to true, then the corresponding application is invoked, passing to it the data in the input template. When the application terminates, the output data returned is stored in the instance table. Then the activity thread evaluates the exit condition of the activity. If it is false, the application is invoked again. If it is true, the activity is considered terminated. Upon successful termination, the outgoing control connectors' transition conditions are evaluated and messages are sent to the appropriate nodes with PUT calls to their queues. The output data is sent to the nodes specified in the process table as outgoing data connectors. Then the entry is removed from the instance table and all messages corresponding to the activity are retrieved from the process queue. Note that each message corresponds to one activity, once the activity successfully terminates there is no need to keep the messages. These operations are performed as an atomic transaction as explained above.

4 Distributed Data Flow

In a distributed environment, application data associated with workflow processes need to "travel" along with the process. However, the application data should not be stored in the workflow management system itself, for reasons of efficiency, and hence a data manager is required. In this section, we describe the relevant aspects of the data flow starting with general document management in Lotus Notes [15, 16] and then describing in some detail its replication capabilities.

4.1 Document and form management

Notes is a document data store with a cross-platform architecture. It has its own specialized storage and indexing subsystem, which is optimized for groupware applications. For our purposes here, a Notes database consists of *documents*, *forms*, and *views*. Documents can be used to store multimedia data types like graphics, voice, attachments, tables, and embedded OLE objects, among others. Forms in Notes include integrated form management capabilities. They are used to create and edit documents. Views in Notes apply selection criteria on the documents in a database, and allow browsing of the documents in a database.

A Notes database contains a set of application documents, and provides functionality to create, list, edit, and delete documents. Each document (basically a record) contains some header information and a set of items. The header information in a document associates the document with a form. This form is used to interpret, display, and edit the document. Many document management systems are tightly coupled with form management systems, as is also the case in Notes. Different documents in the same database can have different sets of items and can be associated with different forms. *Items* in documents are triples consisting of a name, a type, and a data value. This item structure makes documents self-defining. To cross-reference other information sources, doclinks between documents are defined. In the patent example, all application documents will be stored in Notes databases. Each patent application would be a document, *viewable* through different forms (for the person in charge of searching for relevant documentation, for the patent reviewer, for the applicant, for the patent office lawyers, etc.). All references to other documents (like relevant literature or related patents) are stored as doclinks.

4.2 Replication Mechanism

When, as in the patent example, the application runs in a distributed environment and with a significant load, additional mechanisms are needed to provide reasonable performance. If a centralized repository is used, the repository is liable to become a bottleneck and a single point of failure. Alternative solutions include using an imaging system or a distributed database. An imaging system has the problem that documents literally move from one place to the next. This creates very complex problems if a document needs to be used simultaneously at different locations. On the other hand, distributed databases tend to be fairly restrictive. For instance, replication in commercial databases is, in the best cases, limited to primary copy schemas [4], which does not allow to update a document at all locations. To solve this impasse, we propose to use the semantic knowledge embedded in the workflow engine. By exploiting this knowledge, a much "looser" (asynchronous) distributed document management policy can be implemented. For this purpose the replication mechanisms provided in Lotus Notes are used.

Notes' philosophy of replication can be thought of as a lazy exchange of modifications between replicas. Users at different sites can access and modify the same documents in different replicas. Replicas are kept in sync, but only in the course of time. Replicas share a common id, called *replica id*, which is the database id of the original database.[1] Notes allows us to specify the *direction* of replication (uni- or bi-directional), *when* to replicate, and the *contents* of replicas (subset of documents in a database). Replication can occur automatically according to a specified time schedule, or manually through server or client commands. Time scheduled replication is useful for server-to-server replication,

---

[1] The replication id distinguishes a replica from a casual database copy, which has its own different database id.

whereas manually triggered on-demand replication is very appropriate for client/server replication, where the client is a mobile user. Three different types of replicas can be distinguished, depending on the contents of the replica: full replica, partial replica, and replica stub. A *full replica* contains all of a database's documents and design features (such as forms and views), whereas a *partial replica* only contains selected documents specified in a selection criteria.[2] *Replica stubs* contain only the database design but no documents. Replica stubs are only useful to exchange database templates. In addition, Notes Release 4 introduced *field-level replication* which increases the performance of the replication process as only fields that have changed in a document are exchanged when copies are synchronized. As bidirectional replication is supported and concurrent changes are allowed in the replicas, *replication conflicts* can occur. A replication conflict happens when two or more users edit and change the same document in different replicas between replications.[3] Replication conflicts are resolved by determining the document with the most changes as the main document and introducing the other documents as replication conflict documents (responses) to the main document. The replication conflict document can be used to consolidate the different document versions. If a document is edited in one replica and deleted in another, the deletion takes precedence.

Although these concepts are essentially database replication ideas, with a certain choice of the replication parameters the approach can be exploited to implement distributed data flow. This will be illustrated in the next section.

5   Distributed Workflow Data Management

This section describes the overall system combining Exotica/FMQM for control flow and a Lotus Notes-based system for data flow.

5.1   Architecture

The main idea for the integration of the control and data flow consists in establishing the mechanisms necessary to ensure that a message between nodes (on Exotica/FMQM) corresponding to the triggering of an activity also triggers

the underlying data replication mechanisms at the data management level (Lotus Notes). Similar ideas have been introduced in the ActMan approach [23], although on top of a distributed relational database system prototype. The final goal of the approach is that any data required for the execution of the activity will be locally available while still being available at other sites. A *control node* represents the part of the system corresponding to Exotica/FMQM. Hence, it is the part of the system responsible for navigation, persistence of the messages, and interfacing with users and applications. A *data node* is the part of the system corresponding to Notes, i.e., that is in charge of providing access to the data. From an abstract point of view it is easier to treat them as separate entities, but in practice a control node and a data node can reside in the same memory space. Note that it is likely that several control nodes will be working off a single data node. The activities manipulated by the control node do not contain any data per se except a few simple variables (integers, booleans, strings) used to evaluate control flow conditions. Part of these variables will be *references* (documents id's) to data stored in the data node. Thus, control nodes only need to transfer simple variables. These ideas are summarized in Figure 1.

The separation between the control and data nodes presents us with several advantages. First, the data nodes are more likely to be compatible with the existing data management strategies of a company. As a result, the introduction of a workflow management system will not force changes on existing policies. Notes, however, requires the use of its own internal databases. But it must be noted that the data nodes do not need to be solely based on Notes. We have chosen Notes to simplify the explanation and provide details of a particular system. Second, separating the data from the control allows very interesting optimizations and greater flexibility in the handling of complex data. So far, workflow systems have limited themselves to documents but there is no reason to refrain from expanding their capabilities toward multimedia applications. This is only feasible if the control flow is independent of the data which is not the case in most of the existing commercial products. Finally, separating control and data nodes, along with the notion of clusters, allows a much more flexible architecture that will certainly have a significant impact on issues such as scalability, availability and fault tolerance.

5.2   Replication

We have already seen how control flow takes place and how a control node will interact with a data node. It remains to describe how data flow is implemented. In order to do this, it must be first established *when* the data flow should take place. The entire range of possible alternatives can be covered by describing two extreme scenarios: (1)

---

[2] The selection criteria for partial replica are specified in Notes replication formulae. Replication formulae are basically queries in Notes macro language against the database to retrieve the data of interest for replication. *Selective replication* saves local disk space as well as increases the performance of the replication process as only a subset of the data of interest for a site are replicated.

[3] Replication conflicts are comparable to *save conflicts* in Notes. A save conflict happens when two or more users edit the same document in a database on a server at the same time. Notes creates conflict resolution documents to support merging the different versions of a document.

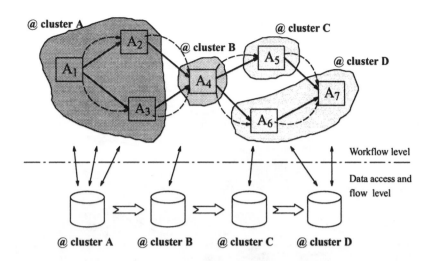

Figure 1. Interaction between a control node and a data node.

data flow takes place simultaneously with the control flow (as a control node sends a message about one activity to a second control node, the corresponding data node forwards the data to the second data node), and (2) data flow happens as soon as the document is accessed on the destination site (that is, the forwarding of the data only takes place upon request). In discussing the two cases, it needs to be kept in mind that an activity becoming ready for execution at a control node does not imply that the activity will be processed right away. Manual activities, for instance, end up in a work list and will not be executed until the user decides to do so, maybe days later. To propagate the data along with the activity is "overprotective" for manual activities. On the other hand, automatic activities (those executed without human intervention) would be unnecessarily delayed if they have to request all the data items one by one. Moreover, the performance of the data system can easily degrade if a series of single documents instead of sets of documents are exchanged between data nodes. These ideas are summarized in Figure 2.

We have opted for an intermediate solution that tries to accommodate the requirements of both types of activities. Since it is known at compile time whether an activity is manual or automatic, when a control node forwards control to another node for an automatic activity, it will also trigger the forwarding of the data. In the case of Notes, this forwarding takes place through replication. When a control node follows a control connector leading to a second control node, it will also prompt the data node to replicate its data at the second data node. We use a manually triggered (by the control node) uni-directional partial replica of the data. The reason for using uni-directional replication is that it matches the way data flows in a workflow environment (from output container to input container). For manual activities, repli-

cation also takes place via a uni-directional partial replica, however the actual transfer can be made manually (if it has not yet taken place at the time the user selects an activity for execution) or automatically as part of *document bundles* exchanged among data servers. The transfer of document bundles is triggered through Notes scheduled agents [15], e.g., once a day. In this way, data exchange can be made more effective by the replication of large amounts of data in one single operation. The size of the data bundles and their frequency are both adjustable parameters of the system. A further advantage of this approach is that if clusters of "equivalent" users exist, as pointed out above, the replication can be delayed until a user selects the activity, thus avoiding sending the data to all the clusters when only one of them will actually use it. To avoid that a user accesses an outdated document during activity execution, we code a timestamp in the work items, when the document on the source site was updated. We compare this timestamp with the timestamp of a possibly existing replica document. If the timestamp are the same, then there is no need for replication. In the other case, we need to replicate the document from the source site before we access it.

What we have presented so far with regard to data replication is fairly generic. The use of Lotus Notes as a concrete data node provides us with additional optimization opportunities. Notes replication, for instance, supports field-level replication which dramatically reduces the amount of data exchanged between node and improves the overall performance. If a user modifies only one field in a 1 Mbyte patent description, Notes transports only the one modified field to all the replicas. In addition, we exploit doclinks supported by Notes in our patent sample application. Patent applications refer to a lot of background information stored in archive databases at remote sites. This information does not

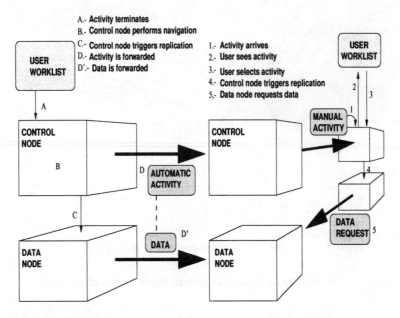

Figure 2. Coordination of distributed workflow and data management.

need to "flow" with the workflow as it is only occasionally accessed on request (following the doclink) by the user. The performance penalty for retrieving this kind of documents from a remote site as opposed to have it locally available is justified by improving the overall workflow performance as less data need to travel with the workflow.

6 Discussion and Future Work

The ideas described above can be divided in two major areas, distributed workflow execution and data management for distributed workflow applications. In both cases, this paper describes a possible architecture based on existing systems but similar ideas can be implemented with other systems. Additionally, in both cases there are a variety of issues that have not been discussed in detail in the paper for reasons of space and not being central to the design. In what follows some of these issues are briefly examined.

There are certain assumptions that must be made when distributing the execution of a workflow system. For instance, the notion of process owner must be changed as there is no centralized entity where the authority of a process owner can be exercised. Similarly, several operations that are trivial in a centralized environment become somewhat complex when implemented in a distributed system. As an example, the problem of detecting process termination could raise some complicated issues similar to those of snapshots and termination detection [5, 19]. To avoid these problems, we assume that each process has a unique starting activity and a unique final activity that can be used to detect where and who starts the process as well as when it completes its execution.

Other interesting aspects of the distributed architecture are the management of work lists and the synchronization problem of ensuring that only one user actually executes an activity, which appears simultaneously on several work lists. In a centralized system, work lists are relatively easy to maintain, and the server handles race conditions so that only the first user performs an activity. These two features are complex to implement in a distributed environment. Our first approach has been to use remote GET calls to allow an activity to appear in several work lists. The first node to GET the message from that queue will be the one to which the activity is assigned. However, today, IBM's MQI does not support remote GET calls and this complicates work list management.

Resilience to failures is ensured by using transactional PUT and GET calls, plus the ability to browse a queue without retrieving messages. When a message is received regarding an activity, it is not retrieved from the queue until the activity has terminated. Messages are kept until they are not needed anymore, and removed from the queue in an atomic operation. In this way, in case of failures which result in the loss of the instance table, a recovering node will restart the process thread which will find the messages still intact in the queue and, based on them, spawn again the appropriate activity threads which will reconstruct the instance table. This is the reason why instance tables do not need to be stored in stable storage and why process tables should be kept in stable storage. For the sake of completeness, it must be mentioned that an audit log is necessary to keep track of which activities have completed execution and to store messages, in case the user decides to restart a finished activity. This audit log can be another queue, checkpointed every so often.

The described distributed data management approach exploiting workflow semantics promises tremendous performance improvements. The document databases are synchronized on a lazy basis depending on the workflow requirements. On the other hand, these databases might be difficult to use for existing non-workflow applications, as, from their perspective, it is not clear how current the data is. This will be a concern in particular, once there are loops in a workflow which result in a loop in the data flow. Problems also arise, once a document is required and updated by different process instances. Although Notes supports the merge of the documents to some extent, but the semantics for the end user might get fuzzy. Services are required, which spread out in a distributed system and find or compose the most current replica of a document in a distributed environment.

7 Related Work

There are many areas that have influenced or are related to workflow management. In Electronic Document Management (EDM), for instance commercial systems like Saros' Document Manager, Intergraph's DM2, Documentum' Documentum Server, IBM's VisualInfo, are concerned with the storage and life cycle of electronic documents. Form management systems can be traced back to early systems like TLA [26] where *form procedures* were proposed to organize the flow of forms. Electronic mail systems like LENS [17] provide means to distribute, forward and track information among individuals. Office automation prototype systems such as SCOOP [28] and DOMINO [13] actively support the automation of office procedures through the exchange of messages and distribution of data. Barbara et al. [2] proposed INCAS for distributed workflow management. In this model, each execution of a process is associated with an *Information Carrier*, which is an object that contains all the necessary information for the execution as well as propagation of the object among the relevant processing nodes. Transaction based applications [25], [18], [24], like the model based on extended nested sagas [8] for coordinating multi-transaction activities, or the Con-Tract model, which provides reliable control flow between transactional activities [27]. In [6] and [7], a specification language and a transactional model for organizing long running activities is developed. Although intended for workflow systems, the primary emphasis is on long running activities in a transactional framework using triggers and nested transactions. The authors present a preliminary design using recoverable queues, which have similar semantics to the message queue interface (MQI) used in this paper.

Most of these early efforts did not address business processes in their full generality, most of them are centralized and fail to address issues such as high availability, failure resilience or scalability. Moreover, they tend to be transactional in nature and too centered around databases, which contrast with the reference model created by the workflow management coalition. For instance, systems like X-Workflow from Olivetti [22], use a central mediator to coordinate the control and data flow of a business process by distributing semi-structured e-mail messages to all users eligible to execute an activity. Once, a user selects an activity, an execution request is sent to the mediator which assigns the activity to the user and sends him/her the context data (input parameters) needed to execute the activity. Also, the mediator informs other users of this fact by sending a message which causes the intelligent mail system to remove the activity from the user's mail folder. This is a highly centralized approach characteristic of most existing commercial systems.

8 Conclusions

This paper has presented an architecture for managing the control and data flow aspects of a workflow system. The main contribution is the combined architecture based on separate systems optimized for different purposes: the workflow engine for the control flow, the data management system for the data flow. We see this architecture as offering significant advantages over existing solutions, as it provides a much better functionality without necessarily penalizing performance. In current commercial workflow systems, data flow is either done externally, with poor coordination and little flexibility, or embedded in the control flow, which has a serious impact on performance. The solution we propose in this paper minimizes the impact on the control flow, i.e. in the workflow engine, while allowing very sophisticated coordination between the activities and the data flow. As part of future work, we plan to enhance the data management features to include complex data types and optimize the data flow in large distributed environments (over WANs instead of over LANs).

Acknowledgments

Many of the ideas described in this paper are the result of the research efforts carried out within the Exotica project (http://www.almaden.ibm.com/cs/exotica/, [20]). We would like to thank Divyakant Agrawal, Amr El Abbadi, Mohan Kamath and Roger Günthör for their help in developing the Exotica/FMQM architecture.

References

[1] G. Alonso, C. Mohan, R. Günthör, D. Agrawal, A. El Abbadi, and M. Kamath. Exotica/FMQM: A Persistent Message-Based Architecture for Distributed Workflow Management. In *IFIP WG8.1 Working Conference on Information System Development for Decentralised Organizations*, pages 1–18, Trondheim, Norway, Aug. 1995. Accessible via http://www.almaden.ibm.com/cs/exotica.

[2] D. Barbara, S. Mehrota, and M. Rusinkiewicz. INCAS: Managing Dynamic Workflows in Distributed Environments. *Journal of Database Management*, 7(1):5–15, Winter 1996.

[3] B. Blakely, H. Harris, and L. J.R.T. *Messaging and Queueing using the MQI: Concepts and Analysis*. McGraw-Hill, 1995.

[4] S. Ceri and G. Pelagatti. *Distributed Databases: Principles and Systems*. McGraw-Hill, 1984.

[5] K. Chandy and L. Lamport. Distributed Snapshots: determining Global States of Distributed Systems. *ACM Transactions on Computer Systems*, 3(1):63–75, Feb. 1985.

[6] U. Dayal, M. Hsu, and R. Ladin. Organizing Long-running Activities with Triggers and Transactions. In *Proceedings of ACM SIGMOD 1990 International Conference on Management of Data*, pages 204–214, June 1990.

[7] U. Dayal, M. Hsu, and R. Ladin. A Transaction Model for Long-running Activities. In *Proceedings of the Sixteenth International Conference on Very Large Databases*, pages 113–122, Aug. 1991.

[8] H. Garcia-Molina, D. Gawlick, J. Klein, K. Kleissner, and K. Salem. Coordinating Multi-transaction Activities. Technical Report CS-TR-247-90, Department of Computer Science, Princeton University, 1990.

[9] D. Hollingsworth. Workflow management coalition: The workflow reference model. Document TC00-1003, Workflow Management Coalition, Dec. 1994. Accessible via http://www.aiai.ed.ac.uk/WfMC/.

[10] IBM. *FlowMark - Managing Your Workflow, Version 2.1*. IBM, Mar. 1995. Document No. SH19-8243-00.

[11] IBM. *FlowMark - Modeling Workflow, Version 2.1*. IBM, mar 1995. Document No. SH19-8241-00.

[12] L. Kawell, S. Beckhardt, T. Halvorsen, R. Ozzie, and I. Greif. Replicated document management in a group communication system. In *Proc. of the Conf. on Computer-Supported Cooperative Work, CSCW (Portland, Oregon)*, 1988.

[13] T. Kreifelts and G. Woetzel. Distribution and Exception Handling in an Office Procedure System. In *Office Systems: Methods and Tools, Proc. IFIP WG 8.4 Work. Conf. on Methods and Tools for Office Systems*, pages 197–208, 1986. October, 22-24, Pisa, Italy.

[14] F. Leymann and W. Altenhuber. Managing Business Processes as an Information Resource. *IBM Systems Journal*, 33(2):326–348, 1994.

[15] Lotus Notes, Cambridge, MA. *Lotus Notes Release 4 Application Developer's Guide*, 1995.

[16] Lotus Notes, Cambridge, MA. *Lotus Notes Release 4 Database Manager's Guide*, 1995.

[17] T. Malone, K. Grant, K. Lai, R. Rao, and D. Rosenblitt. Semistructured Messages Are Surprisingly Useful for Computer-Supported Coordination. *ACM Transactions on Office Information Systems*, 5(2):115–131, 1987.

[18] D. McCarthy and S. Sarin. Workflow and Transactions in InConcert. *Bulletin of the Technical Committee on Data Engineering*, 16(2), June 1993. IEEE Computer Society.

[19] J. Misra. Detecting termination of distributed Computations Using Markers. In *ACM Proceedings of the Symposium on Principles od Distributed Computing*, pages 290–294, 1983.

[20] C. Mohan, G. Alonso, R. Günthör, M. Kamath, and B. Reinwald. An Overview of the Exotica Research Project on Workflow Management Systems. In *Proc. of the Sixth International High Performance Transaction Systems Workshop (HPTS)*, Asilomar, CA, 1995. Accessible via http://www.almaden.ibm.com/cs/exotica.

[21] C. Mohan and R. Dievendorff. Recent Work on Distributed Commit Protocols, and Recoverable Messaging and Queuing. *Bulletin of the Technical Committee on Data Engineering*, 17(1):22–28, Mar. 1994. IEEE Computer Society.

[22] Olivetti Systems & Networks GmbH. *Ibisys X_Workflow-Vorgangssteuerung auf der Basis von X.400*, 1994. Produktbeschreibung.

[23] B. Reinwald and H. Wedekind. Automation of Control and Data flow in Distributed Application Systems. In *Database and Expert Systems Applications (DEXA), Proc. of the Int. Conf. in Valencia, Spain*, pages 475–481, Berlin, 1992. Springer-Verlag.

[24] A. Sheth. On Multi-system Applications and Transactional Workflows, Bellcore's projects PROMP and METEOR, 1994. Collection of papers and reports from Bellcore.

[25] C. Tomlison, P. Attie, P. Cannata, G. Meredith, A. Sheth, M. Singh, and D. Woelk. Workflow Support in Carnot. *Bulletin of the Technical Committee on Data Engineering*, 16(2), June 1993. IEEE Computer Society.

[26] D. Tsichritzis. Form Management. *Communications of the ACM*, 25(7):453–478, July 1982.

[27] H. Waechter and A. Reuter. The ConTract Model. In A. Elmagarmid, editor, *Database Transaction Models for Advanced Applications*, chapter 7, pages 219–263. Morgan Kaufmann Publishers, San Mateo, 1992.

[28] M. Zisman. Representation, specification, and automation of office procedures. Ph.d. thesis, University of Pennsylvania, 1977.

Brokerage Architecture for Stock Photo Industry

Wen-Syan Li   Yoshi Hara   Nancy Fix   Selçuk Candan   Kyoji Hirata   Sougata Mukherjea

C&C Research Laboratories, Multimedia Software Department
NEC USA, Inc., 110 Rio Robles, San Jose, CA 95134
Email: {wen,hara,fix,candan,hirata,sougata}@ccrl.sj.nec.com

Abstract

The Internet has grown to become a major component of the global world-wide network infrastructure, linking millions of users. We first address the need for an electronic market and match-making between consumers and providers on the Internet for the stock photo industry. We discuss business issues and highlight technologies required to support an electronic market for image exchanges on the global Internet, including multimedia databases, visual query interfaces, visualization tools, and watermarking techniques. Finally, we summarize the operational flows and brokerage services provided by the brokerage system.

1   Introduction

As a result of the U.S. government initiative to support the development of an enhanced information infrastructure and rapid advances in computer and communication technologies, we expect a global information system based on the WWW in the near future. In 1995, the Internet reached 148 out of 185 United Nations member countries (86%) compared with 73 out of 159 (46%) in 1991[2]. The number of users and computers is also increasing at a rapid pace, with an annual growth rate of 50%[2]. The combination of computing and communication has rapidly changed our vision of the scope of information systems. With more information, faster communication, world-wide connectivity, many business operations are transforming to take advantages of available technologies.

Information resources and services can be vertically partitioned into three layers: customers, intermediate knowledge-based-modules, and base resources. With access to fast growing information available on the Internet, information providers need modules providing mediation services, such as facilitators, information retrieval, resource allocation, and match makers are needed to avoid data overload and information starvation. We view many of these mediation functionalities as *brokerage* services that provide value-added services to the information. A 1996 survey conducted by Dataquest[3] suggests that 62% of Internet service providers feel that their value-added services differentiate themselves in the Internet business market. With lower usage fee[1] and wide variety of services, the growth rate of on-line service market has exploded in the past few years. This phenomena can be supported by the fact that the number of WEB server computers installed increased worldwide 400% from 1995 to 1996[6]. Many new issues involving electronic commerce and providing brokerage services on the Internet have been raised[11]. Some of the new issues include new ways of payment and fund transfer[12] and publishing models for Internet commerce[13].

Photography, similar to almost every other profession, is undergoing a transition to take advantage of new technologies. Today there are over 1000 agencies in the US; some of the largest stock agencies mange over 10 million images in a variety of media. In the stock photo industry, business is still primarily conducted in the traditional way - browsing through catalogs and face-to-face negotiation and of the largest twenty stock photo agencies in the U.S., only two advertise on the WWW and offer on-line services, registration and photo searching functions as of April, 1996. As a result, stock photo agencies can only reach a small group of customers and customers can only search through a small set of images since no efficient method exists.

This reluctance to on-line full exposure stems from doubts about the efficacy of selling images on-line and concerns about image protection and value. Another factor which plays in the decision of whether to advertise images electronically is the costs of digitizing. With current technology, it costs from $2 to $4 to dig-

---

[1]One survey in 1996 by Dataquest[3] pointed out that the average monthly rate for individual Internet users with 51 to 100 hour usage per month is $0.35 per hour.

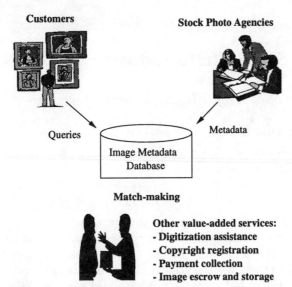

Figure 1: Match-making and Other Functionalities Provided by the Brokerage System

itize images (the cost is dropping). Although it is recognized that digitized images have advantages of image preservation and inspire many new business models and market opportunities, most images are still stored in the format of film. This makes it more difficult to search and market the images to the global electronic market. The other issue is lack of effective visual query interfaces. Because images are semantics richer than textual data, the keyword-based search methods usually yield a low precision.

Many industries recognize phenomenal growth of the Internet and its connectivity to market products to the global market. One example is education brokerages[4] that allow exchanges of pre-designed courses in the electronic format on the Internet and provide many value-added services, such as copyright protection, certification, etc. This paper focuses on information brokerage especially for the stock photo industry. In current stock photo industry, each individual information provider (e.g. photographers and artists) only have small number of images (compared to the total number of images available). It is not cost efficient for these photographers to promote, advertise, register copyrights, and collect usage fees by themselves, As an information consumer (e.g. publisher or stock photo agency), he/she may search a large collection of images and deal directly with many photographers. It is tedious, time consuming, and cost-inefficient to negotiate with each individual photographer. Although today some of the largest stock agencies manage over 10 million images in a variety of media, search and retrieval of images still rely on browsing through catalogs. We argue that there is a

need for a brokerage architecture to provide an electronic market place for images.

The brokerage system is a match-maker in the sense that it receives information consumers' queries and searches the image database to match consumers' query specifications. It provides the information consumers candidate images to select from. For information providers, the brokerage system collect the metadata and store it in a database so that the image metadata can be used to match consumers' queries. In addition to match-making, the brokerage system also provides many value-added services, such as digital image warehousing, digitalization and indexing assistance, and copyright registration. The functionalities of the brokerage system is illustrated in Figure 1. The brokerage system can also provide other services such as copyright protection as value-added services. As a brokerage system over the Internet leverage stock photo agencies' ability to mass-market their products and services to customers around the world, they will be able to reach an economy of scale that will reduce the unit cost of digitization and computer and communication equipments. Other issues related to the database community, such as image indexing, image modeling, query interface and processing, are being focused through development of new database management systems to handle multimedia data. Some of our efforts will be highlighted in a later section.

In this paper, we present an Internet-based framework of brokers for stock photo industry. We discuss architecture and highlight supporting building block techniques for the architecture (some of them are built at NEC, CCRL). We also present a business model of the electronic market for stock photo industry.

The rest of this paper is organized as follows: We first overview the current status and business model of the stock photo industry in Section 2 and discuss the driving force and trend toward an electronic market for images in Section 3. We highlight some building block technologies to support a multimedia information broker architecture in Section 4. In Section 5 we present the development architecture of stock photo brokerages and a business model and its operational flows. Finally we offer our conclusions.

2 Stock Photography Industry and Its Conventional Business Model

The stock photo industry is large and fragmented. There are over 1000 agencies in the US ranging from relatively small, photographer owned companies to the large-scale multinational photography banks which manage over 10 million images. Some are content

Brokerage for Stock Photo Industry		
Business and legal issues: - copyright - pricing - escrow - digitization - usage control - access control - fee collecting	**Business/service infrastructure** business model, services, payment systems...... **Image indexing/search infrastructure** image databases, query processing, query interface, image indexing ..... **Information exchange infrastructure** WWW, EDI..... **Network infrastructure** Internet, networking	**Technical issues:** - image indexing - image retrieval - compression - digitization - image analysis - watermarking - payment protocol - user query interface - image storage ....

Figure 2: Electronic Commerce Framework for Stock Photo Industry

specialized concentrating on editorial news and photo journalism while others are broad-based managing a large variety of stock images. According to data compiled by ASMP (American Society of Magazine Photographers), a third of the stock companies manage around 100,000 to 500,000 images, either in black and white format or color.

The current business model for stock photography involves image providers or photographers who contract with stock agencies for image licensing or "usage". The image providers submit several images on a contractual basis granting rights of usage for commissions. The stock agency receives the images, documents and verifies the contents, caption, remounts and processes the image through his/her client channels, negotiating prices and confirming image releases. Once photos have been categorized and filed, model releases and copyrights are confirmed. In many cases, the stock agent relies on the image provider to provide both. In some cases, the agent will submit the image information to the Copyright office for registration.

The stock agency then sorts the image by market channel and contract usage. The contractual agreement usually stipulates the marketing target for the image, newswire, catalogs, CD-ROM, usage fees and location. Since stock agencies invest heavily in market research and distribution and tracking, they prefer to manage images on an exclusive basis. This means that the the agent will pay higher royalties to the photographer if the contract includes world-wide distribution rights over a variety of marketing channels.

Stock photo agencies provide a bundle of services, including image processing, marketing, invoicing, and registration. In the traditional way, photographers and content providers submit originals or duplicates to the client or stock agency with captions (keywords) indicating the significant features of the image con-

tent and available model releases and copyright registration. Stock agencies advertise their collection of image stock to their client base by catalog and clients usually browse through a number of catalogs. Out of this image group, they select the desired image and pay the stock agency for usage. The ownership rights remained with the original image provider. The stock agency served as the middle-man, receiving a sales commission from the image user and extracting a service commission from the original image provider. However, since many large stock agencies have millions of images, the approach of browsing is not efficient. And since most of business is done in a face-to-face fashion, only a limited number of transactions can be carried out by stock agencies every day. The agencies would like to provide services to a broad-base of image users who would make selections from a larger number of available images. Since stock photo agencies serve as the middle-man to receive sales commissions, they would like to serve more customers and execute more transactions per day.

3 Electronic Stock Photo Brokerage as a New Business Model

The existing business model of the stock photo industry is becoming outmoded and inefficient. New developments in technology and the growth of the image stock and growing problems of media storage, management of complex business transactions and the demand for tighter image security are converging to underscore the need for and integrated approach to stock photo management. Many of the value-added services, such as visual query interfaces, fee collection, copyright registration, escrow and storage for image preservation, can be integrated into one efficient process of image management system. We refer to this new business model as *electronic image brokerage*, a stock photo brokerage architecture that uses the Internet as a channel for distribution.

As shown in Figure 2, our framework of electronic brokerage consists of four layers: the lowest layer, network infrastructure, which provides communication functionalities, the second layer, information exchange infrastructure, that supports information exchange channels, the next layer, image indexing/search infrastructure, that provides common image modeling and indexing methods and search tools across multiple repositories on the Internet, and finally the top layer provides a business model for electronic markets. Lists of business and technical issues across multiple layers are shown in Figure 2.

We have seen the trend toward the "digital age" of

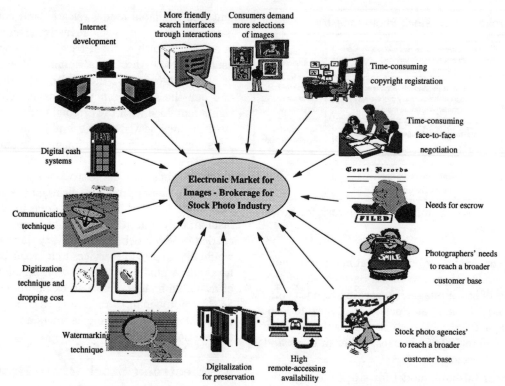

Figure 3: Driving Force of Brokerage for Stock Photo Industry

many industries. Development of new techniques are driving the stock photo industry to a stage of exploring a electronic market for images on the Internet. We illustrate driving forces of brokerages for stock photo industry in Figure 3. In the early stage of development, it is hard to predict the acceptability and applicability of our model from the point of view of stock photo agencies as we see that it is a alternative for transforming the industry toward the "electronic age".

In the next section, we highlight our efforts of development new technologies to support an electronic market for image brokerages.

4 Building Block Technologies for Electronic Global Image Brokerages

In this section, we highlight some important building block technologies that support a general multimedia information broker architecture over a wide-area network or more specifically, the Internet. The development of this architecture is presented in a later section.

4.1 Image Modeling and Registration

Image databases are main components in our architecture. SEMCOG[7] (SEMantics and COGnition-based image retrieval) is an image database management system being developed at NEC, CCRL. When

an image is "registered" at SEMCOG, some image descriptions, such as the image size, image format, registration date, can be automatically extracted, while some metadata, such as image title and semantics of images, can not be extracted fully automatically. We provide a tool, *image semantics editor*, to assist image providers in specifying image semantics through interactions with an image recognition tool, COIR[5], to edit the semantics of an image.

The steps involved in image semantics extraction and editing are as follows: (1) COIR identifies image regions of an image. (2) COIR recommends candidate components and their corresponding semantics by consulting the image component catalog. (3) The user confirms or modifies the results by COIR. (4) The user may select components to store in the image component catalog if he/she thinks these components can be used for "representative samples". The image component catalog is built incrementally in this way. (5) The semantics extracted is then stored in the image semantics database. For more detail on interactions between COIR and the editor, please see [7].

4.2 Object-based Image Retrieval

Because the feature extraction and image matching techniques in our system are object-based, users can query objects with finer granularity than a whole

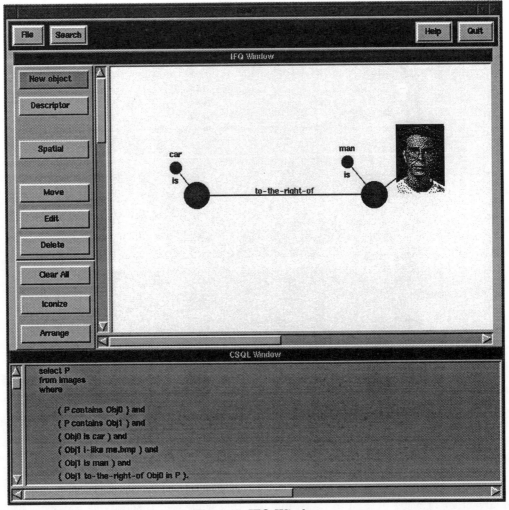

Figure 4: IFQ Window

image and specify spatial relations between objects. SEMCOG[7] allows users to pose a query using both semantics expressions and image examples. In our system, a query, such as "Retrieve all images in which there is a man standing next to a building and the building looks like this sketch", can be posed.

SEMCOG architecture contains five components: a *facilitator*, *COIR*[5], an *image semantics editor*, a *terminology manager*, and a *semantics-based query processor*. The *facilitator* coordinates the interactions between components of SEMCOG. It forwards cognition-based query processing to COIR and non-cognition-based query processing to the *semantics-based query processor*. SEMCOG is considered a hybrid approach to multimedia databases[8]. SEMCOG consists of a database system to store multimedia data and process queries and uses many plug-in modules to handle media-specific functionalities, such image matching. The *image semantics editor* is a tool, described

above, to provide semantics to image objects. The *terminology manager* maintains a knowledge base for query reformulation and relaxation.

The image retrieval language used in our system is called CSQL (Cognition and Semantics-based Query Language). The image retrieval related predicates include: *is* (e.g. man vs. man), *is_a* (e.g. car vs. transportation, man vs. human), *s_like* for "semantics like" (e.g. car vs. truck), *i_like* for "image like" that compares visual signatures of two arguments, *contains*, *to_the_right_of in*, and etc.

4.3 Visual Query User Interface

There are two major directions for image retrieval interface development. One direction is manipulation through query languages, which is more precise to computers but not user friendly since users need to know database schema and query languages. Another direction is to develop a more natural interface, such as

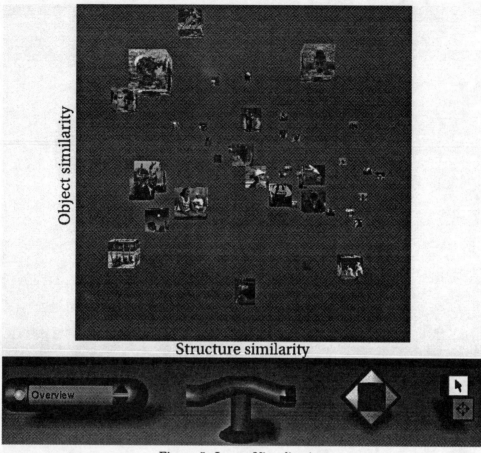

Figure 5: Image Visualization

query by image or sketch examples. This type of interfaces has an advantage of being natural to users, but it has disadvantage of low precision because queries are ambiguous to computers.

IFQ (In Frame Query)[9] is a visual interface for SEMCOG. IFQ is designed to bridge the gap between users' mental models and precise database access languages. In IFQ, objects are represented as bullets and *descriptors* are represented as small bullets, attached to these objects to describe the properties of the corresponding objects. Figure 4 shows an IFQ query "Retrieve all images in which there is a man to the right of a car and he looks like this image". The IFQ query is posed as follows: The user introduces the first object in the image. and then further describes the object by attaching "i_like $< image >$" and "is *man*" descriptors. After a user specifies a image path or provide a drawing, the interface automatically replaces the descriptor with the thumbnail size image the user specifies. Then, the user introduces another object and describes it using the "is *car*" descriptor. Finally, the user describes the spatial relationship between these two objects by drawing a line, labeled by *to-the-right-*

of, from the man object to the car object. Please note that while user is specifying the query using IFQ, the corresponding CSQL query is automatically generated in the CSQL window. Users simply pose queries by clicking buttons and drag-and-drop icons representing entities and descriptors. Please note that in Figure 4 we only show IFQ generating the corresponding CSQL query.

Users can also specify the following query parameters: (1) ratio of color importance to shape importance (used by COIR for image matching), (2) ratio of object matching importance to structure matching importance (used to rank images), (3) filtering parameters, such as a minimum degree of relevancy and a maximum number of image retrieved, and (4) image related parameters, such as titles and authors.

4.4 Result Visualization

The candidate images' thumbnail size images are first presented to the user through visualization since a lot of photos would be retrieved by the search in many cases. If the results are shown to the user in traditional forms, for example as a scrolled list, it be-

96

comes very difficult for the user to understand the results. Visualization is useful in this case because it can convert large amounts of information into meaningful and interpretable visual representations thus allowing people to use perceptual rather than cognitive reasoning in carrying out tasks[14].

Visualizations can be used for presenting image search results[10] as shown in Figure 5, in which cubes are used to represent retrieved images. Texture mapping is used to show the respective images on the cube. Please note that in Figure 4 users can specify the importance of object matching versus structural matching. In this visualization, the structural similarity has been mapped to the X axis and the object similarity to the Y axis. The size of the cubes indicate the overall degree of the relevancy of retrieving the pictures. The visualization gives the user a better understanding of the search results. For example, images on the top-right corner are more relevant images having large values for both x and y. Figure 5 shows the results for a query in which the user specify object matching is more important so that the size of the cubes on the top-left corner is bigger.

The user can use various tools provided by the image browser (and shown at the bottom of the figure) to navigate through the space. For example, the Joystick control allows the users to walk around in a scene by moving forward, back, left, and right. The user is also allowed to click and zoom on any interesting point of the space.

4.5 Watermarking Technique

Copyright issues are a real concern of image providers. With the improvement of scanners, photocopying devices and advances in digital technologies, it has become easier for images to be misappropriated, retouched and reassembled. There are various means of safeguarding images, some involving the use of *watermarking* techniques[1] which embeds information such as electronic signatures or serial numbers directly within images and other creative property. Watermarking technologies not only secure the ownership of the image but can also verify copyright ownership, detect alterations, trigger digital-cash meters or it can track black-market distribution. "Watermarking technology" can be incorporated into our stock photo brokerage system by encoding watermarks onto valuable photos, films, videos, and manuscripts.

4.6 Image Preservation and Escrow Services

The digitized images have advantages of better utilization and transmission. Another advantage is that digitized media is easier to preserve because the life of image data that is film based is short because it falls prey to fading and discoloration. Estimated time before perceptible color change in dark storage ranges from 3 years to 100 years depending on the temperature, humidity, and photographic materials[2]. Digitized images would allow users to store data and extend the life of their valued images captured on film. It also serves as a way of preserving masterpieces from years. Digitalization also make escrow service more feasible since storage environments for all digital data are the same unlike storage environments for physical media.

Although the cost of storage systems is dropping dramatically, the equipments for digitizing really high quality images are still expensive. Digital cameras, powerful workstations, storage, lenses and lighting is currently priced at $15,000 to $35,000[3]. We are studying possible business models to assist the stock photo industry to digitize images and store in electronic form so computerized search and retrieval can be implemented. One possible solution to this is to lease digitization equipments and charge usage fee. We can also provide tools for specifying image semantics as part of image on-line registration.

5 Development Architecture for Electronic Stock Photo Industry

Figure 6 shows our development architecture for stock photo brokerage. The main box indicates the brokerage scope. Figure 6 contains 4 types of entities. In this section, we explain the roles and functionalities of these entities:

Image providers: Image providers are artists or stock photo agencies. After the providers decide to put a particular set of images on the market, they send copies of the original images, along with usage fee specifications, to the image broker. We believe that in order to make information search effective and efficient, information sources should be responsible for providing metainformation. This way, the information search problem can be transferred to match making, a more trackable problem. Our system provides an image semantics editing tool that can interact with users to help specifying semantics of images. More details are reported in [7]. The usage fee, royalties, and licensing fee for the images are transferred to the providers through a third party, such as a digital cash bank[12].

---

[2]Source: Eastman Kodak publications, ASMP, 1990, p 172
[3]Source: MacWeek Jan 8, 1996, v.10 p.97

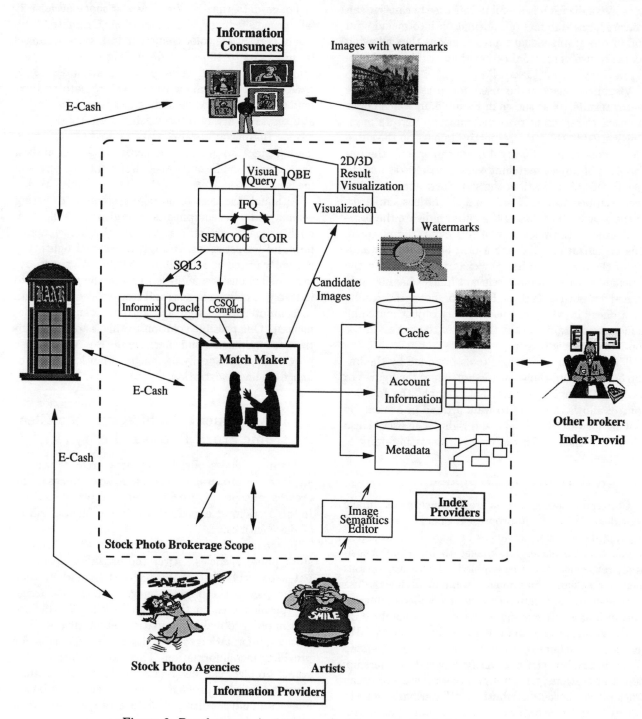

Figure 6: Development Architecture for Electronic Stock Photo Industry

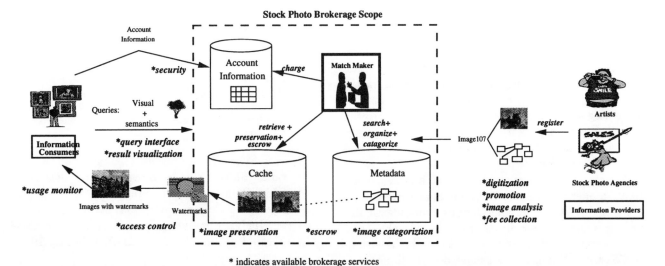

Figure 7: Stock Photo Brokerage Operational Flows

Image consumers: Our architecture allows image consumers to pose semantics-based queries and/or cognition-based queries to search images using the visual query interface (IFQ), or to pose similarity based queries by providing an image or drawing example to retrieve similar images, as in QBE. When a user submits a query, the match-maker executes the query by using the information stored in the image metadata database. After the query is executed, the candidate images are presented to the user through a 2D/3D result visualization interface. The user can browse through the candidate images and select the best-matches to her query among them. The broker, then, provides watermarked copies of the selected images to the user, and it charges the corresponding usage fee to his/her account. Note that, to be able to access the broker, a consumer must have an active account. Consumers pay their balances using digital cash.

Brokerage system: The broker contains a match-maker which matches consumers' queries with image semantics in the metadata database. The information necessary for brokerage is managed by index providers. This information includes user account information (e.g. copyright information, usage fee), metadata (e.g. feature and color information for image match, image semantics for semantics-based query processing), thumbnail size images, and frequently accessed images in the cache. The metadata storage can be viewed as a warehouse for image indexes. Given the fact that the number of images in the brokerage can be as large as millions, the broker must benefit from suitable data warehousing techniques to organize image metadata.

The match-making functionalities are provided matching consumers' image query specifications with the metadata in the database. Given there may not be an image that exactly matches the consumer's query specification, visualization is used to present candidates to the consumer. The consumer can select from the candidates or re-formulate the query specification. The consumer can also pose queries with "fuzzier" specifications, such as using "is-a" or let the query processor to relax the query. In either case, the system acts as a match-maker to find the best-matched images for the consumers. Additional functionalities provided by the brokerage system include visual query interface, query result visualization, image transmission (some with watermarks), and image semantics editing.

Index providers: Index providers keep the necessary information for match making. A broker can serve as an index provider for an other broker. An example to the index providers is *specialized image brokers* (e.g. stock photo agencies for medical images).

6 Operational Flows and Brokerage Services

Figure 7 shows the operational flows and brokerage services (* indicates the service provided) in our system. We highlight the brokerage services as follows:

First of all, for image providers, the brokerage system provides services (digitizing and analyzing images) to extract image semantics. Based on the extracted semantics, the system categorizes images and make them available for various markets. The broker provides storage for image preservation, escrow services, and fee collection. Besides these, for image providers, the brokerage system also provides access control and usage monitoring (using watermarking), as well as security through consumer account information management.

The image consumers, on the other hand, first need to establish their accounts. The account information includes user profiles, preferences, and payment methods (e.g. E-cash). The brokerage system maintains and categorizes image metadata for quick processing of consumers' image retrieval requests. The brokerage system provides services of visual query interfaces and result visualization.

For the brokerage system, the match maker is actually a query processor. It organizes and categorizes image metadata by building hierarchical indexes. To process a query, it searches the metadata database and then present candidates to users through the visualization tool. When the consumer decides to use particular sets of images, the match maker retrieve the images and send them to the consumers with watermarks. At the same time, the match maker charges the consumers' account for usage fee and credit the corresponding accounts of image providers. Other functionalities the broker provides include escrow and image preservation.

7 Conclusions

In this paper, we point out the driving forces and the need for an electronic market for the stock photo industry. We present a pioneering model for electronic market for stock photo industry as well as its building block technologies. Each building block of this model contributes the specialized technologies required, such as digital-cash, watermarking, visual query interfaces, visualization tools, and image databases. We believe the maturity of these building blocks are driving our model to a more applicable stage.

References

[1] H. Berghel and L. O'Gorman. Protecting Ownership Rights Through Digital Watermarking. *IEEE Computer*, 29(7):101–103, July 1996.

[2] Kilnam Chon. Internet In Roads. *Communications of the ACM*, pages 59–60, June 1996.

[3] Dataquest. On-Line Strategies Worldwide. June 1996.

[4] Matti Hamalainen, Andrew B. Whinston, and Svetlana Vishik. Electronic Markets for Learning: Education Brokerages on the Internet. *Communications of the ACM*, page 51, June 1996.

[5] Kyoji Hirata, Yoshinori Hara, H. Takano, and S. Kawasaki. Content-Oriented Integration in Hypermedia Systems. In *Proceedings of 1996 ACM Conference on Hypertext*, March 1996.

[6] Dataquest. On-Line Strategies Worldwide. October 1996.

[7] Wen-Syan Li, K. Selçuk Candan, and K. Hirata. SEMCOG: An Integration of SEMantics and COGnition-based Approaches for Image Retrieval. In *Proceedings of 1997 ACM Symposium on Applied Computing Special Track on Database Technology*, San Jose, CA, USA, February 1997.

[8] Wen-Syan Li, K. Selçuk Candan, K. Hirata, and Y. Hara. *Lecture Notes in Computer Science - Worldwide Computing and Its Applications*, A Hybrid Approach to Multimedia Database Systems through Integration of Semantics and Media-based Search. Springer-Verlag, New York, March 1997.

[9] Wen-Syan Li, K. Selçuk Candan, K. Hirata, and Yoshi Hara. IFQ: A Visual Query Interface for Object-based Image Retrieval. In *Proceedings of the 1997 ACM CHI Conference (Demonstration Session)*, Atlanta, GA, March 1997.

[10] Sougata Mukherjea, K. Hirata, and Y. Hara. Visualizing the Results of Multimedia WWW Search Engines. In *Proceedings of 1996 IEEE Information Visualization Symposium*, San Francisco, California, USA, October 1996.

[11] N. R. Adam and Yelena Yesha (editors). *ACM Computing Surveys*, Electronic Commerce and Digital Libraries: Towards a Digital Agora. 28(4). ACM, December 1996.

[12] Patiwat Panurach. Money in Electronic Commerce: Digital Cash, Electronic Fund Transfer, and Ecash. *Communications of the ACM*, pages 45–50, June 1996.

[13] Tim O'Reilly. Publishing Models for Internet Commerce. *Communications of the ACM*, pages 79–86, June 1996.

[14] Vincente, K.J. and Rasmussen, J. The Ecology of Human Machine Systems: II. Mediating Direct Perception in Complex Domain. *Ecological Psychology*, 2:207–249, 1990.

On Disconnected Browsing of Distributed Information*

Anupam Joshi

Department of Computer Engineering and Computer Science
University of Missouri
Columbia, MO 65211
joshi@ece.missouri.edu

Sanjiva Weerawarana and Elias N. Houstis
Department of Computer Sciences
Purdue University
West Lafayette, IN 47907-1398
E–mail:{saw,enh}@cs.purdue.edu

Abstract

The software and protocols associated with information browsing systems are largely designed with static access points and wired networks in mind, HTTP and the Web are a case in point. Static hosts are connected to wired, high bandwidth networks, and are capable of transmitting and receiving large amounts of data without significant delays. As such, the size and format of the data files being received by the browser/client has never been a concern. However, this causes problems when information access is desired on mobile hosts (MH), since data transmission over a wireless network is much slower than on a wired network. Mobile computers are also relatively resource-poor, compared to their desktop counterparts. This fact is ignored by HTTP servers, and large data files are transmitted to computers that cannot properly display them. Also, mobile computers operate in constantly changing network environments. It is possible for a mobile computer to become temporarily disconnected from a network when it changes base stations or goes out of range of a base station. A mobile host may also doze off to preserve battery power and thus be disconnected. The information browsing system and protocols assocaiated with mobile computers should thus be able to tolerate the fault of temporary disconnection. This work focuses on addressing these problems in the context of web browsing from a mobile host. The current model of Web browsing is inherently sequential, and wasteful of bandwidth. This paper investigates an efficient model for browsing and describes the design of a smart Web browsing application which performs transactions based on the user's available resources and manages disconnection.

1. Introduction

Recent years have seen a significant increase in interest generated by mobile computing. With the advent of the World Wide Web[3], browsing (surfing) the web is becoming an increasingly common activity for computer users. The current model of browsing the web, however, is sequential, and one that leaves most of the burden of finding the relevant information on the user and his computer. In other words, a user is expected to know starting points, and then search through documents and follow links to find the information s/he needs. Clearly, this means that while the user is searching for information, a network connection needs to be constantly maintained. Moreover, a lot of (potentially) useless information is transmitted over the (wireless) network, wasting precious bandwidth. This mode of information access is clearly not suited for web browsing from a mobile platform. Mobile platforms, for one, are connected over wireless links. Even the best of such networks provides far lower bandwidth than run of the mill wired networks. Wireless LANs typically provide a total bandwidth of 2Mbps, and throughputs in the hundreds of Kbps range. Wide area wireless networks (mostly cellular) operate at tens of Kbps. Moreover,

---
*This work was supported in part by NSF awards ASC 9404859 and a grant from the Intel Corporation.

unlike wired networks, disconnections are a frequent phenomenon in wireless networks. These occur while a host is between base-stations, or when it falls in a "radio-shadow" area. Disconnections in the mobile environment can also be elective. In other words, the mobile host may chose to "switch off" certain part(s) of its functionality in order to preserve battery power. We refer the reader to [5] for details of the mobile computing scenario. A related problem is the capability of the mobile platform. Web servers do not take into consideration the network connection between them and their clients. Rather, the server merely returns whatever document was asked for. Furthermore, users are routinely creating multimedia-rich pages. In fact, so heavily is multimedia used that often "text only" versions of these pages have to be made available for users accessing them across WANs. Wireless networks do not have the data transmission speeds of wired networks, so downloading large files over wireless networks, even local area ones, consumes a longer time. Not only does it take longer to download large files, but more battery power is consumed, reducing the time the mobile computer can be used. Web servers also have no notion of the resources available at the client's end, and blindly assume that the client is capable of properly displaying the data that it receives. For example, a user may follow a hyperlink to a sound file on an X terminal which is not capable of playing sound. The server will blindly supply this data to the client, consuming time and network bandwidth to deliver a sound file that cannot be used. Such problems are especially acute on mobile computers, which are not as resource-rich as their desktop counterparts. Text only pages, while helpful in this context, force an unnecessary all or none choice on the user.

While we have articulated these problems in the context of web, they generally relate to information access from mobile platforms to distributed data. The Internet protocols are primarily designed for static networks where changes are rare and disconnections catastrophic. HTTP is a typical such protocol, and has no knowledge about the state of the system, including the underlying network. HTTP/1.0, the version of the protocol used most widely today, establishes a new TCP connection for every GET request. The three way handshake involved in establishing the TCP connection can be a significant overhead on a wireless link. HTTP/1.1 has addeddressed this problem, and the proposed HTTP-NG[19], presently being discussed, will go farther by having some notion of the context of the request.

The attempt in this work is to add some intelligence to the present http client server system in a manner

that will be interoperable with HTTP-NG. Providing a reasonable level of performance in the face of frequent disconnections, restricted bandwidth and limited resources is a major issue in mobile computing. In context of information access, we refer to this problem as *disconnected browsing*. Note that our use of this term is in a much broader sense than in some commercial products. In these products, the only concern is to be able to operate in a mode where predictable disconnections from the network occur in an otherwise high bandwidth connection. An argument can be made that these bandwidth and resource related problems are transient, and eventually wireless network speeds as well as the resources available on mobile platforms will increase. That may well be the case, yet the speeds on wired networks and the resources (memory, CPU speed, etc.) on static hosts will also increase. Existing (and novel) applications will evolve and be dependent on these enhanced capabilities. Thus while the absolute performance measures of mobile systems will undoubtedly improve, what we call the *bandwidth gap* and *resource gap* will remain. In this paper, we describe a software architecture to support disconnected browsing, and present preliminary implementations of two component systems called *Mowser* and *WebIQ*.

2. Related Work

There is little existing work in the area of web browsing from mobile platforms. There is little existing work in the area of web browsing from mobile platforms. The two major ongoing efforts in this area are MOWGLI and Glomop. Mowgli[12] is a comprehensive project to design Mobile Office Workstations using GSM Links (hence the acronym). One of the efforts in this direction is a web browser. This is accomplished by putting a proxy on the support station, and an agent on the mobile host. Mowgli Web browser's primary strengths is its use of a single TCP connection to handle multiple GETs over the wireless link. This reduces the massive overhead of establishing a new TCP connection for multiple get requests within a document, which requires a three way handshake. It also caches the incoming documents at the proxy end. Glomop[6] has an approach similar to the mowser component[9] of our system. Glomop scales the images down to a smaller size before transmitting them to the mobile user. This is an instance of what the authors call type specific distillation. This reduces the bandwidth requirement between the mobile platform and static host, and allows for faster transmission times. It also allows the user to re-request parts of the distilled document at greater resolution. However, it does not have a notion of asynchronous operation. Another initial effort was the Teleweb project[17] by Schilit et. al., which proposed a reactive architecture to control the costs of information access. Faced with a GET request, the proxy would either get the document, or depending on the network connection, defer the request till a better connection could be obtained. The user could override the proxy's decision. In addition, it cached documents at the proxy end.

The two mutually distinct areas of related research are offline browsing and dynamic browsing. The first is the perusal of information available on the WWW, while being disconnected from the network. Most current work in this area involves downloading entire documents to the mobile platform and caching them for later browsing. We believe this approach does not suit a resource-poor platform as it poses additional burdens in the form of larger disk requirements. Dynamic browsing, on the other hand involves integrating location information to the query being sent. This information is used to retrieve information relevant to the user's current location. While these projects suggest interesting uses for the WWW, they are based on additions to the current protocols, and do not address the problem of viewing the information that is currently available on the WWW, from a resource-poor mobile platform that is frequently disconnected.

Several offline browsers are commercially available. WebWhacker[21] , and Grab-a-Site[7] are offline browsers that download documents into a local disk for later viewing. WebWatch[20] is a similar product, that in addition, periodically looks for changes on the cached sites. Milktruck[13], another offline browser, runs a proxy web server on the portable machine to deliver the cached documents. The common feature of these products is that they propose to conserve one scarce resource (connection bandwidth) by using up another scarce resource (disk space). Furthermore, none of the mobile platform's resource limitations are considered in these systems. We believe this is a very narrow view of "disconnected operation".

Mobisaic[18] is a system that extends the current WWW protocols to encode location information in the URL. It uses a "dynamic environment" introduced by Xerox PARC[16] to deduce the mobile user's current location and create a "dynamic URL". Dynamic documents[10] are another example of mobile access to the WWW. In this case, the burden of processing location dependent information is placed on the mobile computer, thereby using more of its resources. Another location-dependent information service is described in [1], with a description of a building navigator application. These applications propose extensions to the

current WWW and its protocols, in order to deliver information relevant to a mobile platform (i.e. location information). However, they do not deal with the issues of disconnectivity, and resource-scarcity of mobile platforms.

Some prior work, in unrelated contexts, has been done on searching for information on the Internet. Locating specific information in the Internet is becoming more difficult due to the its explosive growth and diversity. Many search engines and research papers have attempted to address this problem. However, these works for the most view this as a pure information retrieval problem. The reader is likely familiar with several "crawler" based search engines such as Yahoo, AltaVista, Lycos, InfoSeek, etc. etc.

3. Software Architecture

Our proposed software architecture builds on the widely accepted model for mobile computing [2]. In essence, it assumes that the wired network is a high bandwidth pipe. Failures of either the network or host machines on this part of the infrastructure are rare and catastrophic events. The mobile hosts, on the other hand, can frequently disconnect, either electively to preserve resources, or otherwise due to a dropping of the wireless connection. The mobile hosts (MH) are supported by mobile support stations (MSSs) which act as gateways between the wired and wireless networks. Each MSS supports MHs within its cell, similar to how cellular phones are organized. MHs within a cell can directly communicate with each other, otherwise they must communicate through their MSS, which in turn talks to other hosts and MSSs on the wired network.

Our architecture adds a proxy server on each MSS to the basic MSS-MH model. This functions as the gateway to the Web for browsers running on MHs. All information requests will be routed through this proxy, which will operate in a manner transparent to the user. The MHs will be able to still run the user's favorite Web browser, as long as it is forms capable and allows the provision of a proxy mechanism. The proxy will implement the new model we are proposing for disconnected browsing. Essentially, the objective is to provide some state information which will enable us to handle the constraints imposed by mobility. In other words, we are adding some intelligence to the network, so that it adapts to changing resources available. A more general vision of such a proxy, suited to computational rather than information access tasks, can be found in our prior work[4]

Running a proxy server allows us to push all the intelligence into this unit, and also have it maintain needed state information. This allows us to use existing IP based systems as is, and allows retention of popular tools and software such as Web browsers and servers. In other words, legacy stateless protocols effectively become statefull. For disconnected browsing, the proxy has two distinct but related functionalities, which we call Media Transformation and Asynchronous operation respectively. Mowser[9] performs media data transformation on the documents being served to the browser on the MH, changing their granularity to better reflect the available bandwidth and resources. For example, it will notice that the image being sent to an MH with an 8 bit color display has 24 bit data, and will transform it so as to not make the user wait an inordinate time after the request due to the low bandwidth available. The functionality represented by Asynchronous operation is broader, and is implemented as the WebIQ[11] proxy. HTTP at the moment is a synchronous protocol. In other words, once a request has been made, the connection is maintained till such a time as the response returns. In the mobile scenario, disconnections are frequent, and so the existing protocol does not serve us well. We instead use WebIQ to make the process asynchronous. The user connects to the proxy, makes the request, and disconnects. When the user connects next, the result of his prior request(s) is available. S/he can then fetch this, and disconnect again. The user can connect again to provide the system feedback about the usefulness of this information. Thus the system manages disconnection. Another aspect of Asynchronous Operation is to allow the user to specify requests as queries, rather than explicit URLs. In other words, the burden of locating appropriate information is taken away from the user to facilitate asynchronicity. In the synchronous mode, the user has to explicitly follow links to locate the right information, which, as mentioned earlier, is wasteful of bandwidth. To obtain the results of the queries, the WebIQ proxy first looks at its own cache, then queries its peer proxies, and only as a last recourse uses brute force search engines (Yahoo, Lycos etc.) available on the Internet. So our state information consists of data about the QOS from the network (bandwidth, latency), capabilities of the hardware in the MH, and the preferences and information requests of the user.

Proxy servers also have peer to peer protocols to exchange state information as MHs travel from the cell of one MSS to another. Essentially, our method employs an active join, passive leave technique[2] to initiate transfer of information. This means that when an MH decides (based on, say, signal beacons) that it should switch its MSS, it sends a message to the new MSS signaling a join with its own id and the id of its previous MSS. The new MSS can then request the profile of this MH/User, in terms of the information required by Mowser and WebIQ, from the old MSS. The other advantage of such peer protocols is that information about the state of the world obtained by one peer can be shared by the others. In fact, we view these multiple proxies as a distributed multiagent system which cooperates to solve certain problems.

The proposed software architecture allows us to address research issues such as

- The information needed by a user is spread across heterogeneous and geographically distributed systems. To expect the user to provide the location where the information resides is clearly not correct. Further, the response to a query from the user could involve aggregating information obtained from a variety of sources.

- The current models of information retrieval assume that the browsing software is operational after a request for information has been made. This is clearly not justifiable in the mobile scenario, where disconnections are a fact of life.

- While wired networks are capable of sending and receiving large amounts of data without significant delay, this is clearly not the case in the mobile scenario. In addition to network bandwidth limitations and variability, mobile hosts also have relatively less resources than their static counterparts. These include smaller screen resolution and color capability, and limited or no sound capability.

Most existing approaches to disconnected browsing do not deal with these problems. They limit themselves to essentially caching information locally so as to be able to continue operation even if the network connection goes down. Our approach addresses these issues by augmenting information at each site with ancillary structures storing metadata about the state of the network, the capabilities of the MH and the preferences of the user. The cooperative retrieval process[15] can then use a combination of knowledge–rich and knowledge–poor techniques. In our asynchronous model, the system "dynamically" creates Web pages based on the client requests by locating and retrieving information from across the network. In this sense, our architecture can be viewed as a system to develop multilevel models of hypertext [14] that are appropriate for disconnected browsing. We use the next two sections to further describe the Mowser & WebIQ preliminary implementations.

4. Mowser

Mowser (Mobile Browser) allows a mobile user to set his or her viewing preferences, based on the network connection and available resources. Each mobile host's preferences are known to the proxy server. They are stored according to the mobile host's IP address, allowing the MH to access them from anywhere. The only requirement placed on the browser is that it be able to support proxy servers.

4.1 Servers

Logically, the functionality of Mowser can be split along the lines of a preferences server and a caching server. The preferences server has two functions, to get the preferences for a MH at the start of a browsing session, and to update them whenever the user requests so. A browsing session is started on a MH by the Web browser contacting a preference server and saving preferences. These preferences may also be updated anytime during the browsing session. Such changes could reflect a change in network connection or availability of different resources during different sessions. Once the preferences are stored, the proxy server starts the browsing session by loading the starting URL defined in the preferences. All HTTP *GET* & *POST* requests from that point are handled by the proxy server. If a file requested by the MH does not meet the requirements described in the preferences, the proxy server can modify the file before sending it to the MH. The proxy server identifies the file type by means of its MIME type header. Depending on the type of the file, different conversions can be performed on it to meet the MH preferences. If a file does not meet the size requirement for its type, the proxy server will not send it to the MH. Files that cannot be properly displayed by the MH will not be sent either. This granularity reduction is easy to achieve in some cases; for example, image files can be compressed by sacrificing quality without sacrificing semantics. In particular, the size of the image, and the number of colors can be reduced, resulting in a smaller image that conveys the same information. Whenever a file is modified by the proxy server, a URL will be provided to retrieve the original unmodified file, if the user so requires. Figure 1 illustrates the conversion done by Mowser on the homepage of one of the authors. The current implementation handles images, with ongoing work adding in other data types such as video.

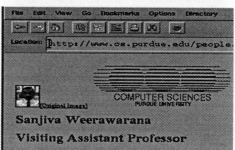

Figure 1. Original and Converted pages using Mowser

5. WebIQ

In our asynchronous model, we view Web access as a sequence of small, atomic transactions. The connection between the MH and the proxy system need only be maintained during such transactions; there is no need for a continuous connection. These transactions involve retrieving information and providing metadata about the information. The WebIQ proxy minimizes the bandwidth it uses over the mobile link as well as the power it forces the MH to consume. This is done by weeding out information which has a low probability of interest using user profiles. User profiles are thus important in determining what information will be useful. Users explicitly rate the URLs provided by the system, based on how useful they were. This gives the user control over the kind of information he or she would like retrieved, and allows the system to infer the user's profile. From another perspective, the user feedback allows the system to infer a *semantic* match between the user's query and the information in the document. Oft-repeated actions of users, e.g. fetching the stock market URLs every morning before 9 am, should be detected and automated. This would enable the MH to receive data during periods of low activity, saving time and CPU cycles.

WebIQ[11] uses existing information resources in a cooperative manner to find information. Each proxy will maintain a ranking of its peers, as well as external information brokers, based on the volume of information requested, quality value required for the results, and quality of previous responses etc [8]. Such information can be used to guide a query to a particular search engine, based on past information, or to a proxy which might be caching relevant URLs in response to a query by another user. Reusing previously obtained (and cached) URLs which were ranked highly by the user prevents a brute force keyword based search for every query. It also allows our metadata to indirectly capture the semantic content of the URL. In general, the proxy will contain the notion of user groups and use these to direct queries. Specifically, let us say that a user asks for URLs related to *football*. When rating the returned URLs, the rankings will be different depending on whether the user was European/Asian or American, since this word means different things to these two groups. Which rankings should a system use when another user queries for information related to football. Obviously, knowing what group the new user belongs to can help the proxy return appropriate cached URLs. This notion of groups and sharing information brings up the question of security and privacy. While we are interested in these issues, they are beyond the scope of the work discussed here.

6. Conclusion and Ongoing Work

In this paper, we present techniques that facilitate disconnected browsing – browsing the web from wirelessly connected, resource limited hosts typical of mobile systems. A software architecture suited for this task in particular, and for mobile information access in general, is described. Two components of this architecture are presented in detail, and their preliminary implementations described. One, called Mowser, handles the automatic transformation for multimedia data from the server to a form that the client can handle. The other, WebIQ, makes Web access an asynchronous operation which is relatively oblivious to disconnections. It also reduces the amount of useless (from the user's point of view) information that needs to be transmitted on the wireless link.

Our ongoing work has three major thrusts. The first relates to software improvement. We are trying to rewrite our software in Java/Jeeves and Oracle NCA to make it platform independent. While at present this adds a performance penalty, it should not be so in the near future with the availability of native Java compilers for many machines. Along the same lines, we are trying to convert the file system based database used by WebIQ to use a commercial system such as Oracle. We are also enhancing the various media types that

Mowser can handle and convert to bandwidth saving formats. An interesting question arises in this context in terms of the active components of the web, such as applets. There is at present no characterization of the compute capabilities that an applet needs, nor its functionality. As such, there is no easy way to filter out applets that are not suited for a mobile host. We are presently engaged in trying to come up with ways of characterising these. The second thrust is to implement the peer–peer protocols for these systems. While we have defined these, the implementation is still not complete. Finally, we are currently deploying these systems internally and testing them with users. We would like to make them available more widely and conduct detailed studies of their utility in terms of ease of use, as well as the tradeoffs involved in our design choices.

References

[1] A. Acharya, B. Badrinath, T. Imielinski, and J. Navas. *A WWW-based Location-Dependent Information Service for Mobile Clients.* http://www.caip.rutgers.edu/ navas/loc_dep_mosaic/ Overview.html 1995.

[2] B. Badrinath, A. Acharya, and T. Imielinski. Impact of Mobility on Distributed Computations. *Op. Sys. Rev.*, 27:15–20, 1993.

[3] T. Berners-Lee, R. Cailliau, J.-F. Groff, and B. Pollermann. World Wide Web: The Information Universe. *Electronic Networking: Research, Applications, and Policy*, 2(1):52–58, 1992.

[4] T. Drashansky, S. Weerawarana, A. Joshi, R. WeeraSinghe, and E. Houstis. Software architecture of ubiquitous scientific computing environments. *ACM - Baltzer Mobile Networks and Nomadic Applications*, 1(4), 1996.

[5] G. Forman and J. Zahorjan. The Challenges of Mobile Computing. *IEEE Computer*, 27:38–47, 1994.

[6] Glomop. *Glomop description.* http://HTTP.CS.Berkeley.EDU/ fox/glomop/, 1995.

[7] Grab-a-Site. *Grab-a-Site product description.* http://www.bluesquirrel.com/store/116p.htm, 1995.

[8] A. Joshi. To learn or not to Learn .... In *Lecture Notes in AI: Proc. IJCAI '95 Workshop on Learning and Adaptation in Multiagent Systems*. Springer-Verlag, 1995.

[9] A. Joshi, R. Weerasinghe, S. McDermott, B. Tan, G. Bernhardt, and S. Weerawarana. Mowser: Mobile platforms and web browsers. Bulletin of the IEEE Technical Committee on Operating Systems and Application Environments, 1996. Vol 8, no. 1.

[10] F. Kaashoek, T. Pinckney, and J. Tauber. Dynamic documents: Mobile wireless access to the www. Workshop on Mobile Computing Systems and Applications, December 1994.

[11] R. Kavasseri, T. Keating, M. Wittman, A. Joshi, and S. Weerawarana. Web intelligent query - disconnected web browsing using cooperative techniques. In *Proceedings of the First Intl. Conf. on Cooperative Information Systems*, pages 167–174. IEEE Press, 1996.

[12] M. Liljeberg, T. Alanko, M. Kojo, H. Laamanen, and K. Raatikainen. Optimizing world-wide web for weakly connected mobile workstations: An indirect approach. In *Proc. 2nd International Workshop on Services in Distributed and Networked Environments*, June 1995.

[13] Milktruck. *Milktruck delivery description.* http://www.milktruck.com/cpsisv/index.htm, 1995.

[14] J. Myfield and C. Nicholas. Snitch: Augmenting hypertextdocuments with a semantic net. *Intl. Journal of Intelligent and Cooperative Information Systems*, 2:335–351, 1993.

[15] T. Oates, M. Nagendraprasad, and V. Lesser. Cooperative Information Gathering: A Distributed Problem Solving Approach. Technical Report TR-94-66, UMASS, 1994.

[16] B. Schilit, N. Adams, R. Gold, M. Tso, and R. Want. The parctab mobile computing system. pages 34–39. Proceedings of the Fourth Workshop on Workstation Operating Systems, October 1993.

[17] B. Schilit, F. Douglas, D. Kristol, P. Krzyzanowski, J. Sienicki, and J. Trotter. Teleweb: Loosely connected access to the world wide web. *Computer Networks and ISDN Systems*, 28(711):1431, 1996.

[18] G. Voelker and B. Bershad. Mobisaic: An information system for a mobile wireless computing environment. Workshop on Mobile Computing Systems and Applications, December 1994.

[19] W3 Consortium. Http-ng problem statement. http://www.w3.org/, 1995.

[20] WebWatch. *WebWatch product description.* http://www.specter.com/, 1996.

[21] WebWhacker. *WebWhacker product description.* http://www.ffg.com/whacker.html, 1995.

SESSION :5

CHALLENGES IN SCALABILITY OF DATABASE SYSTEMS

INVITED TALK

Generalization and Decision Tree Induction:
Efficient Classification in Data Mining

Micheline Kamber   Lara Winstone   Wan Gong   Shan Cheng   Jiawei Han
Database Systems Research Laboratory
School of Computing Science
Simon Fraser University, B.C., Canada V5A 1S6
{*kamber, winstone, wgong, shanc, han*}@*cs.sfu.ca*

Abstract

Efficiency and scalability are fundamental issues concerning data mining in large databases. Although classification has been studied extensively, few of the known methods take serious consideration of efficient induction in large databases and the analysis of data at multiple abstraction levels. This paper addresses the efficiency and scalability issues by proposing a data classification method which integrates attribute-oriented induction, relevance analysis, and the induction of decision trees. Such an integration leads to efficient, high-quality, multiple-level classification of large amounts of data, the relaxation of the requirement of perfect training sets, and the elegant handling of continuous and noisy data.

1. Introduction

Computational efficiency and scalability are two important and challenging issues in data mining. Data mining is the automated discovery of non-trivial, previously unknown, and potentially useful patterns embedded in databases [9]. The increasing computerization of all aspects of life has led to the storage of massive amounts of data. Large scale data mining applications involving complex decision-making can access billions of bytes of data. Hence, the efficiency of such applications is paramount.

Classification is a key data mining technique whereby database tuples, acting as *training samples*, are analyzed in order to produce a model of the given data [5, 8, 23]. Each tuple is assumed to belong to a predefined class, as determined by one of the attributes, called the *classifying attribute*. Once derived, the classification model can be used to categorize future data samples, as well as provide a better understanding of the database contents. Classification has numerous applications including credit approval, product marketing, and medical diagnosis.

A number of classification techniques from the statistics and machine learning communities have been proposed [7, 25, 26, 30]. A well-accepted method of classification is the induction of decision trees [3, 25]. A decision tree is a flow-chart-like structure consisting of internal nodes, leaf nodes, and branches. Each internal node represents a decision, or test, on a data attribute, and each outgoing branch corresponds to a possible outcome of the test. Each leaf node represents a class. In order to classify an unlabeled data sample, the classifier tests the attribute values of the sample against the decision tree. A path is traced from the root to a leaf node which holds the class predication for that sample. Decision trees can easily be converted into IF-THEN rules [26] and used for decision-making.

The efficiency of existing decision tree algorithms, such as ID3 [25] and CART [3], has been well established for relatively small data sets [16, 22, 29]. Efficiency and scalability become issues of concern when these algorithms are applied to the mining of very large, real-world databases. Most decision tree algorithms have the restriction that the training tuples should reside in main memory. In data mining applications, very large training sets of millions of examples are common. Hence, this restriction limits the scalability of such algorithms, where the decision tree construction can become inefficient due to swapping of the training samples in and out of main and cache memories.

The induction of decision trees from very large training sets has been previously addressed by the SLIQ [20] and SPRINT [27] decision tree algorithms. These propose pre-sorting techniques on disk-resident data sets that are too large to fit in memory. While SLIQ's scalability, however, is limited by the use of a memory-resident data structure, SPRINT removes all memory restrictions and hence can handle data sets that are too large for SLIQ [27]. Unlike SLIQ and SPRINT, which operate on the raw, low-level data, we address the efficiency and scalability issues by proposing a different approach, consisting of three steps: *1) attribute-oriented induction* [11, 13], where concept hierarchies are used to generalize low-level data to higher level concepts, *2) relevance analysis* [10], and *3) multi-level mining*, whereby decision trees can be induced at different levels of abstraction.

Attribute-oriented induction, a knowledge discovery tool which allows the generalization of data, offers two major advantages for the mining of large databases. First, it allows the raw data to be handled at higher conceptual levels. Generalization is performed with the use of attribute concept hierarchies, where the leaves of a given attribute's concept hierarchy correspond to the attribute's values in the data (referred to as primitive level data) [13]. Generalization of the training data is achieved by replacing primitive level data (such as numerical values for a *GPA*, or *grade point average* attribute) by higher level concepts (such as ranges $3.6 - 3.8$, $3.8 - 4.0$, or categories *good* or *excellent*). Hence, attribute-oriented induction allows the user to view the data at more meaningful abstractions. In many decision tree induction examples, such as in [25], the data to be classified are presented at a relatively high concept level, such as "mild" (temperature) and "high" (humidity). This implies that some preprocessing may have been performed on the primitive data to bring it to a higher concept level. Attribute-oriented induction is useful in that it allows the generalization of data to *multiple-level* generalized concepts. This is particularly useful for continuous-valued attributes.

Furthermore, attribute-oriented induction addresses the scalability issue by compressing the training data. The generalized training data will be much more compact than the original training set, and hence, will involve fewer input/output operations. As we will illustrate in section 4, the efficiency of the resulting decision tree induction will be greatly improved.

The second step of our approach aids scalability by performing attribute relevance analysis [10] on the generalized data, prior to decision tree induction. This process identifies attributes that are either irrelevant or redundant. Including such attributes in the generalized data would slow down, and possibly confuse, the classification process. This step improves classification efficiency and enhances the scalability of classification procedures by eliminating useless information, thereby reducing the amount of data that is input to the classification stage.

The third and final step in our approach is multi-level mining. We propose two algorithms which allow the induction of decision trees at different levels of abstraction by employing the knowledge stored in the concept hierarchies. Furthermore, once a decision tree has been derived, the concept hierarchies can be used to generalize or specialize individual nodes in the tree, allowing attribute rolling-up or drilling-down, and reclassification of the data for the newly specified abstraction level. This interactive feature executes in our DBMiner data mining system [14] with fast response.

This paper is organized as follows. Section 2 describes the attribute-oriented induction, relevance analysis, and multi-level mining components of our proposed approach.

Each component has been implemented in DBMiner [14]. Section 3 presents MedGen and MedGenAdjust, our proposed multi-level decision tree induction algorithms. A performance evaluation is given in Section 4. Section 5 addresses related issues, such as classification accuracy. Conclusions and future work are discussed in Section 6.

2. Proposed approach: generalization-based induction of decision trees

We address efficiency and scalability issues regarding the data mining of large databases by proposing a technique composed of the following three steps: *1)* generalization by attribute-oriented induction, to compress the training data. This includes storage of the generalized data in a multi-dimensional data cube to allow fast accessing, *2)* relevance analysis, to remove irrelevant data attributes, thereby further compacting the training data, and *3)* multi-level mining, which combines the induction of decision trees with knowledge in concept hierarchies. This section describes each step in detail.

2.1. Attribute-oriented induction

In real-world applications, data mining tasks such as classification are applied to training data consisting of thousands or millions of tuples. Applying attribute-oriented induction prior to classification substantially reduces the computational complexity of this data-intensive process [14].

Data are compressed with a *concept tree ascension* technique which replaces attribute values by generalized concepts from corresponding attribute concept hierarchies [11]. Each generalized tuple has a *count* associated with it. This registers the number of tuples in the original training data that the generalized tuple now represents. The *count* information represents statistical data and is used later in the classification process, and enables the handling of noisy and exceptional data.

Concept hierarchies may be provided by domain experts or database administrators, or may be defined using the database schema [11]. Concept hierarchies for numeric attributes can be generated automatically [12]. In addition to allowing the substantial reduction in size of the training set, concept hierarchies allow the representation of data in the user's vocabulary. Hence, aside from increasing efficiency, attribute-oriented induction may result in classification trees that are more understandable, smaller, and therefore easier to interpret than trees obtained from methods operating on ungeneralized (larger) sets of low-level data (such as [20, 27]). The degree of generalization is controlled by an empirically-set *generalization threshold*. If the number of distinct values of an attribute is less than or equal to this threshold, then further generalization of the attribute is halted.

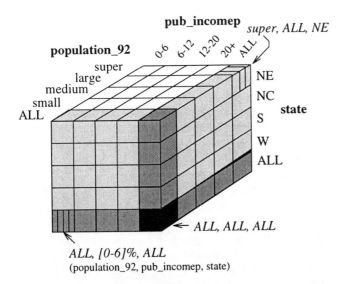

pub_incomep

super, ALL, NE

population_92

ALL, [0-6]%, ALL
(population_92, pub_incomep, state)

Figure 1. A multi-dimensional data cube.

$\{$ USA $\} \subset \{$ ANY $\}$
$\{$ North_East, North_Central, South, West $\} \subset \{$ USA $\}$
$\{$ New_England, Middle_Atlantic $\} \subset \{$ North_East $\}$
$\{$ Mountain, Pacific_East, Pacific_West $\} \subset \{$ West $\}$
... $\{$ Alaska, Hawaii $\} \subset \{$ Pacific_West $\}$

$\{$ small_city, medium_city, large_city, super_city, other $\} \subset$
$\{$ ANY $\}$
$\{$ 10000~20000, 20000~30000, 30000~40000,
40000~50000 $\} \subset \{$ small_city $\}$
... $\{$ 1000000~9999999 $\} \subset \{$ super_city $\}$

Figure 2. Concept hierarchies for attributes *state* **and** *population_92* **of the CITYDATA database.**

Attribute-oriented induction also performs generalization by *attribute removal* [11]. In this technique, an attribute having a large number of distinct values is removed if there is no higher level concept for it. Attribute removal further compacts the training data and reduces the bushiness of resulting trees.

In our approach, the generalized data are stored in a *multi-dimensional data cube* [14], similar to that used in data warehousing [15]. This is a multi-dimensional array structure. Each dimension represents a generalized attribute, and each cell stores the value of some aggregate attribute, such as the *count* information described earlier. Consider a *CITYDATA* database consisting of statistics describing incomes and populations, collected for cities and counties in the United States. Attributes in the database include *state*, *population_92* (city population in 1992), and *pub_incomep* (percentage of population receiving public assistance). A multi-dimensional data cube, *citydata*, is depicted in Figure 1. The original values of *state* have been generalized to *NE* (North_East), *NC* (North_Central), *S* (South), and *W* (West), while *population_92* has been generalized to *small_city, medium_city, large_city* and *super_city*, and *pub_incomep* has been generalized to *0-6%, 6-12%, 12-20%*, and *20+%*. Each dimension includes a value *ALL*, representing the aggregate sum of the entire dimension. The advantage of the multi-dimensional structure is that it allows fast indexing to cells (or slices) of the cube. For instance, one may easily and quickly access the total count of cities for which *0-6%* of the 1992 population received public assistance, for all states and population sizes, combined (i.e., cell *<ALL, 0-6%, ALL>*).

We illustrate the ideas of attribute-oriented induction with an example using the described database. The data mining task is to classify the data according to the database attribute *median_income* (median family income), based on the attributes *city_area* (in square miles), *state, population_92*, and *pub_incomep*. This task is specified in our data mining query language, DMQL [14], as shown below in Example 2.1.

Example 2.1: *Classification task.*

```
classify CITYDATA
according to median_income
in relevance to city_area, state,
              population_92, pub_incomep
from INCOME, POPULATION
where INCOME.place = POPULATION.place
  and INCOME.state = POPULATION.state
```

Prior to applying attribute-oriented induction, the above query retrieves the task-relevant data by performing a relational query on *CITYDATA*. Tuples not satisfying the *where* clause are ignored, and only the data concerning the relevant attributes specified in the *in relevance to* clause, and the class attribute, *median_income*, are collected. An example of such task-relevant training data is shown in Table 1.

city_area	state	population_92	pub_incomep	median_income
20.2	Alabama	27115	10.8	26067.0
...	...	...	...	...
11.3	Wisconsin	62149	5.3	36085.0
20.6	Wyoming	47800	5.9	33366.0

Table 1. Task-relevant data from the CITYDATA database (ungeneralized).

Attribute-oriented induction is performed on the set of relevant data. An intermediate generalized relation, achieved by concept ascension using the concept hierarchies of Figure 2 for the attributes *state* and *population_92*, is displayed in Table 2. Owing to the attribute removal technique, *city_area* does not appear in the resulting table because it has many distinct values and no concept hierarchy with which it could be further generalized. Identical tuples for Table 1 were merged while collecting the count (*cnt*) information. In practice, the resultant table will be substantially smaller than the original database, as well as the ungeneralized task-relevant data.

state	popula-tion_92	pub_incomep	median_income	cnt
North_East	large_city	0%-6%	45Ks-	1
North_East	small_city	0%-6%	30Ks-45Ks	14
...	...	...	...	...
West	large_city	6%-12%	30Ks-45Ks	27

Table 2. Task-relevant data, generalized to an intermediate concept level, with count (*cnt*).

How high a level should each attribute be generalized prior to the application of relevance analysis and multi-level mining? There are at least three possibilities. First, generalization may proceed to the *minimally generalized concept level*, based on the attribute generalization thresholds described above. A relation is minimally generalized if each attribute satisfies its generalization threshold, and if specialization of any attribute would cause the attribute to exceed the generalization threshold [11]. A disadvantage of this approach is that, if each database attribute has many discrete values, the decision tree induced will likely be quite bushy and large.

On the other extreme, generalization may proceed to very high concept levels. Since the resulting relation will be rather small, subsequent decision tree induction will be more efficient than that obtained from minimally generalized data. However, by overgeneralizing, the classification process may lose the ability to distinguish interesting classes or subclasses, and thus may not be able to construct meaningful decision trees.

A trade-off, which we adopt, is to generalize to an intermediate concept level. Such a level can be specified either by a domain expert, or by a threshold which defines the desired number of distinct values for each attribute (such as "4-8 distinct attribute values"). For example, one may generalize the attribute values for *state* to {*North_East, North_Central, South, West*}. It is possible, however, that an intermediate level derived from a predefined concept hierarchy may not best suit the given classification task. In such cases, a level-adjustment process should be introduced to im-

prove the classification quality. In section 2.3, we describe a technique for level-adjustment that is integrated with the induction of decision trees.

2.2. Relevance analysis

In the second step of our approach, we apply attribute relevance analysis to the generalized data obtained from attribute-oriented induction. This further reduces the size of the training data.

A number of statistical and machine learning-based techniques for relevance analysis have been proposed in the literature [2, 10, 17]. We employ an information-theoretic asymmetric measure of relevance known as the *uncertainty coefficient* [19]. This coefficient is based on the information gain attribute selection measure used in C4.5 [26] for building decision trees.

The relevance analysis is performed as follows. Let the generalized data be a set P of p data samples. Suppose the classifying attribute has m distinct values defining m distinct classes P_i (for $i = 1, \ldots, m$). Suppose P contains p_i samples for each P_i, then an arbitrary sample belongs to class P_i with probability p_i/p. The expected information needed to classify a given sample is given by,

$$I(p_1, p_2, \ldots, p_m) = -\sum_{i=1}^{m} \frac{p_i}{p} log_2 \frac{p_i}{p}. \quad (2.1)$$

An attribute A with values $\{a_1, a_2, \cdots, a_k\}$ can be used to partition P into $\{C_1, C_2, \cdots, C_k\}$, where C_j contains those samples in C that have value a_j of A. Let C_j contain p_{ij} samples of class P_i. The expected information based on the partitioning by A is given by,

$$E(A) = \sum_{j=1}^{k} \frac{p_{1j} + \cdots + p_{mj}}{p} I(p_{1j}, \ldots, p_{mj}). \quad (2.2)$$

Thus, the information gained by branching on A is,

$$gain(A) = I(p_1, p_2, \ldots, p_m) - E(A). \quad (2.3)$$

The uncertainty coefficient for attribute A, i.e., $U(A)$, is obtained by normalizing the information gain of A so that $U(A)$ ranges from 0 (meaning statistical independence between A and the classifying attribute) to 1 (strongest degree of relevance between the two attributes),

$$U(A) = \frac{I(p_1, p_2, \ldots, p_m) - E(A)}{I(p_1, p_2, \ldots, p_m)}. \quad (2.4)$$

The user has the option of retaining either the n most relevant attributes, or all attributes whose uncertainty coefficient value is greater than a pre-specified uncertainty threshold, where n and the threshold are user-defined. Note that it is much more efficient to apply the relevance analysis to the generalized data rather than to the original training data. Such analysis on large sets of (ungeneralized) data can be computationally expensive. Hence, by applying attribute-oriented induction in step one in order to reduce the size of the training data, we reduce the amount of computation required in step two of our approach. Furthermore, relevance analysis contributes to step 3 by removing attributes that would otherwise slow down and possibly confuse the classification process.

2.3. Multi-level mining

The third and final step of our method is multi-level mining. This combines decision tree induction of the generalized data obtained in steps 1 and 2 (attribute-oriented induction and relevance analysis) with knowledge in the concept hierarchies. In this section, we introduce two algorithms for multi-level mining. A detailed description of each algorithm follows in Section 3.

In section 2.1, the degree to which attribute-oriented induction should be applied in order to generalize data was discussed. Generalization to a minimally generalized concept level can result in very large and bushy trees. Generalization to very high concept levels can result in decision trees of little use since overgeneralization may cause the loss of interesting and important subconcepts. It was determined that it is most desirable to generalize to some *intermediate* concept level, set by a domain expert or controlled by a user-specified threshold.

We also noted that generalization to an intermediate level derived from a predefined concept hierarchy may not best suit the given classification task. Thus to improve classification quality, it can be useful to incorporate a concept level-adjustment procedure into the process of inducing decision trees. Hence, we propose two algorithms: MedGen and MedGenAdjust. Each algorithm operates on training data that have been generalized to an intermediate level by attribute-oriented induction, and for which unimportant attributes have been removed by relevance analysis. Med-Gen simply applies decision tree induction to the resulting data. MedGenAdjust applies a modified decision tree algorithm which allows the adjustment of concept levels for each attribute in an effort to enhance classification quality. Since both algorithms confine their processing to relatively small generalized relations, rather than repeatedly accessing the (initially large) raw data, both algorithms should have a reasonable processing cost.

3. Proposed algorithms: MedGen and MedGenAdjust

This section describes the MedGen and MedGenAdjust algorithms for classification of large databases in greater detail. Both algorithms apply attribute-oriented induction to generalize data to an intermediate level, followed by relevance analysis, as means of compressing the original large training set. Both MedGen and MedGenAdjust induce decision tree classifiers from the generalized relevant data. While MedGen directly applies a decision tree algorithm to the generalized data, MedGenAdjust allows for dynamic adjustment between different levels of abstraction during the tree building process.

The decision tree induction algorithm on which Med-Gen and MedGenAdjust are based is C4.5 [26] (an earlier version of which is known as ID3 [25]). C4.5 was chosen because it is generally accepted as a standard for decision tree algorithms, and has been extensively tested. It has been used in many application areas ranging from medicine [18] to game theory [24], and is the basis of several commercial rule-induction systems [25]. Furthermore, C4.5 allows the use of an attribute selection measure known as *information gain* [25]. In a comparative study of selection measures, information gain was found to produce accurate and small trees [4]. C4.5 has been repeatedly shown to perform well on relatively small data sets [16, 22, 29]. Section 3.1 outlines the C4.5 algorithm. MedGen and MedGenAdjust are described in Sections 3.2 and 3.3, respectively.

3.1. C4.5 overview

The C4.5 method [25, 26] is a greedy tree growing algorithm which constructs decision trees in a top-down recursive divide-and-conquer strategy. The tree starts as a single node containing the training samples. If the samples are all of the same class, then the node becomes a leaf and is labeled with that class. Otherwise, the algorithm uses equations 2.1 – 2.3 to select the attribute with the highest information gain. This attribute becomes the "decision" or "test" attribute at the node. A branch is created for each value of the decision attribute, and the samples are partitioned accordingly. The algorithm uses the same process recursively to form a decision tree for each partition. The recursive partitioning stops only when all samples at a given node belong to the same class, or when there are no remaining attributes on which the samples may be further partitioned.

3.2. The MedGen algorithm

The MedGen algorithm integrates attribute-oriented induction and relevance analysis with a slightly modified version of the C4.5 decision tree algorithm [26].

MedGen introduces two thresholds which are not part of C4.5. These are an *exception threshold* and a *classification threshold*. A criticism of C4.5 is that, because of the recursive partitioning, some resulting data subsets may become so small that partitioning them further would have no statistically significant basis. The maximum size of such "insignificant" data subsets can be statistically determined. To deal with this problem, MedGen introduces an exception threshold. If the portion of samples in a given subset is less than the threshold, further partitioning of the subset is halted. Instead, a leaf node is created which stores the subset and class distribution of the subset samples.

Moreover, owing to the large amount, and wide diversity, of data in large databases, it may not be reasonable to assume that each leaf node will contain samples belonging to a common class. MedGen addresses this problem by employing a classification threshold, κ. Further partitioning of the data subset at a given node is terminated if the percentage of samples belonging to any given class at that node exceeds the classification threshold. Our classification threshold is similar to the precision threshold introduced by [1]. Use of such thresholds for dynamic pruning may be more efficient than traditional tree pruning strategies [21] which first fully grow a tree and then prune it. The MedGen algorithm is outlined below.

Algorithm 3.1 (MedGen) *Perform data classification using a prespecified classifying attribute on a relational database by integration of attribute-oriented induction and relevance analysis with a decision tree induction method.*

Input. *1)* a data classification task which specifies the set of relevant data and a classifying attribute in a relational database DB, *2)* a set of concept hierarchies on attributes A_i, *3)* τ_i, a set of *attribute (generalization) thresholds* for attributes A_i, *4)* an exception threshold ϵ, and *5)* a classification threshold κ.

Output. A classification of the set of data and a set of classification rules.

Method.
1. Data collection: Collect the relevant set of data, R_0, by relational query processing.
2. Attribute-oriented induction: Using the concept hierarchies, perform attribute-oriented induction to generalize R_0 to an intermediate level. The resultant relation is R_1. The generalization level is controlled by τ_i, a set of *attribute thresholds* associated with attributes A_i.
3. Relevance analysis: Perform relevance analysis on the generalized data relation, R_1. The information theoretic-based uncertainty coefficient [19] is used for this purpose, although other methods, such as those suggested in [2, 17] could be used. The resulting data relation is R_2.

4. Decision-tree generation
   (a) Given the generalized and relevant data relation, R_2, compute the information gain for each candidate attribute using the equations $(2.1) - (2.3)$. Select the candidate attribute which gives the maximum information gain as the decision or "test" attribute at this current level, and partition the current set of objects accordingly. Although information gain is used here, as in C4.5 [25], alternatively other selection measurements (such as the gini-index [20, 30]) could be used.
   (b) For each subset created by the partitioning, repeat Step 4a to further classify data until either (1) all or a substantial proportion (no less than κ, the classification threshold) of the objects are in one class, (2) no more attributes can be used for further classification, or (3) the percentage of objects in the subclass (with respect to the total number of training samples) is below ϵ, the exception threshold.

5. Classification-rule generation: Generate rules according to the decision tree so derived (as in [26]).
   □

Rationale of Algorithm 3.1. Step 1 is relational query processing. Step 2 has been verified in [11, 13]. Step 3 eliminates irrelevant attributes from the generalized data. Step 4 is essentially the C4.5 algorithm whose correctness has been shown in [25, 26]. Our modification uses quantitative information collected in Step 1 to terminate classification if the frequency of the majority class in a given subset is greater than the classification threshold, or if the percentage of training objects represented by the subset is less than the exception threshold. Otherwise, further classification will be performed recursively. Step 5 generates rules according to the decision tree which reflect the general regularity of the data in the database.   □

3.3. The MedGenAdjust algorithm

The MedGenAdjust algorithm performs the same steps as the MedGen algorithm, yet it replaces the **decision-tree generation** step (Step 4) by **level-adjusted decision-tree generation**, an integration of the decision tree generation process with abstraction-level adjustment. This allows the generalization and/or specialization of the abstraction level of individual decision nodes in the tree.

The level-adjustment process consists of *node-merge*, *node-split*, and *split-node-merge* operations. We say that a node *largely* belongs to a given class if the number of class samples it contains exceeds the classification threshold, κ. In *node-merge*, if some child nodes at a selected concept level share the same parent, and largely belong to the same

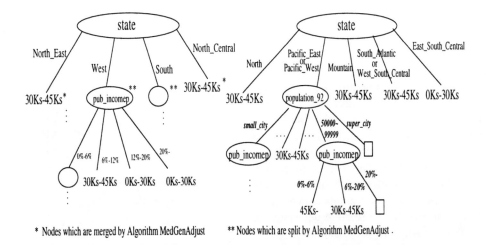

* Nodes which are merged by Algorithm MedGenAdjust   ** Nodes which are split by Algorithm MedGenAdjust .

Figure 3. Decision trees obtained for *median_income* **from** MedGen **(left), and** MedGenAdjust **(right).**

class, then these nodes can be merged into one. A set of nodes representing numeric ranges should be merged together if such a merge would result in a range extension. In *node-split*, if a node does not largely belong to a class, but some of its sub-nodes do, then the node can be split based on the grouping of its sub-nodes. In *split-node-merge*, some split nodes may share the same parent and largely belong to the same class, so these nodes can be merged together. Moreover, certain split nodes may be further merged with neighboring nodes. Node-merging can reduce the number of disjunctions in the derived classification rules, simplifying the classification results.

For example, consider the classification task of Example 2.1, as well as the generalized *CITYDATA* of Table 2, and the concept hierarchies of Figure 2. To classify data according to *median_income*, the attribute *state* can be examined at an intermediate level, consisting of values {*North_East, North_Central, South, West*}. If *North* is made up of *North_Central* and *North_East*, and most cities in these regions have a high median income, then *North_Central* and *North_East* can be merged into a single node, designated as *North* (Figure 3). On the other hand, if cities in the *West* show no obvious median income class, then this category may be split. Recall from Figure 2 that *West* consists of three subregions, namely {*Mountain, Pacific_East, Pacific_West*}. If the *Mountain* subregion shows an obvious class of 30Ks - 45Ks for *median_income*, while the other two subregions show no obvious class, then the node *West* should be split into two sub-nodes, *Mountain* and *Pacific_East_or_Pacific_West*. The *South* node may be split in a similar fashion. Figure 3 shows the resulting tree.

The level-adjustment process can be performed on each candidate attribute. The level-adjusted attribute with the largest information gain is selected as a decision node and is used to partition the training data into subsets. The algorithm

is recursively applied to each subset, using the same stopping condition as for MedGen. The level-adjustment procedure (Step 4 of MedGenAdjust) is outlined below.

Step 4. Level-adjusted decision-tree generation.

1. For each attribute A_i, do $level\_adjustment(A_i)$.

   The level-adjustment procedure finds a partitioning for each A_i by performing *node-merge* (generalization), *node-split* (specialization) and *node-split-merge* (generalization and specialization), and can be performed on all relevant attributes in parallel.

2. Compute the information gain for each candidate attribute's adjusted partitioning (obtained in 1). Select one candidate attribute as the decision attribute based on the calculated information gains obtained.

3. Recursively perform Step 4 for each subclass (node) created by the partitioning until either (1) all or a substantial proportion (no less than κ) of the objects are in one class, (2) no more attributes can be used for further classification, or (3) the size of the node falls below the specified exception threshold ϵ.

The result of **level-adjustment** may be a partition that occurs at multiple levels of abstraction, with the principal motivating factor being improved classification through dynamic adjustment.

4. Performance Evaluation

This section describes experiments conducted to study the efficiency and scalability of our proposed approach to the classification of large databases. Recall that prior to decision tree induction, the task relevant data can be generalized to a number of different degrees, e.g.,

117

1. No generalization: The training data are not generalized at all. This is the case for typical applications of decision tree classifiers, such as C4.5 [26]. We call such an algorithm NoGen.

2. Minimal-level generalization: The training data are generalized to a minimally generalized concept level (see Section 2.1). Subsequently, decision tree induction is applied. We call such an algorithm MinGen.

3. Intermediate-level generalization: The training data are generalized to an intermediate concept level before decision tree induction. This is the case for the proposed MedGen and MedGenAdjust algorithms.

4. High-level generalization: The training data are generalized to a high concept level before decision tree induction. We call such an algorithm HiGen.

Since the generalized data induced in HiGen will typically be much smaller than that in the other algorithms listed here, we would expect it to be the most efficient. However, as discussed earlier, we do not expect such classifications to be meaningful due to overgeneralization. Hence, we do not include it in our study. Furthermore, we expect NoGen to be the least efficient of all methods. The NoGen approach involves working on a very large set of raw data, and thus entails heavy data accessing. In contrast, classification on generalized data will be faster since it will be working with a smaller generalized relation. Our strategy of storing data in a multi-dimensional data cube results in increased computation efficiency. Granted, some overhead is required to set up the cube. However, the subsequent advantage of stored data in a data cube is that it allows fast indexing to cells (or slices) of the cube. Recall that C4.5 requires the calculation of information gain for each attribute, considering each attribute value, at each node [26]. This results in heavy computation from the calculation of memory addresses and subsequent accessing of the raw data. Fast accessing and quick calculation of addresses are a feature of the data cube's storage and indexing system [14, 15]. Hence, our experiments focus on comparing the efficiency of MinGen, MedGen, and MedGenAdjust. Classification accuracy is discussed in Section 5.

All experiments were conducted on a Pentium-166 PC with 64 MB RAM, running Windows/NT. The algorithms were implemented in DBMiner [14] using MicroSoft Visual C++. (DBMiner is accessible on the web at http://db.cs.sfu.ca/DBMiner). The results were obtained from the execution of a query from the *CITYDATA* database. The query was executed ten times, and the average CPU time in milliseconds was calculated. The database consists of over 29 MB, and was described in Section 2.1. Figure 4 graphs the execution time, in CPU milliseconds, for each algorithm with various classification threshold settings. As expected, the execution time for each algorithm generally increases with the classification threshold. The algorithms

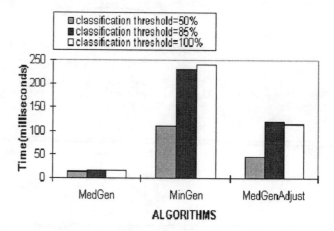

Figure 4. Average execution time (in CPU milliseconds) per algorithm for various classification threshold settings.

were tested with the exception threshold set at 0.5%. All threshold values were empirically-determined. There were 1071 tuples in the task-relevant, ungeneralized data relation, 855 tuples in the minimal concept level generalized relation (for MinGen), and 97 tuples in the intermediate level generalized relation (processed by MedGen and MedGenAdjust).

In order to generalize the data to an intermediate concept level, MedGen and MedGenAdjust must spend more time than MinGen on attribute-oriented induction. Yet, because the generalized intermediate level data are much smaller than the generalized minimal level data, both algorithms require much less time to induce decision trees than does MinGen. Hence, MinGen is the least efficient of the three algorithms. Thus, we see that generalizing training data to an intermediate level does improve the efficiency of decision tree induction. As expected, MedGen is more efficient than MedGenAdjust due to the extra processing time incurred by MedGenAdjust for level-adjustment. However, with MedGenAdjust, a balance is struck between user-desired levels and automatic refinement of the abstraction level to ensure classification quality. On average, trees induced by MinGen, MedGen, and MedGenAdjust had 72, 36, and 37 leaves, respectively. Thus, generalization also reduces the average size of the induced decision trees, thereby contributing to improved understandability of the classification results. MedGen with dynamic pruning (using an empirically set classification threshold of 85% to control the growth of branches during construction of the tree) was compared with MedGen with post-pruning (employing a classification threshold of 100% to avoid pre-pruning). The error-cost complexity post-pruning algorithm [3] was used since it has been shown to produce small and accurate decision trees [21]. Although post-pruning requires greater computational effort since it must grow the tree fully, and then generate and examine variations of the tree pruned to different degrees in order to find the most accurate tree, we found no statistically significant difference in the accuracy of the decision trees obtained from the dynamic and post-pruning strategies.

Finally, the user can perform additional multi-level mining on a displayed tree by clicking on any nonleaf node to expand it (showing all of the node's children) or shrink it (collapsing all of the node's descendants into the node itself). Storage of the generalized data in the multi-dimensional data cube allows for fast attribute rolling-up or drilling-down, and reclassification of the data for the newly specified abstraction level. This interactive feature of DBMiner is fast, executing in real time, and allows the user to gain additional insight into the classified data.

5. Discussion

Classification accuracy. In classification problems, it is commonly assumed that all objects are uniquely classifiable, i.e., that each training sample can belong to only one class. In addition to efficiency, classification algorithms can then be compared according to their accuracy. Accuracy is measured using a *test* set of objects for which the class labels are known. Accuracy is estimated as the number of correct class predictions, divided by the total number of test samples. To classify an object, a path is traced (based on the attribute values of the object) from the root of the tree to a leaf node. The majority class at that node is deemed the class prediction of the given object. For each test object, the class prediction is compared to the known class of the object. If the two match, the class prediction is counted as correct. Otherwise, it is counted as incorrect.

However, owing to the wide diversity of data in large databases, it is not reasonable to assume that all objects are uniquely classifiable. Rather, it is more probable to assume that each object may belong to more than one class. How then, can the accuracy of classifiers on large databases be measured? The accuracy measure is not appropriate, since it does not take into account the possibility of samples belonging to more than one class. This problem has not yet been adequately solved in the literature.

A *second guess* heuristic has been used to address this situation [28] whereby a classification prediction is counted as correct if it agrees with the majority class of the leaf at which the object "falls", or if it agrees with the second class in majority at that leaf. Class predictions that disagree with the first two classes in majority at the leaf, are counted as incorrect. Although this method does take into consideration, in some degree, the non-unique classification of objects, it is not a complete solution.

It is difficult to compare the accuracy of decision trees that are based on the same classifying attribute, yet that use different levels of abstraction. For example, given *population_92* as the classifying attribute, one tree may use the values from, say, a low level of the attribute's concept hierarchy as class values (e.g., 10000~20000, ..., 1000000~9999999), while another may use the values from a higher level (e.g., small_city, ..., super_city). This situation can make it difficult to compare decision trees obtained from MedGen and MedGenAdjust. In these cases, the user plays an important role in judging the classification quality.

As we have seen, it is difficult to assess the accuracy of classifiers on large databases. Presently, we are investigating some form of *weighted* accuracy measure which considers the correctness of objects belonging to multiple classes.

Additional issues. An inherent weakness of C4.5 is that the information gain attribute selection criterion has a tendency to favor many-valued attributes [25]. Quinlan offers a solution to this problem in [26]. Attribute-oriented induction is yet another solution since it results in the generalization of many values into a small set of distinct values.

By creating a branch for each decision attribute value, C4.5 encounters the overbranching problem caused by unnecessary partitioning of the data. Various solutions have been proposed for this problem [6, 20, 27]. MedGenAdjust also addresses this problem since it allows node merging, thereby discouraging overpartitioning of the data.

6. Conclusions and future work

We have proposed a simple but promising method for data classification which addresses efficiency and scalability issues regarding data mining in large databases. We have proposed two algorithms, MedGen and MedGenAdjust. Each algorithm first generalizes the data to an intermediate abstraction level by attribute-oriented induction. This compresses the data while allowing the data to be used at more meaningful levels of abstraction. Relevance analysis is then applied to remove irrelevant data attributes, thereby further compacting the generalized data. The resulting data are much smaller than the original training set. MedGen then applies a modified version of the C4.5 algorithm [26] to extract classification rules from the generalized relation by inducing a decision tree. MedGenAdjust is a refinement of MedGen since it allows for level-adjustment across multiple abstraction levels during decision tree construction. With MedGenAdjust, a balance is struck between user-desired levels and automatic refinement of the abstraction level to promote quality classification.

Generalization of the training data, and the use of a multi-dimensional data cube make the proposed algorithms scalable and efficient since the algorithms can then operate on a smaller, compressed relation, and can take advantage of fast data accessing due to the indexing structure of the cube.

Our future work involves further refinement of the level-adjustment procedure of MedGenAdjust. For example, we plan to consider the merging of cousin, niece/nephew nodes in addition to the merging of siblings in *node-merge*.

References

[1] R. Agrawal, S. Ghosh, T. Imielinski, B. Iyer, and A. Swami. An interval classifier for database mining applications. In *Proc. 18th Intl. Conf. Very Large Data Bases (VLDB)*, pages 560–573, Vancouver, Canada, 1992.

[2] H. Almuallim and T. G. Dietterich. Learning with many irrelevant features. In *Proc. 9th Nat. Conf. on Artificial Intelligence*, volume 2, pages 547–552, Menlo Park, CA, July 1991. AAAI Press.

[3] L. Breiman, J. Friedman, R. Olshen, and C. Stone. *Classification of Regression Trees*. Wadsworth, 1984.

[4] W. Buntine and T. Niblett. A further comparison of splitting rules for decision-tree induction. *Machine Learning*, 8:75–85, 1992.

[5] U. Fayyad, G. Piatetsky-Shapiro, and P. Smyth. Knowledge discovery and data mining: Towards a unifying framework. In *Proc. 2nd Intl. Conf. on Knowledge Discovery and Data Mining (KDD'96)*, pages 82–88, Portland, Oregon, 1996.

[6] U. M. Fayyad. Branching on attribute values in decision tree generation. In *Proc. 1994 AAAI Conf.*, pages 601–606, AAAI Press, 1994.

[7] U. M. Fayyad, S. G. Djorgovski, and N. Weir. Automating the analysis and cataloging of sky surveys. In U. Fayyad, G. Piatetsky-Shapiro, P. Smyth, and R. Uthurusamy, editors, *Advances in Knowledge Discovery and Data Mining*, pages 471–493. AAAI/MIT Press, 1996.

[8] U. M. Fayyad, G. Piatetsky-Shapiro, P. Smyth, and R. Uthurusamy. *Advances in Knowledge Discovery and Data Mining*. AAAI/MIT Press, 1996.

[9] W. J. Frawley, G. Piatetsky-Shapiro, and C. J. Matheus. Knowledge discovery in databases: An overview. In G. Piatetsky-Shapiro and W. J. Frawley, editors, *Knowledge Discovery in Databases*, pages 1–27. AAAI/MIT Press, 1991.

[10] D. H. Freeman, Jr. *Applied Categorical Data Analysis*. Marcel Dekker, Inc., New York, NY, 1987.

[11] J. Han, Y. Cai, and N. Cercone. Data-driven discovery of quantitative rules in relational databases. *IEEE Trans. Knowledge and Data Engineering*, 5:29–40, 1993.

[12] J. Han and Y. Fu. Dynamic generation and refinement of concept hierarchies for knowledge discovery in databases. In *Proc. AAAI'94 Workshop on Knowledge Discovery in Databases (KDD'94)*, pages 157–168, Seattle, WA, 1994.

[13] J. Han and Y. Fu. Exploration of the power of attribute-oriented induction in data mining. In U. Fayyad, G. Piatetsky-Shapiro, P. Smyth, and R. Uthurusamy, editors, *Advances in Knowledge Discovery and Data Mining*, pages 399–421. AAAI/MIT Press, 1996.

[14] J. Han, Y. Fu, W. Wang, J. Chiang, W. Gong, K. Koperski, D. Li, Y. Lu, A. Rajan, N. Stefanovic, B. Xia, and O. R. Zaiane. DBMiner: A system for mining knowledge in large relational databases. In *Proc. 1996 Intl. Conf. on Data Mining and Knowledge Discovery (KDD'96)*, pages 250–255, Portland, Oregon, August 1996.

[15] V. Harinarayan, A. Rajaraman, and J. D. Ullman. Implementing data cubes efficiently. In *Proc. 1996 ACM-SIGMOD Int. Conf. Management of Data*, pages 205–216, Montreal, Canada, June 1996.

[16] L. B. Holder. Intermediate decision trees. In *Proc. 14th Intl. Joint Conf. on Artificial Intelligence*, pages 1056–1062, Montreal, Canada, Aug 1995.

[17] G. H. John. Irrelevant features and the subset selection problem. In W. W. Cohen and H. Hirsh, editors, *Proc. 11th Intl. Conf. on Machine Learning*, pages 121–129, San Fransisco, CA, July 1994. Morgan Kaufmann.

[18] M. Kamber, R. Shinghal, D. L. Collins, G. S. Francis, and A. C. Evans. Model-based 3D segmentation of multiple sclerosis lesions in magnetic resonance brain images. *IEEE Transactions on Medical Imaging*, 14(3):442–453, 1995.

[19] H. J. Loether and D. G. McTavish. *Descriptive and Inferential Statistics: An Introduction*. Allyn and Bacon, 1993.

[20] M. Mehta, R. Agrawal, and J. Rissanen. SLIQ: A fast scalable classifier for data mining. In *Proc. 1996 Intl. Conf. on Extending Database Technology (EDBT'96)*, Avignon, France, March 1996.

[21] J. Mingers. An empirical comparison of pruning methods for decision-tree induction. *Machine Learning*, 4(3):227–243, 1989.

[22] R. Mooney, J. Shavlik, G. Towell, and A. Grove. An experimental comparison of symbolic and connectionist learning algorithms. In *Proc. 11th Intl. Joint Conf. on Artificial Intelligence*, pages 775–787, Detroit, MI, Aug 1989. Morgan Kaufmann.

[23] G. Piatetsky-Shapiro and W. J. Frawley. *Knowledge Discovery in Databases*. AAAI/MIT Press, 1991.

[24] J. R. Quinlan. Learning efficient classification procedures and their application to chess end-games. In M. et al., editor, *Machine Learning: An Artificial Intelligence Approach, Vol. 1*, pages 463–482. Morgan Kaufmann, 1983.

[25] J. R. Quinlan. Induction of decision trees. *Machine Learning*, 1:81–106, 1986.

[26] J. R. Quinlan. *C4.5: Programs for Machine Learning*. Morgan Kaufmann, 1993.

[27] J. Shafer, R. Agrawal, and M. Mehta. SPRINT: a scalable parallel classifier for data mining. In *Proc. 22nd Intl. Conf. Very Large Data Bases (VLDB)*, pages 544–555, Mumbai (Bombay), India, 1996.

[28] R. Uthurusamy, U. Fayyad, and S. Spangler. Learning useful rules from inconclusive data. In G. Piatetsky-Shapiro and W. J. Frawley, editors, *Knowledge Discovery in Databases*, pages 141–157, Menlo Park, CA, 1991. AAAI/MIT Press.

[29] S. M. Weiss and I. Kapouleas. An empirical comparison of pattern recognition, neural nets, and machine learning classification methods. In *Proc. 11th Intl. Joint Conf. on Artificial Intelligence*, pages 781–787, Detroit, MI, Aug 1989. Morgan Kaufmann.

[30] S. M. Weiss and C. A. Kulikowski. *Computer Systems that Learn: Classification and Prediction Methods from Statistics, Neural Nets, Machine Learning, and Expert Systems*. Morgan Kaufman, 1991.

SESSION :6

DISTRIBUTED FILE STRUCTURE AND MULTIMEDIA SYSTEMS

Batching and Dynamic Allocation Techniques for Increasing the Stream Capacity of an On-Demand Media Server *

Divyesh Jadav & Chutimet Srinilta
ECE Department & CASE Center
Syracuse University , Syracuse, NY 13244
{divyesh,csrinilt}@cat.syr.edu

Alok Choudhary
ECE Department & Technological Institute
Northwestern University, Evanston, Illinois 60208.
choudhar@ece.nwu.edu

Abstract

A server for an interactive distributed multimedia system may require thousands of gigabytes of storage space and high I/O bandwidth. In order to maximize system utilization, and thus minimize cost, the load must be balanced among the server's disks, interconnection network and scheduler. Many algorithms for maximizing retrieval capacity from the storage system have been proposed. This paper presents techniques for improving server capacity by assigning media requests to the nodes of a server so as to balance the load on the interconnection network and the scheduling nodes. Five policies for request assignment are developed. The performance of these policies on an implementation of a server model developed earlier is presented.

1. Introduction

Digitalization of traditionally analog data such as video and audio, and the feasibility of obtaining networking bandwidths above the gigabit-per-second range are two key advances that have made possible the realization, in the near future, of interactive distributed multimedia systems. Multimedia data differs from unimedia data in the diversity of data sizes and the need to provide real-time guarantees for playback (video and audio data). One of the most pervasive interactive multimedia applications is *media-on-demand* which refers to the possibility of a consumer interactively retrieving multimedia data over high-speed networks from geographically distributed media servers. It is anticipated that a distributed media-on-demand (MOD) system will be built in a hierarchical manner,

with clients connected to neighbourhood servers, which are connected to metropolitan servers, which in turn are connected to massive archive servers. This hierarchy of servers is similar to the memory hierarchy in a computer system. When the processor issues a request for data, the time penalty for retrieving the data is directly proportional to the hierarchical distance of the data from the processor, which constitutes the apex of the hierarchy. In a hierarcical MOD system, a similar relationship exists in this case with regard to the time delay for data retrieval by a client. On account of the real-time and storage capacity requirements of multimedia data, the servers are high-end machines with gigabytes of storage space and high I/O bandwidth. Moreover, higher up the hierarchy is the server, the higher its storage and I/O capacity. In order for the entire system to be cost effective, each server must be cost effective. Hence, it is essential to maximize the utilization of each resource type of the server. This paper deals with techniques to maximize the utilization of one of the resource types of a MOD server.

1.1. Related work

Researchers have proposed various approaches for the storage and retrieval of multimedia data. [1, 2] have proposed a disk arm scheduling approach for multimedia data, and characterized the disk-level tradeoffs in a multimedia server. [3] proposed a model based on constrained block allocation, which is basically non-contiguous disk allocation in which the time taken to retrieve successive stream blocks does not exceed the the playback duration of a stream block. Storing a stream on a single disk restricts the retrieval bandwidth to the data transfer bandwidth of the disk. [4] get around this problem by striping media data across several disks in a round robin fashion. The effective retrieval bandwidth is then proportional to the number of disks used. Our server model (section 2) is simi-

---

*This work is supported by Intel Corporation and NSF grants CCR-9357840 and CCR-9509143. The authors thank the Caltech CCSF facilities for providing access to the Intel Paragon.

lar to this model. Issues in designing MOD servers are discussed in [6]. [5, 14] studied efficient memory allocation and utilization techniques to maximize the number of supported users. [5] also studied cost trade-offs and scalability issues in high performance MOD servers. Techniques for improving reliability and availability of the storage subsystem are studied in [13]. A component-wise instrumentation of the delays in a MOD [7], showed that variable delays become performance bottlenecks at high loads. Techniques for balancing the load on the storage devices of a MOD server were developed in [8] .Given the fact that a high performance MOD server consists of multiple processors (nodes) connected by an interconnection network, not much work has been reported on efficient use of the interconnection network so as to maximize server capacity. In this paper we address this issue by developing five policies - round robin (RR), minimum link allocation (MLA), minimum contention allocation (MCA), weighted minimum link allocation (WMLA) and weighted contention allocation (WMCA). We have developed and implemented a logical model for a MOD server [7]. Performance results of the five policies under this model implemented on the Intel Paragon parallel computer are presented.

The rest of this paper is organized as follows : Section 2 explains the server and data scheduling model. Section 3 presents the five allocation strategies. Section 4 discusses various striping tradeoffs for distributing file data across storage nodes. We present and analyze performance results in Section 5. Conclusions and future work are presented in Section 6.

2. Server and scheduling model

At the heart of the system is a high-performance server optimized for fast I/O. A parallel machine is a good candidate for such a server because of its ability to serve multiple clients simultaneously, its high disk and node memory, and the parallelism of data retrieval that can be obtained by data striping. We assume that (a) the server is connected to clients by a high-speed wide-area network, which delivers data to clients reliably and at the required bandwidth. (b) Clients have *hard* deadlines i.e. they cannot tolerate jitter. (c) The data are stored at the server in compressed digital form, with the decompression being done at the client end. The server consists of multiple nodes interconnected by a network. Each node is a computer in its own right, with a CPU, RAM and secondary storage. There are three types of nodes, **interface (I) nodes**, **storage (S) nodes** and the **object manager (O) node**. The object manager receives all incoming requests for me-

Symbol	Description	Units
R_{pl}	Required playback rate	bytes/sec
P_I	Size of packets sent by an I node	bytes
δ_I	Duration of a packet sent by an I node	sec
B_I	Buffer size at an I node	bytes
P_S	Size of packets sent by a S node	bytes
δ_S	Duration of data in B_I	sec
SF	Stripe factor	-

Table 1. The parameters used in this paper

dia objects, and *delegates the responsibility* of serving a request to one of the interface nodes. I nodes are responsible for scheduling and serving stream requests that have been accepted. Storage nodes *store* multimedia data on their secondary storage devices in a striped fashion, and *retrieve* and transmit the data to an interface node on request. The assumption about the architecture of the interconnection network is that any node can transfer data to and from any other node with approximately the same latency, under conditions of light load. For the purposes of this paper, we assume that the interconnection network is a *direct* network[9].

The data is compressed and striped across the storage nodes in a round-robin fashion. The number of nodes across which a data object is striped is called the *stripe factor (SF)*. The collection of SF storage nodes that store an object is called a *striping group*. The data stored at a storage node consists of chunks of the object. The collection of chunks is called a *subobject*. Note that the collection of chunks of a subobject do not constitute a contiguous portion of the object; however the data *within* a chunk is a contiguous part of the entire object. This contiguous data is called a *stripe fragment*. Note that each storage node may have a single high-performance disk, or an array of slower, but cheaper disks. The point to note is that a storage node represents a *virtual disk* to an interface node. Since the stripe fragments on any given storage node's disk are not consecutive fragments, it is not necessary to store them contiguously. Disk scheduling algorithms to optimize retrieval from the disk surface have been proposed [1, 11, 5], and can be used in our model. We are concerned with harnessing the parallelism provided by striped storage and balancing the load across the server subsystems.

Table 1 shows the parameters used by our model. δ_I is the time for which a packet sent by an I node to a client will last at the client. Hence this is also the deadline by which the next packet from the I node must be received at the client. Its value is given by:

$$\delta_I = \frac{P_I}{R_{pl}} \qquad (1)$$

Once the requested SF stripe fragments from the S nodes have arrived at the destination I node, the latter arranges them in the proper sequence and continues sending packets of size P_I to the client no less than every δ_I seconds. The buffer at the I node will last for δ_S time, before which the next set of stripe fragments must have arrived from the S nodes. The average time to retrieve P_S bytes from a S node is given by

$$\delta_{io} = \delta_{rq} + \delta_{avg_{seek}} + \delta_{avg_{rot}} + \delta_{tr_{P_S}} + \delta_{nw_{P_S}} \quad (2)$$

where δ_{rq} is the time delay for a request from an I node to reach a S node, $\delta_{avg_{seek}}$ and $\delta_{avg_{rot}}$ are the average seek and rotational latencies for the disks being used, $\delta_{tr_{P_S}}$ is the disk data transfer time for P_s bytes, and $\delta_{nw_{P_S}}$ is the network latency to transport P_s bytes from a S node to an I node. Note that equation 2 uses average seek and rotational latencies for disk accesses, for reasons explained in[7].

3. Stream assignment policies

In a given server configuration, only a finite number of nodes (interface nodes) would be connected to the high speed wide area network. Moreover, their position in the server architecture would be fixed a-priori. Secondly, since the secondary storage capacity for a given server configuration is finite, only a finite number of media objects can be stored in the secondary storage system at a time. In order to maximize the pool of potential clients, there would exist a tertiary storage system from which the most frequently requested objects are materialized on the secondary storage subsystem. However, the number of objects stored on secondary storage would be a slowly changing set. Given the fact that the position of the I nodes and the storage pattern of data on S nodes is fixed, the problem is one of assigning accepted media requests to I nodes so as to minimize the incremental workload due to the new requests on the server's resource types. This allows the server to maximize the number of streams that it can source. The network communication time is the sum of two factors - the network latency in the absence of blocking, and the blocking time due to link contention in the interconnection network i.e.,

$$\delta_{nw_{P_S}} = \delta_{nw_{comm}} + \delta_{nw_{bl}} \quad (3)$$

For a given message size and interconnection network, the former is fixed; while the latter depends on the network traffic. There is another variable delay in the retrieval time : when multiple requests arrive at a S node, only a finite number of them can be served at a given time; this causes a queueing delay at the S nodes. If δ_{S_Q} denotes this queueing delay, equation 2 requires

to be modified to :

$$\delta'_{io} = \delta_{rq} + \delta_{seek} + \delta_{rot} + \delta_{tr_{P_S}} + (\delta_{nw_{comm}} + \delta_{nw_{bl}}) + \delta_{S_Q}$$
$$(4)$$

The effect of the variable delays $\delta_{nw_{bl}}$ and δ_{S_Q} on total retrieval time at various workloads was studied in[7]. At heavy workloads, these delays become the limiting factors on stream capacity. Any mechanism that reduces either or both of these quantities improves performance. In this paper we show that techniques that reduce $\delta_{nw_{bl}}$ by minimizing link contention translate into the ability to support more streams.

3.1. RR assignment policy

This is the simplest policy. If n is the total number of interface nodes, and the ith request was assigned to interface node k, then the $(i + 1)$th request will be assigned to interface node $(k + 1)$ mod n. This policy is simple, requiring $O(1)$ time to execute. The maximum workload imbalance in terms of number of streams served per I node is at most 1. However, this policy does not balance or minimize the load imposed on the interconnection network.

3.2. MLA policy

This policy aims to minimize the total number of links that the data for an object has to travel from the SF storage nodes on which it is stored to the I node which sends it to the outside world. If l_{I_i, S_j} denotes the number of links between interface node I_i and storage node S_j, then the cost of assigning a stream request to interface node I_i under this policy is :

$$CA_{MLA}(I_i) = \sum_{j=1}^{SF} l_{I_i, S_j} \quad (5)$$

This policy will assign a request to interface node p,

$$p = i : (\min(CA_{MLA}(I_i)) \qquad i = 1, 2, ..., n) \quad (6)$$

i.e., the request is assigned to that interface node which is closest in terms of the total number of links that need to be traversed from the S nodes to the I node. This policy tries to minimize the number of streams using a given link. But, it does not take into account the pre-existing link load. Nor does it balance the total stream load among all the interface nodes.

3.3. MCA policy

In this policy, state information is maintained about the usage of each link. Specifically, whenever a new request is assigned to an interface node, the load imposed on the interconnection network by data traffic due to that stream is calculated and the total load on the network due to all streams is updated. When a stream terminates, the load due to it is decremented from the total network load. If $c_{I_i,S_j}[k]$ is the cost of using the kth link on the path from storage node S_j to interface node I_i, then the cost of assigning a stream request to interface node I_i under this policy is :

$$CA_{MCA}(I_i) = \sum_{j=1}^{SF} \sum_{k=1}^{l_{I_i,S_j}} c_{I_i,S_j}[k] \qquad (7)$$

This policy will assign a request to interface node p,

$$p = i : (\min(CA_{MCA}(I_i)) \qquad i = 1, 2, ..., n) \qquad (8)$$

The cost of using a link is directly proportional to the traffic that the link carries. The link traffic due to accepting a new request is updated as follows :

$$
\begin{aligned}
&\text{for } (\ j = 1 \text{ to } SF \ ) \\
&\quad \text{for } (\ k = 1 \text{ to } l_{I_p,S_j}) \\
&\qquad c_{I_p,S_j}[k] = c_{I_p,S_j}[k] + ld \qquad (9)
\end{aligned}
$$

where ld is a scalar that reflects the load imposed by the new stream on link k. Its value is implementation-dependent : it depends on the network, the size of packets being transferred and the playback rate of the stream. The premise behind this policy is that the load should be distributed evenly over the interconnection network. If some links are more heavily used than others, contention in these links increases network blocking effects, which in turn degrades server performance. Note that since the traffic pattern in the interconnection network for data packets consists of storage nodes sending data to interface nodes, there is a possibility of hot spots developing at the links around the interface nodes. This policy tries to prevent the formation of such hot spots by allocating requests to interface nodes so that aggregate link traffic is distributed as evenly as possible over the entire interconnection network.

3.4. WMLA and WMCA policies

The MLA policy tries to minimize the total number of links that data for a stream will have to travel, while the MCA policy tries to minimize link contention by distributing traffic over more lightly used links. However, neither of them tries to balance the load across the interface nodes. An interface node can source only a finite number of streams; beyond this limit client deadlines may be missed due to excessive scheduling overhead. The weighted MLA and MCA policies try to balance the load across both the network and the

I nodes. This is done by factoring in the number of streams that a candidate I node is serving in the cost equation. Specifically, if M_{I_i} is the number of streams being served by interface node I_i, then the cost of assigning to it the responsibility of serving a request under WMLA and WMCA (respectively) is :

$$CA_{WMLA}(I_i)\prime = \alpha * M_{I_i} + \beta * CA_{MLA}(I_i) \qquad (10)$$

$$CA_{WMCA}(I_i)\prime = \alpha * M_{I_i} + \beta * CA_{MCA}(I_i) \qquad (11)$$

where α and β are fractions that sum to 1, and $CA_{MLA}(I_i)$ and $CA_{MCA}(I_i)$ are given by equations 5 and 7 respectively. The criterion for selecting a candidate I node is similar to that for the respective unweighted cases (equations 6 and 8 respectively); so are the running times. The value to assign to the weight is a design choice that depends on the network size and topology, routing strategy and the maximum number of streams that an I node can source. Note that WML(C)A with $\alpha = 1$, $\beta = 0$ is equivalent to RR, while WML(C)A with $\alpha = 0$, $\beta = 1$ is equivalent to ML(C)A.

4. Concurrency of retrieval

An important factor that affects data retrieval time is the stripe factor (SF). We differentiate between *wide striping*, in which a media object is striped across all the storage nodes of a server, and *narrow striping*, in which an object is striped across a fraction of the total storage nodes in a server. Each approach has its advantages and disadvantages. In the latter case, a striping group containing a frequently accessed object can become a bottleneck for the server in the absence of object replication. For example, in a video-on-demand case, it is but natural that some videos will be more frequently accessed than others : newly released videos are likely to be more frequently accessed than older videos. Wide striping avoids the formation of such bottlenecks by striping an object across all the storage nodes, which has the effect of balancing the load across all storage nodes even for skewed access patterns. However, wide striping also has some drawbacks. In wide striping, there is only one striping group; this complicates system reconfiguration. Since each storage node has some data for all objects stored in the server, most of the chunks of all the objects may have to be moved. This may lead to an undesirable reconfiguration load on *all* storage nodes. In contrast, in narrow striping, only the storage nodes in the striping group where the object is stored incur the penalty. Secondly, the larger the size of a striping group (i.e. the wider the striping), the lower is the reliability, and also the availability, of the entire

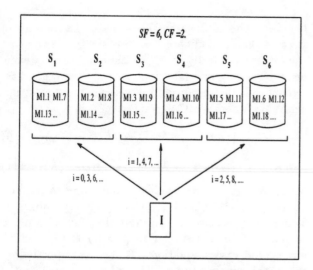

Figure 1. Concurrency Factor (*CF*). Figure shows one object, M_1, striped across 6 storage nodes (*SF* = 6), with a concurrency factor of 2 (*CF* = 2).

Description	Value
Required playback rate (R_{pl})	1.5 Mbits/sec
Size of packets sent by an I node (P_I)	80 Kbytes
Size of packets sent by a S node (P_S)	160 Kbytes
Minimum disk seek time	4 msec
Maximum seek time	30 ms
Time for one rotation	10 ms
Disks per storage node	2
Disk data transfer rate	10 MBytes/sec
Stripe Factor (SF)	4
Concurrency Factor (CF)	4
Num. of Interface nodes	11
Num. of Storage nodes	36
Num. of media objects	100
Evaluation machine	Intel Paragon

Table 2. The parameter values used

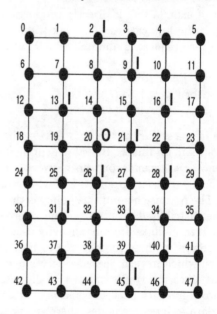

Figure 2. Distribution of I, S and O nodes

system [12, 13] in the event of a single disk failure. In this paper we consider only narrow striping.

We mentioned earlier that a storage node represents a virtual disk to an interface node. Whether wide striping or narrow striping is used to store data files, the important parameter for data rtrieval and delivery at runtime is the degree of parallelism seen by an interface node. We define now a new parameter, the *concurrency factor (CF)*. This is an integer, $1 \leq CF \leq SF$, and denotes the degree of parallelism employed by an interface node in requesting data from the storage nodes. For example, figure 1 shows a media object, $M1$, with a stripe factor of 6 and concurrency factor of 2. In the figure, the interface node (I) *concurrently* retrieves data from S_1 and S_2 in service rounds 0,3,6,.., from S_3 and S_4 in service rounds 1,4,7,..., and from S_5 and S_6 in service rounds 2,5,8,.....

5. Performance evaluation

We have implemented our logical server model on the Intel Paragon parallel computer [16]. The Intel Paragon is a mesh-based architecture with Intel i860XP microprocessors. Interprocessor communication is done using *wormhole routing* [9]. The data access pattern is assumed to follow a Zipfian distribution with parameter 0.271[10]. Due to storage space and availability of real-world data limitations, the disk access part was simulated by elapsing the system timer on each storage node. Disk retrieval was simulated by

assuming that the stripe fragments are stored on the disk using a random placement model [15]. Table 2 shows the values of the parameters defined in table 1 that we used for our simulation. The traffic was generated as follows. Initially, requests for videos are sent to the object manager at random times, with average inter-arrival time of 2 seconds. Each video lasts for about 10 minutes. As soon as a video terminates, a new request for a video is sent to the object manager. Figure 2 shows the distribution of I nodes and S nodes used[1]. The value of the parameter ld for the MCA policy (subsection 3.3) we used was 1, since the value of P_S

---

[1]Numerous tradeoffs are possible with respect to the data partitioning strategy, which are well reported in [4]. However, these are not the subject of this paper.

Policy	Average streams per I node	Standard (σ_i) Deviation
RR	51.36	0.48
MLA	57.27	33.75
MCA	57.27	22.49
WMLA $(\alpha = \beta = 0.5)$	57.27	8.85
WMCA $(\alpha = \beta = 0.5)$	57.27	4.07

Table 3. Standard Deviation of stream load per I node

and R_{pl} is the same for all streams. The load on the server was increased by incrementally increasing the number of object requests. The same data distribution and request pattern were used for each experiment.

5.1. Comparison of load balancing ability

In order to compare the distribution of stream requests to the I nodes, the number of streams served by each interface node was measured for the same total number of streams served for each policy. Figure 3 illustrates these values for each I node in figure 2 for a total server load of 565 streams for the RR policy and for a load of 630 streams for the other four policies. (the maximum number of streams supported by RR was only 565. Each of the other 4 policies supported at least 630 streams). We first compare the RR, MLA and MCA policies. We note from the figure that the RR policy performs best in terms of balancing stream load across the interface nodes. A measure of the degree to which a request assignment policy balances stream load across the interface nodes is the standard deviation of the number of streams per interface node, σ (Table 3). The standard deviation of the number of requests per I node for MLA, σ_{MLA}, is the worst among the standard deviations of RR, MCA and MLA. The reason for this is the skewed data access pattern. Consider now the WMLA and WMCA policies. The graphs in figure 3 for the WMLA and WMCA policies are for values of α and β of 0.5 each. In this case too, the load balancing of WMCA is better than that of WMLA. Although σ_{WMLA} (8.85) is lesser than σ_{MLA} (33.75), it is still greater than σ_{WMCA} (4.07). In summary, the weighted assignment policies improve the load balancing ability at the I nodes as compared to the pure schemes; however MCA gives better performance than MLA, and WMCA gives better performance than WMLA.

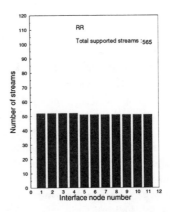

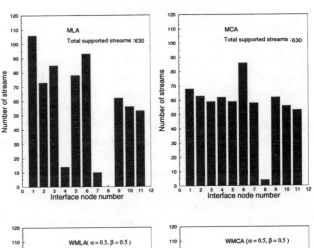

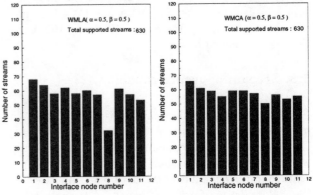

Figure 3. Comparison of request assignment of RR, MLA, MCA, WMLA and WMCA policies

5.2. Comparison of network blocking time

With reference to equation 4, the networking blocking time for each packet requested by an I node from a S node, $\delta_{nw_{bl}}$, was measured as follows : δ_{seek} and δ_{rot} were measured at run time. Given a disk and a value of P_S, $\delta_{tr_{P_S}}$ can be computed. δ_{S_Q} is given by $\delta_{S_Q} = \Delta_t - (\delta_{seek} + \delta_{rot} + \delta_{tr_{P_S}})$, where Δ_t is the time interval between arrival of the packet request at the S node, and the time when the packet is sent to the requesting I node. $\delta_{nw_{comm}}$ is a known when P_S and network bandwidth in the absence of blocking is fixed. The round trip time for the sequence of events represented by equation 4, $\delta_{io'}$, is measurable at run time. Hence, the only unknowns in equation 4 are δ_{rq} and $\delta_{nw_{bl}}$, from which the latter can be approximated (by neglecting δ_{rq}). Figure 4 shows the distribution of packet network blocking time, $\delta_{nw_{bl}}$, for the 5 policies. Bins of size 10 ms each (horizontal axis) were used to count the distribution of network blocking time for each packet. The vertical axis shows the percentage of packets that fell in each bin. For real-time retrieval of data with a high quality of service (QOS), it is desirable that the variable components in equation 4 be bounded and of minimal value. The higher the cumulative percentage of packet blocking times falling in the leftmost bins, the better is the performance of the policy. Accordingly, the performance of the policies with respect to this metric (in ascending order) is RR, MCA, WMCA, WMLA and MLA. The frequency distribution of blocking times for the last four are not very different from each other, suggesting that the the number of supportable streams for (W)MLA and (W)MCA policies should be nearly the same. However, this is not the case, as shown below.

5.3. Stream sourcing capacity

We now compare the policies with respect to the more important metric of stream sourcing capacity. Table 4 shows the maximum number of streams that were supported by each policy, together with the percentage improvement over the RR policy. As expected, the RR policy performs the worst. Although it best balances the stream among the I nodes (minimum σ), it makes no effort to balance the load on the interconnection network. At the other end of the spectrum are the MLA and MCA policies : they try to reduce load on the interconnection network by minimizing link contention; however, they do not try to balance the load across the I nodes. In spite of this, they outperform RR by 12.0 % and 14.5 %, respectively. In between RR, on the one hand, and MLA and MCA, on the

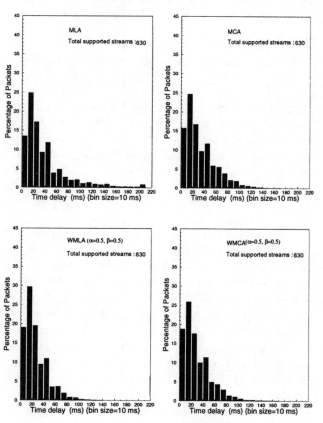

Figure 4. Frequency distribution of packet network blocking time for RR, MLA, MCA, WMLA and WMCA policies

Policy	Max. # of streams	improvement over RR
RR	565	-
MLA	633	12.0 %
MCA	647	14.5 %
WMLA ($\alpha = 0.5$, $\beta = 0.5$)	736	30.3 %
WMCA ($\alpha = 0.5$, $\beta = 0.5$)	757	34.0 %

Table 4. Maximum streams supported.

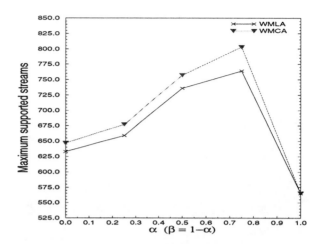

Figure 5. Effect of changing weight values on performance (maximum streams supported) of WMLA and WMCA policies.

other, are the WMLA and WMCA policies that try to balance the load on both the network as well as the I nodes. This translates into superior performance over RR, MLA and MCA. The WMCA policy with $\alpha = 0.5$ gave the highest throughput of 757 streams among the 5 cases shown, corresponding to a 34.0 % improvement over RR. In summary, although the performance of (W)MLA is similar to that of (W)MCA as far as network blocking time is concerned, the load imbalance on the I nodes is much higher for the former than for the latter (table 3). This explains why (W)MCA consistently outperforms (W)MCA.

6. Conclusions

In this paper we developed five policies for assigning requests to the interface nodes in a high-performance multimedia server. MLA, MCA, WMLA and WMCA each outperformed RR in terms of number of streams. RR best balances inter I node load, followed by WMCA and WMLA. WMCA with proper choice of weights gave highest throughput. The (W)MCA policy is a global one, as it takes into account the load on a link due to the existing traffic. (W)MLA, on the other hand is a local optimization that is oblivious of the load imposed by other nodes. This explains why WMCA gave the best throughput. Figure 5 shows the effect of varying the weight values on the maximum number of supported streams, while figure 6 shows the effect of varying weight values on standard deviation of stream load per I node for the five policies. For the parameters and data access pattern considered in this paper, $\alpha = 0.75$, $\beta = 0.25$ gave the best performance (in terms of maximum sustainable streams) for both WMLA and WMCA policies. The optimum values to assign to the weights is an implementation-dependent problem that depends on the network topology, routing strategy and the maximum streams that an I node can source. However, changing the ratio values of α and β in one direction makes the assignment criterion tend to RR (α $= 1$, $\beta = 0$), while changing the ratio in the opposite direction will make it tend to ML(C)A ($\alpha = 0$, $\beta = 1$). We have shown that values in between give better performance than these extremes. This is so because such values try to balance both the load on the I nodes and the load on the interconnection network, unlike the extreme cases, which balance one or the other.

In this paper, the experiments that we conducted were for the case when the stripe factor of an object is equal to the concurrency factor when the object is being retrieved. It was reported in [17] that for a given stripe factor and buffer size at an interface node, the maximum number of concurrent streams that could be supported had an inverse relation to the concurrency factor. We are currently evaluating the performance of the allocation policies when the concurrency factor is not equal to the stripe factor.

References

[1] A. Reddy and J. Wyllie. Disk-scheduling in a multimedia I/O system. *Proceedings of the 1st ACM Intl. Conference on Multimedia*, August 1993, pg. 225.

[2] A. Reddy and J. Wyllie. I/O issues in a multimedia system. *IEEE Computer*, vol. 27, No. 3, pp. 69-74, March 1994.

[3] P. V. Rangan and H. Vin. Efficient storage techniques for digital continuous multimedia. *IEEE Transactions on Knowledge and Data Engineering*, Vol. 5, No. 6, August 1993.

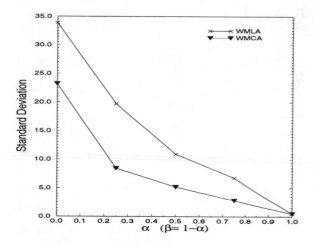

Figure 6. Effect of changing weight values on performance (standard deviation of stream load per I node) of WMLA and WMCA policies.

[4] S. Ghandeharizadeh and L. Ramos. Continuous retrieval of multimedia data using parallelism. *IEEE Trans. on Knowledge and Data Engineering*, Vol. 5, No. 4, August 1993.

[5] C. S. Freedman and D. J. DeWitt. The SPIFFI Scalable Video-on-Demand System. *Proceedings of the ACM 1995 Intl. Conference on the Management of Data*, pp. 352-363, May 1995.

[6] D. Jadav and A. Choudhary. Design issues in high performance media-on-demand servers. *IEEE Parallel and Distributed Technology Systems and Applications*, Summer 1995.

[7] D. Jadav, A. Choudhary, P. Bruce Berra and C. Srinilta. An evaluation of design tradeoffs in a high performance media-on-demand server. *CASE Center Technical Report # 9502*, CASE Center at Syracuse University, February 1995).

[8] A. Dan and D. Sitaram. An Online Video Placement Policy based on Bandwidth to Space Ratio. *Proceedings of the ACM 1995 Intl. Conference on the Management of Data*, pp. 376-385, May 1995.

[9] L. Ni and P. McKinley. A survey of wormhole techniques in direct networks. *IEEE Computer*, vol. 26, No. 2, pp. 62-76, February 1993.

[10] A. Dan, D. Sitaram and P. Shahabuddin. Scheduling Policies for an On-Demand Video Server with Batching. *Proceedings of ACM Multimedia '94*, pp. 15-23, 1994.

[11] P. S. Yu, M.-S. Chen, and D. D. Kandlur. Design and Analysis of a Grouped Sweeping Scheme for Multimedia Storage Management. *Proceedings of the Third Intl.*

Workshop on Network and Operating System Support for Digital Audio and Video, pp. 44-55, November 1992.

[12] A. Dan, M. Kienzle and D. Sitaram. A Dynamic Policy of Segment Replication for Load Balancing in Video-on-Demand Servers. *ACM Multimedia Systems Journal*, pp. 93-103, Vol. 3, Number 3, 1995.

[13] S. Berson, L. Golubchik and R. R. Muntz. Fault Tolerant Design of Multimedia Servers. *Proceedings of the ACM 1995 Intl. Conference on the Management of Data*, pp. 364-375, May 1995.

[14] B. Ozden, R. Rastogi and A. Silberschatz. Demand Paging for Video-on-Demand Servers. *Proc. of the Second IEEE Intl. Conf. on Multimedia Computing and Systems*, pp. 264-272, May 1995.

[15] M. McKusick, W. Joy, S. Leffler and R. Fabry. A fast file system for UNIX. *ACM Transactions on Computer Systems*, 2(3), August 1984.

[16] Intel Corporation. *Paragon OSF/1 User's Guide*, Intel Supercomputer Systems Division, February 1993.

[17] C. Srinilta. Storage and Retrieval Strategies for a multi-session multimedia server. *Master's Thesis, ECE Dept., Syracuse University*, December 1995.

Stochastic Performance Guarantees for Mixed Workloads in a Multimedia Information System *

Guido Nerjes[†], Peter Muth[‡], Gerhard Weikum[‡]

[‡]University of the Saarland
Department of Computer Science
D-66041 Saarbrücken, Germany

[†]Swiss Federal Institute of Technology (ETH)
Institute of Information Systems
CH-8092 Zurich, Switzerland

E-mail: {nerjes, muth, weikum}@cs.uni-sb.de, WWW: http://www-dbs.cs.uni-sb.de/

Abstract

We present an approach to stochastic performance guarantees for multimedia servers with mixed workloads. Advanced multimedia applications such as digital libraries or teleteaching exhibit a mixed workload with accesses to both 'continuous' and conventional, 'discrete' data, where the fractions of continuous-data and discrete-data requests vary over time. We assume that a server shares all disks among continuous and discrete data, and we develop a stochastic performance model for the resulting mixed workload, using a combination of analytic and simulation-based modeling. Based on this model we devise a round-based scheduling scheme with stochastic performance guarantees: for continous-data requests, we bound the probability that 'glitches' occur, and for discrete-data requests, we bound the probability that the response time exceeds a certain tolerance threshold. We present early results of simulation studies.

1. Introduction

Multimedia applications such as news-on-demand for the home market or digital library access over the Internet pose challenging performance demands on the underlying storage servers [14, 7]. Previous research in this area has very much focused on the performance issues for *continuous data* only (i.e., video and audio), assuming that all client requests refer to movies or video clips. However, advanced applications such as digital libraries or teleteaching will rather exhibit a *mixed workload* with massive access to conventional, *discrete data* such as HTML text documents and images as well as index-supported searching in addition to the requests for continuous data. Furthermore, with unrestricted 24-hour world-wide access over the Web, such multimedia servers have to cope with a dynamically evolving workload where the fractions of continuous-data vs. discrete-data requests vary over time and cannot be reliably predicted in advance. Thus, for a good price/performance ratio it is mandatory that such a server operates with a *shared resource pool* rather than statically partitioning all resources (disks, memory, etc.) into two pools for continuous and discrete data.

This paper addresses some of the critical performance issues that arise in the disk scheduling for mixed workload servers with a shared disk pool. A well known requirement is that continuous data calls for *performance guarantees* in terms of data delivery time to ensure 'hiccup-free' display at the client site. In addition, quality-conscious applications require that the response time of discrete-data requests stay below some user-tolerance threshold as well. This requirement has been ignored in prior work on mixed multimedia workloads [25] where the performance of discrete-data requests seems to be an afterthought. In fact, given that video viewing is commonly perceived as a higher-class service compared to the bread-and-butter access to 'standard' discrete data, it is likely that users will accept an admission control policy for resource-intensive continuous-data requests and may be turned away when the system saturates, whereas slow service for the vanilla requests to discrete data would be considered as unacceptable. Admission control for discrete-data requests, on the other hand, is out of the question from the user's viewpoint (although some WWW servers resort to this solution upon high load, but this is exactly perceived as non-responsive service).

Research on multimedia storage systems has put emphasis on deterministic worst-case guarantees for continuous data. Worst-case guarantees may indeed be reasonable in specific video-only applications such as movie-on-demand or in extremely critical real-time applications such as tele-surgery. However, in the more general setting considered here, deterministic worst-case guarantees are infeasible and we argue that *stochastic guarantees* are more appropriate for the following reasons:

- The load imposed by the discrete-data requests can be characterized only in a stochastic manner (typically as a Poisson arrival process with a certain probability distribution for the service demands). In more technical terms [18], this fraction of the load is better captured by an open system model whereas the continuous-data requests can indeed be adequately modeled as a closed system with

* This work has been supported by the ESPRIT LTR project HERMES.

a fixed multiprogramming level and periodic service demands.

- The resource demands of both discrete- and continuous-data requests cannot be realistically modeled in a deterministic manner. Important performance factors like disk controller caches or masking of transient failures (e.g., in a RAID) can be captured only stochastically at best. In order to employ a deterministic model, one would have to assume very conservative service-time bounds (e.g., with no disk caching at all) so that scheduling policies may end up with substantially underutilized resources. Alternatively, a deterministic model could be based on mean values only (e.g., average disk seek time), but then it is impossible to give hard performance guarantees.

In this paper, we will therefore pursue stochastic guarantees for both continuous- and discrete-data requests. For discrete-data requests we aim to guarantee good response time with high probability by bounding the tail of their response time distribution (e.g., the 95th percentile). For continuous-data requests, on the other hand, we aim to bound the probability that data portions are behind their delivery deadline according to the real-time display requirements. Our approach is based on coarse-grained striping of the data across the server's disks and a disk scheduling scheme that operates in *rounds* similar to the schemes in [2, 6, 11, 23]. Each round (of say a few seconds duration) is divided into two periods, a *C-period* and a *D-period*, during which the continuous-data and the discrete-data requests are served. The length ratio of the two periods is a degree of freedom that is dynamically adapted to the current workload based on a prediction of the near-future response time of the discrete-data requests. Whenever the specified response time guarantees (in the order of a few seconds) can no longer be satisfied, it is attempted to shorten the length of the C-period and extend the D-period correspondingly. This in turns triggers an admission control and scheduling problem for the continuous-data requests within the C-period of a round.

Our approach uses an analytic model for stochastically estimating the 'glitch' rate, i.e., probability that a data portion does not meet its display deadline, for a given multiprogramming level of continuous-data streams between clients and the server. When a request arrives to open a new continuous-data stream, it is admitted only if the predicted glitch rate for the new multiprogramming level does not exceed a specified tolerance threshold. To estimate the response time distribution of the discrete-data requests, we investigate the use of analytic queueing models, specifically M/G/1 vacation server models. However, as it turns out that we can (so far) not derive a model that is both accurate and computationally inexpensive, we finally resort to using a carefully constructed simulation model that is evaluated off-line and can efficiently drive the system's run-time decisions.

We are not aware of any previous work that pursues an approach to mixed workloads along these lines. A prototype system based on this new approach is being built by extending the FIVE experimental file system [29, 30, 32].

The rest of the paper is organized as follows. Section 2. introduces our system architecture. Section 3. develops an approach towards a performance prediction model, for both continuous-data and discrete-data requests. Finally, Section 4. discusses the admission control and the adaptation of the disk scheduling to the workload dynamics, based on precomputed results of the performance model.

2. System Architecture

In this section, we discuss assumptions on the workload and the architecture of our system. In general, we assume that clients submit requests for both *continuous data* and *discrete data*, in short: *C-data* and *D-data*, to the server. Objects consisting of C-data, e.g., videos, audios or animation data, are composed of sequences of *fragments* and constitute data *streams* that are consumed by the client in a time-constrained way according to the display bandwidth of the object. In contrast, D-data such as text, images, or metadata, has no explicit time constraints. For C-data requests, in short *C-requests*[1], we assume that each client provides a certain amount of memory as a buffer for incoming fragments. The buffer size may vary among clients according to the local resources available. The buffer size must not be below a certain minimum allowing the server to deliver a fragment before the previous one is consumed by the client. We assume a fast and reliable network with a performance capacity well above our bandwidth requirements, and thus disregard network issues in this paper.

2.1. Data Layout

We consider a single server with D disks. Since video and audio compression techniques reduce the bandwidth of videos and audios substantially, we assume that the display bandwidth $r_{display}$ of a continuous object is always smaller than the bandwidth r_{disk} of a single disk.

C-data is split into fragments. Fragments are assigned to disks in a round robin fashion, similarly to the coarse-grained striping approach of [23] and the simple/staggered striping approach of [2] specialized to the case with cluster size 1 and stride 1. The salient properties that we share with these approaches are twofold:

- The load is balanced across the disks, assuming that continuous objects are sufficiently large to be spread across all disks and that most users consume complete objects (as opposed to fast-forwarding a video or viewing only a short prefix).

- The server can sustain more concurrent (but time-wise unrelated) streams on the same continuous object than it

---

1. Likewise, requests to D-data will henceforth be called *D-requests*.

would be possible by multiplexing the service of a single disk in case the entire object resided on this disk. With D disks, disk bandwidth r_{disk}, and object display bandwidth $r_{display}$, the server can, in principle, support up to $D * r_{disk} / r_{display}$ streams on the same or different objects (under the optimistic assumption that multiplexing does not lead to a reduction of the effective disk bandwidth).

We do not assume the display bandwidth of a continuous object to be constant, as compression techniques such as MPEG-2 result in a variable bandwidth over time. In our scheme, all data fragments stored by the server have the same display time [9, 3], i.e., the time it takes a client to consume a fragment (e.g., a few seconds). As a consequence, fragments vary in size. By 'normalizing' all fragments to the same time length, we induce a periodic access pattern with a uniform period across all continuous objects regardless of the display bandwidth differences between objects and the variation within an object. This type of fragmentation requires parsing a continuous object before it is laid out on the server's disks, but this is straightforward and inexpensive given that continuous objects are never modified after their initial insertion.

Discrete objects are allocated to disk such that the expected I/O load on behalf of this data is balanced across the disks; this involves coarse-grained striping for large objects and simple but effective load balancing heuristics along the lines of [30]. In what follows we do, however, not rely on any specific assumptions on the storage layout for discrete objects.

C-data and D-data both reside on the same shared disk pool, as this provides a much better resource utilization than a partitioned scheme with dedicated disks, from both a disk space and a disk bandwidth point of view:

- For a partitioned server, new disks have to be added when the space for one of the two data categories becomes exhausted. A server with shared disks requires additional disks only if it runs out of space for both kinds of data together. The difference becomes important when the ratio of space used by C-data and D-data varies over time. This is the case, for example, for many Web servers with evolving sets of HTML documents.

- The advantage of a shared disk pool is even more important from a disk bandwidth viewpoint. For many multimedia applications it is likely that the ratio of C-requests and D-requests varies over time. For example, teleteaching lectures in the morning may be mostly based on videos, whereas working on assignments in the afternoon requires more lookups of reference data such as text. A partitioned server needs enough disk performance capacity on each data type in order to sustain all workloads. On a shared server, the aggregate bandwidth of all disks can be used anytime to serve both C- and D-requests. Thus, sharing disks may yield a substantial cost saving.

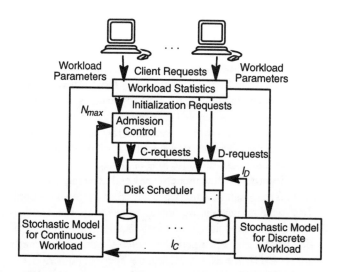

Figure 1: Architecture of the Mixed Workload Server

2.2. Admission Control and Disk Scheduling

The scheduling is composed of an admission control and a separate disk scheduler for each disk, as illustrated in Figure 1. D-requests are immediately submitted to the responsible disk schedulers for those disks on which the requested object resides. For simpler explanation, we will assume that all D-requests are served by exactly one disk as it would indeed be the case with non-striped objects. *Initialization requests* for opening a new continuous data stream have to pass the admission control first. As C-requests are deadline-oriented, only a limited number of concurrent streams can be sustained. Therefore, the admission control rejects new initialization requests when the server load becomes too high (as computed by the stochastic model of Section 3.1.). D-requests are not subject to admission control because we assume that this is not acceptable to the applications that consider such requests as a bread-and-butter workload. If D-requests were rejected by some form of admission control, they would have to be queued until they are eventually accepted. From the application point of view, the queueing time just adds to the response time perceived by the user.

Now consider the actual disk scheduling. The periodic pattern of the C-requests for the admitted streams suggests a cyclic scheduling scheme that proceeds in rounds, with a round length, l_{round}, equal to the display time of a fragment, which is uniform across all fragments. The round length is a configuration parameter of our architecture; changing it would require all C-data to be re-fragmented. During a round, all C-requests of the admitted streams have to be served. Given that a fragment always resides on a single disk, there are no dependencies among the requests of one round, so that we can schedule the requests of each disk separately, as long as we complete all requests by the end of the round. In order to minimize disk seeks, we use the SCAN algorithm for the disk arm movement [28, 4] (also known as the 'elevator' algorithm). With this algorithm, all requests of one round are sorted according to their seek position on the disk and are served with one sweep of the disk arm.

So far we have disregarded the scheduling of D-requests. Since the round length would be at most a few seconds, which is a tolerable delay for most applications, an intriguing idea would be to schedule the D-requests after all C-requests of a round are served. However, since this unused time at the end of a round can become arbitrarily small depending on the C-request load, the response time of D-requests may degrade significantly. Discrete requests may end up being queued for several rounds, unless the scheduler takes additional actions. To avoid this situation, we further refine the approach and divide a disk scheduling round into two periods of pre-specified length: In the first period, denoted *C-period*, C-requests are served by the SCAN algorithm. The second period, denoted *D-period*, is used to serve D-requests, with an FCFS policy for fairness reasons. The ratio l_C/l_D of the lengths of both periods is a scheduling parameter and has to be adjusted to reflect changes in the overall workload. A longer *C-period* is needed if a higher number of continuous data streams must be sustained, and a longer *D-period* is needed when the arrival rate of D-requests increases. As the overall round length $l_{round} = l_C + l_D$ is constant, it is impossible to support both request categories in an optimal way. Our approach to finding an adequate compromise is based on two stochastic model components, as shown in Figure 1:

(1) For the discrete requests, based on the assumption of a Poisson arrival process with a given arrival rate λ_D and a certain, observable distribution of the service time, the length l_D is derived such that the response time for the majority of discrete requests, say the 95th percentile, is below a certain threshold (which would typically be in the order of a few seconds).

(2) Then, given the length $l_C = l_{round} - l_D$ of the C-period, we derive the maximum number, N_{max}, of concurrent C-data streams that can be served during a C-period such that the probability, p_{late}, of missing a display deadline stays below a specified threshold, say 99 percent. The computed value of N_{max} is then used to drive the admission control in that only up to N_{max} streams can be admitted.

Using both models gives us stochastic guarantees for C-requests not missing their deadlines and for discrete request not exceeding a given response time threshold. The stochastic models themselves are discussed in the next section.

3. Performance Guarantees

This section develops stochastic models that allow us to give stochastic guarantees for the glitch rate of C-requests and the response time of D-requests. These guarantees are derived as Chernoff bounds [19, 22] for the tail of the underlying probability distributions. Throughout the section we consider only one disk and its corresponding load, which is feasible as there are no scheduling dependencies among different disks (see Section 2.). Thus, all workload parameters like the multiprogramming level of continuous streams and the arrival rate of D-requests are on a per disk basis, assuming that the load is uniformly distributed across disks.

3.1. Performance Guarantees for C-Requests

The goal of this section is to derive, for a C-period of length l_C, an upper bound, N_{max}, for the number N of concurrent streams such that the probability of not being able to serve all N requests within time l_C is below a certain threshold p_{late}, say 1 percent. From this probability, p_{late}, we derive the probability mass function f_{glitch} for the number of 'glitches', i.e., late data deliveries, within an entire stream of duration n_R rounds as follows:

$$f_{glitch}(k) = P[\# \, of \, glitches = k] = \binom{n_R}{k} \, p_{late}{}^k \, (1 - p_{late})^{n_R - k}$$

Note that this is actually a pessimistic upper bound for the glitch rate of an individual stream, as a late round would affect only a subset of the active streams. We will later use these probabilistic considerations in the admission control for newly arriving initialization requests (see Section 4.), with a specified bound on p_{late} or, equivalently, the tail of f_{glitch}.

The key problem to be solved here is to estimate the total service time for the N requests of one round's C-period, using a SCAN policy for the disk arm movement. Prior work on this problem used constant worst case values for the seek and rotational delays between successive data transfers [12], or assumed that the total (i.e., accumulated) seek time of one sweep over the disk equals the maximum seek time of the disk [23]. This yields a deterministic but unrealistic estimate since it ignores the stochastic nature of rotational delays and the non-linearity of the disk arm movement [26]. The only work that addresses this problem by a stochastic model are [5, 8]. [5] assumes independent seeks for the N requests rather than the much better SCAN policy, and arrives at a relatively coarse bound based on the Tschebyscheff inequality. [8] is also based on independent seeks and assumes that N is sufficiently large to apply the central limit theorem (i.e., consider only the limit $N \to \infty$) and thus assume that the total service time is normally distributed, which is not always justified for realistic values of N (e.g., 10 to 50 streams per disk). In the following we derive a much more accurate stochastic model and a much tighter bound using a recent result on the total seek time of the SCAN policy [24] and the method of Chernoff bounds [19, 22].

Let T_C denote the total service time for a C-period with N requests. Then we have

$$T_C = T_{seek} + \sum_{i=1}^{N} T_{rot,i} + \sum_{i=1}^{N} T_{trans,i}$$

where T_{seek} is the accumulated seek time for one sweep of the SCAN policy, $T_{rot,i}$ is the rotational delay and $T_{trans,i}$ is the transfer time of the ith request.

According to [24] T_{seek} is maximized, under a realistic function for the seek time, for equidistant seek positions of the N requests. The seek time function itself is assumed to be proportional to the square root of the seek distance for small distances below a disk-specific constant, and a linear function of the seek distance for longer distances, which is in accordance with the studies of [26]. Thus, for given disk parameters, the maximum total seek time of a sweep can be easily computed by assuming the N seek positions to be at cylinders $i*CYL/(N+1)$ for $i=1, ..., N$ where CYL is the total number of the disk's cylinders, and applying the seek time function. This computation yields an upper bound for T_{seek} which, other than depending on N, can now be viewed as a constant, denoted $SEEK$ in the following.

The N random variables $T_{rot, i}$ are independently and identically distributed with a uniform distribution between 0 and the time for one disk revolution, ROT. Similarly, the random variables $T_{trans,i}$ are independently identically distributed. This distribution depends on the distribution of data fragments and the disk's transfer rate (which in turn is a function of the revolution speed and the head switch time). For the sake of a simpler explanation, we assume in the following that $T_{trans,i}$ is exponentially distributed with a mean value $TRANS$. (The same derivation could be carried out also with other common distributions, e.g., a more realistic hyperexponential distribution, but this would complicate the formulas.)

So T_{seek} is equal to the constant $SEEK$, and the probability density functions of $T_{rot,i}$ and $T_{trans,i}$ are given by

$$f_{rot}(x) = \frac{1}{ROT} \quad \text{and} \quad f_{trans}(x) = \frac{1}{TRANS} \, e^{-\frac{x}{TRANS}},$$

and their Laplace-Stieltjes transforms [1, 22] are given by

$$L_{seek}(s) = e^{-s\,SEEK}, \, L_{rot}(s) = \frac{1 - e^{-s\,ROT}}{s\,ROT}, \text{ and}$$

$$L_{trans}(s) = \frac{1}{1 + s\,TRANS}.$$

The Laplace transform of T_C, which involves the N-fold convolution of the convolution of $T_{rot,i}$ and $T_{trans,i}$, is given by

$$L_C(s) = e^{-s\,SEEK} \left(\frac{1 - e^{-s\,ROT}}{s\,ROT} \right)^N \left(\frac{1}{1 + s\,TRANS} \right)^N,$$

and the corresponding moment generating function $M_C(s)$ equals $L_C(-s)$. Now we are ready to apply Chernoff's theorem to bound the tail of the random variable T_C. Namely, the following inequation holds [19, 22]:

$$P[T_C \geq t] \leq inf_{\theta \geq 0} \left\{ e^{-\theta t} \, M_C(\theta) \right\} = inf_{\theta \geq 0} \left\{ g(\theta) \right\}$$

with

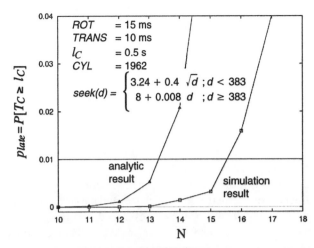

Figure 2: Analytically Predicted vs. Simulated 'Lateness' Distribution

$$g(\theta) = e^{-\theta t} \, e^{\theta\,SEEK} \left(\frac{e^{\theta\,ROT} - 1}{\theta\,ROT} \right)^N \left(\frac{1}{1 - \theta\,TRANS} \right)^N.$$

For the given form of g, differentiating g and solving $g' = 0$ for θ yields the optimum value of θ to obtain the sharpest bound in the Chernoff inequation. While we did not manage to obtain a closed form expression for this result, solving $g' = 0$ numerically is straightforward and very efficient.

So finally p_{late} is obtained by

$$p_{late} = P[T_C \geq l_C] \leq g(solution \ of \ g' = 0 \ using \ t = l_C)$$

For example, for $l_C = 0.542$, $ROT = 0.015$, $TRANS = 0.01$, $SEEK = 0.12282$, $N = 15$, the derived upper bound for p_{late} is approximately 0.01 . In other words, we can guarantee with probability at least $1 - p_{late} = 0.99$ that all N C-requests of one round can be served within the C-period of length l_C. So for a given value of l_C and a threshold δ for p_{late}, we can derive the maximum number of concurrent streams as $N_{max} = \max \{N \mid p_{late} \leq \delta\}$. For example, if $l_C = 0.2$ and p_{late} should be at most 1 percent, then N_{max} would be 3, and for $l_C = 0.4$, N_{max} would be 9.

We compared the predictions of this model with results obtained from detailed simulations. Figure 2 shows the analytically predicted and the simulated values for p_{late} as a function of N_{max}. The analytic model is conservative in that it always overestimates the lateness probability. For example, for a p_{late} threshold of 0.01, the analytic model allows a maximum of 13 streams whereas the simulation shows that a value of 15 for N_{max} is possible.

Now that we have the probability p_{late} for not being able to complete all N requests within time l_C, we can apply the method of Chernoff bounds also to the probability mass function f_{glitch} of the number of glitches within an entire stream of n_R rounds. As derived above, the number of glitches is binomially distributed. For this important case, the following Chernoff bound, derived in [HR89], can be applied to our scenario under the constraint that $k / n_R > p_{late}$:

$$p_{error} = P[\# \ of \ glitches \geq k]$$

$$\leq \left(\frac{n_R \, p_{late}}{k}\right)^k \left(\frac{n_R - n_R \, p_{late}}{n_R - k}\right)^{n_R - k}$$

For example, using $p_{late} = 0.01$ and $n_R = 1200$, the probability p_{error} for more than 24 glitches is at most 1 percent. Conversely, for a specified upper bound for the number of glitches per stream (the k value above) and the corresponding probability that this bound is not exceeded, we can again derive the maximum number of streams, N_{max}, that the system can sustain within a C-period of length l_C under these conditions.

For example, for $l_C = 0.5$, $n_R = 1200$, $k = 12$ and the other parameters as given in figure 2, simulations show that at most 17 streams can be accepted. The analytic evaluation restricts N_{max} to a maximum value of 12.

3.2. Performance Guarantees for D-Requests

3.2.1. Applicability of M/G/1 Vacation Server Models

In this section we explore the use of M/G/1 vacation server models for predicting the response distribution of the D-requests. In applications with a large number of clients, the arrival of requests can be stochastically described as a Poisson process. As a consequence, the time between the arrival of two successive D-requests is exponentially distributed with mean $1 / \lambda_D$, where λ_D is the average arrival rate of the Poisson process. Because of this stochastic behavior it is not feasible to provide 'hard', deterministic performance guarantees to every single request (e.g. every request is served within 0.1 seconds). Rather it is common (see, e.g., database and transaction system benchmarks [13]) to require that a specified percentage of requests will finish within a given time, e.g., 95 percent of the D-requests will have a response time below 1 second.

As described in Section 2. the service of requests is performed in a cyclic manner. During each round of constant length l_{round} a D-period of length l_D is dedicated to the service of D-requests. D-requests that arrive outside the D-period are queued and served in FCFS order in the subsequent D-periods. This situation is illustrated in Figure 3. The performance measure that we aim to predict in this section is the response time of D-requests, which depends on the arrival rate λ_D, the length of the D-period $l_D = l_{round} - l_C$, and the service time distribution of the D-requests.

An analytic approach to the estimation of the response time of D-requests is to build on *vacation-server queueing models* [31, 10]. In an M/G/1 queueing model with vacations the arriving requests form a Poisson process with exponen-

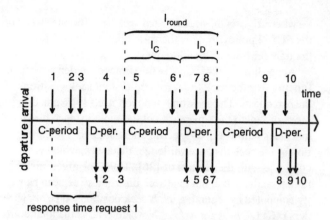

Figure 3: Arrivals and Departures of D-Requests

tially distributed interarrival time, the service time can be arbitrarily distributed, and the requests are served by a single server in FCFS order. The speciality of vacation-server models is that the server occasionally suspends its service for a certain 'vacation period'; in our setting the 'vacation' corresponds to the C-period during which the server pauses serving D-requests. In the following we discuss the suitability of specific vacation-server models for which analytic results can be found in the literature.

In vacation models with exhaustive service, the server takes a vacation (i.e., stops serving requests) for a certain time whenever its queue of waiting requests becomes empty. When the server returns from a vacation it takes another vacation (following a so-called 'multiple vacation model') if no request has arrived during the vacation and the queue is still empty [31]. A possible sequence of service and vacation periods is shown in Figure 4 (where service and vacation times are assumed to be constant).

Our cyclic service strategy of serving C-requests and D-requests can be coarsely mapped to the sketched M/G/1 vacation-server model with exhaustive service and multiple vacations: D-periods correspond to the service periods, C-periods to vacations of the server. Note that this is an approximation since our actual service policy does not take another vacation when the D-request queue is empty at the beginning of the D-period. Despite this discrepancy it seems intriguing

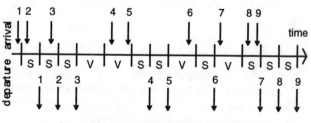

S = constant service time (single request)
V = constant vacation time

Figure 4: Service and Vacation Periods in the Vacation Server Model

to apply such a model for an approximate performance prediction as follows.

The response time of a D-request, T_{resp}, is composed of the time T_{wait} the request spends in the server queue until service starts and the time T_{svc} that is needed for service.

$$T_{resp} = T_{wait} + T_{svc}$$

For a simple presentation, it is assumed that the service time T_{svc} is exponentially distributed with mean $E[T_{svc}] = SVC$ (other distributions such as normal or hyper-exponential could be handled as well). The vacation time T_{vac} is constant with value $E[T_{vac}] = VAC = l_{round} - l_D$. The Laplace-Stieltjes transforms of the service time, vacation time, and waiting time [31] distributions are given by

$$L_{svc}(s) = \frac{1}{1 + s\,SVC}, \; L_{vac}(s) = e^{-sVAC}, \text{ and}$$

$$L_{wait}(s) = \frac{1 - L_{vac}(s)}{s\,E[T_{vac}]} \frac{s\,(1 - \lambda\,E[T_{svc}])}{s - \lambda + \lambda\,L_{svc}(s)}.$$

The Laplace-Stieltjes transform of T_{resp} is then obtained as the product of the waiting and service time transforms:

$$L_{resp}(s) = L_{wait}(s) * L_{svc}(s) =$$

$$\frac{1 - e^{-sVAC}}{s\,VAC} \frac{s\,(1 - \lambda\,SVC)}{s - \lambda + \lambda\,(1 + s\,SVC)^{-1}} \frac{1}{1 + s\,SVC}$$

Now, analogously to Section 3.1., it is possible to apply Chernoff's theorem to bound the tail of the random variable T_{resp}. Let $M_{resp}(s) = L_{resp}(-s)$ be the moment generating function of T_{resp}. Then the following inequation holds:

$$P[T_{resp} \geq t] \leq \inf_{\theta \geq 0}\left\{e^{-\theta t}\,M_{resp}(\theta)\right\} = \inf_{\theta \geq 0}\{h(\theta)\}$$

with

$$h(\theta) = e^{-\theta t} \frac{e^{\theta VAC} - 1}{\theta\,VAC} \frac{\theta\,(1 - \lambda\,SVC)}{\theta + \lambda - \lambda\,(1 - \theta\,SVC)^{-1}} *$$

$$\frac{1}{1 - \theta\,SVC}$$

Given a fixed response time threshold ρ, the probability that a request has a response time of at least ρ can be calculated using

$$p_{delay} = P[T_{resp} \geq \rho] \leq h(\text{solution of } h' = 0 \text{ with } t = \rho)$$

For example, for $SVC = 0.01s$, $VAC = 0.3s$, $\lambda = 30s^{-1}$ and $\rho = 0.338$ seconds, p_{delay} is bounded by 0.05. This means that with probability $1 - p_{delay} = 0.95$ a request will finish within a time interval of 0.338 seconds. If, on the other hand, both the response threshold ρ and a bound δ for p_{delay} are given, then the maximum feasible vacation time T_{vac} or, equivalently, the minimum length of the D-period, $l_D = l_{round} - VAC$, can be determined for a certain arrival rate λ.

As noted before, the multiple vacation model with exhaustive service does not capture the periodic nature of our scheduling policy. Under light load, i.e., when the arrival rate is low and the waiting queue is often empty, the vacation model predicts more vacations than our policy which would actually take a vacation only once in a round. Under heavy load, i.e., when the waiting queue is rarely empty, the vacation model predicts only few vacations, which is in contrast to our actual policy where the server is definitely on vacation once in a round and the vacation length is not affected by the load. These discrepancies lead to deviations between the predicted performance as derived analytically and the results of a detailed simulation. Unfortunately, the large error we found renders the analytic model unacceptable for practical use.

Better approximations could be obtained by applying the more sophisticated models described in [20, 21]. These models assume that the length of a service period, in our case l_D, is limited. Whenever the server expires this limited service time, a vacation period is started regardless of whether the request queue is empty or not. In [20] the request in service is preempted when the service time expires and resumed directly after the vacation; in [21] the request in service is first completed before the vacation period starts. Unfortunately, however, these models incur substantial mathematical difficulties; there are no closed-formula results, and even approximative derivations involve a high computational complexity. Studies on improving the computational complexity of the solution methods of [20, 21] while retaining an acceptable accuracy are left for future work.

3.2.2. Simulation-Based Guarantees

Although the analytic model of Section 3.2.1. does provide better insight into the performance of D-requests, its inaccuracy, on the one hand, and the computational complexity of more accurate models, on the other hand, prevent us from adopting an analytic model for run-time scheduling decisions. So we rather resort to estimations based on off-line simulations. Assuming that the service time distribution, the round length l_{round}, and the user-tolerated response time percentile are fixed at the system configuration time, we can pre-compute by simulation the minimum value of l_D that is necessary to meet the requirements, over a spectrum of λ values. These values would then be stored in a table that can be efficiently looked up at run-time.

Although this approach may appear less elegant than an analytic model, it serves its purpose well in that it allows us to predict the response time distribution of the D-requests as a function of the two parameters l_D and λ. The reduction of the parameter space to these run-time-relevant parameters is what makes this approach feasible. Note that we can control the accuracy and statistical confidence of the predictions, without incurring any additional run-time costs, as the simulations are carried out off-line.

4. The Scheduling Algorithm

Our disk scheduling algorithm is driven by the control parameters N_{max}, l_C, and l_D, where $l_C + l_D = l_{round}$ and l_{round} is fixed. In the previous section we have presented a stochastic model and a simulation approach to derive the values of l_C, l_D and N_{max} from given workload parameters:

(1) The arrival rate of D-requests, λ_D, and the specified threshold for the tail of the response time distribution determine the value of l_D and, with fixed l_{round}, also the value of l_C.

(2) The value of l_C and the specified threshold for the probability of missing a delivery deadline (or, equivalently, the glitch rate of a C-data stream) determine the maximum sustainable multiprogramming level of concurrent C-data streams, N_{max}.

These control parameters are adjusted whenever a change in the workload takes place. In principle, this can happen at the beginning of each round. But we expect that shifts in the workload are not that frequent, and the parameters remain stable over several rounds. The computation of the parameters is based on the analytic model of Section 3.1 and off-line simulations for the problem of Section 3.2. In both cases the results are precomputed and stored in tables that merely need to be looked up at run-time. These tables are very compact, as we can assume that service time distributions are stationary (as they are determined by disk and data properties) and thus do not have to be considered as variable parameters. Thus, the table for the l_D values has one entry for each value of λ_D within a range of expected values, say from 1 arrival per second through 10000, and could even be organized as a sparse table using interpolation for missing values. The table for N_{max} needs one entry for every possible setting of l_C and would be in the order of a thousand entries. Altogether, the run-time overhead of the approach is in the order of 10 KBytes of memory.

Figure 5 presents the complete admission control and disk scheduling algorithm in a pseudo-code notation. In addition to the tables discussed above, the main data structures are three queues, denoted *C-queue*, *D-queue*, and *I-queue*, for the C-requests, D-requests, and initialization requests, respectively. The algorithm is invoked at the beginning of each round, i.e., every l_{round} time units. The first step analyzes the current load conditions by inspecting the workload statistics and looking up the tables for the control parameters of the round. In the second step, it is attempted to admit new streams that may be waiting in the *I-queue*. However, for each disk, a limit of N_{max} streams must not be exceeded. Note that invoking the admission control at the start of each scheduling round implies an average startup latency for newly arriving

```
step 1 (analysis):
    determine currently expected  lD from
    workload statistics;
    look up the appropriate values of lD, lC, and Nmax in
    the corresponding tables;
step 2 (admission control):
    let N be the current number of continuous requests
    that need to be served per round and per disk on
    behalf of the active streams;
    while (N <= Nmax) {
        admit first stream from the I-queue;
        insert the first request of each newly admitted
        stream into the C-queue;
        N++
    };
step 3 (overload management):
    if (N > Nmax)
    case (policy)
        kill: kill N-Nmax streams;
        adapt QoS: reduce quality of service of all
        streams by N/Nmax;
        wait: delay adjustment of lC until N-Nmax streams
        have terminated;
step 4 (disk service):
    while (current_time < start_of_current_round + lC) {
        process requests of the C-queue according to the
        SCAN policy;
    }
    while (current_time < start_of_current_round + lround) {
        process next request from the D-queue
        in FCFS order;
    };
```

Figure 5: Pseudo Code for the Admission Control and Disk Scheduling Algorithm

riving initialization requests of half a round length. Given a typical round length of a few seconds, the startup delay appears to be tolerable.

The third step, overload management, is necessary because of the evolving load incurred by the D-requests. It may turn out that the C-round duration l_C has to be shortened in order to accommodate an increased discrete load. In such a situation, the system could have admitted already more streams than it can now sustain. The problem is how to drive the system back to a state where it is able to sustain the current load. There are at least three pragmatic options, iterated until, for each disk, the number of C-requests to be served in each round is again below N_{max}:

(1) Kill active streams

(2) Reduce the quality of service for active streams [16, 8], e.g., by dropping some video frames

(3) Keep the old length of the C-period until enough streams are finished

In cases (1) and (2), C-requests suffer from the increased load incurred by D-requests. In case (3), D-requests suffer until the load of C-requests is eventually reduced. Combinations of the above approaches are possible, but they remain pragmatic, as during the overload phase the performance guarantees are not met. In practice, this might be less of a problem as in most cases the arrival rate λ_D of D-requests will change slowly, causing only slight changes in the scheduling parameters. However, we will address this problem in more detail in our future work.

The fourth and final scheduling step is the actual processing of the requests in the C- and D-queues. The processing of the C-queue should be finished l_C time units after the start of the round. C-requests that cannot be served until then cause a glitch in the corresponding data stream. If the last C-request to be served in the round finishes before the end of the C-period, the remaining time is dedicated to the D-queue, which makes the D-period longer.

5. Conclusions

In this paper, we have presented an approach towards stochastic performance guarantees for multimedia servers with workloads consisting of both continuous-data and discrete-data requests. This work is part of the Esprit long-term research project HERMES [15]. The architecture of our server in terms of data placement and load balancing is based on experiences with the FIVE prototype [29, 30, 32], an experimental file system for parallel disk systems. We are currently extending FIVE to support the presented admission control and scheduling method for both continuous and discrete data, using the stochastic model components developed in this paper. We plan to integrate the extended FIVE system with an already implemented prototype multimedia server for a 'News on Demand' application [27] (which is currently based on staggered striping).

Future work includes extensions of the architecture in order to make it more flexible. In particular, we have disregarded buffering issues so far, and we want to exploit caching opportunities especially at the client sites. In the advanced multimedia applications that we are aiming at, many clients are quite powerful PCs or workstations that have memory and also local disk resources that substantially exceed the minimum buffering capabilities of a client as opposed to a set-top unit in a home market setting. This allows the server to deviate from the usual just-in-time-delivery paradigm for the continuous data, and rather preload fragments into the client ahead of time depending on the client's available cache space, thereby saving resources for heavy-load periods later. On the other hand, with a more complex architecture, the complexity of the stochastic models increases, too. Therefore, the approach of pre-computing performance prediction results by off-line simulations (as pursued in Section 3.2) and using these results in an efficient table-lookup manner for run-time scheduling decisions may become more intriguing.

References

[1] Arnold O. Allen, *Probability, Statistics and Queueing Theory with Computer Science Applications*, 2nd edition, Academic Press, 1990.

[2] Steven Berson, Shahram Ghandeharizadeh, Richard Muntz, *Staggered Striping in Multimedia Information Systems*. Proceedings ACM SIGMOD Conference 1994, International Conference on Management of Data, Minneapolis, Minnesota, pp.79–90, May 1994.

[3] Ariel Cohen, Walter A.Burkhard, P. Venkat Rangan, *Pipelined Disk Arrays for Digital Movie Retrieval*, Proceedings of the International Conference on Multimedia Computing and Systems, ICMCS '95, Washington D.C., May 1995.

[4] Edward G. Coffman, Jr., Micha Hofri, *Queueing Models of Secondary Storage Devices*, In Hideaki Takagi, editor, Stochastic Analysis of Computer and Communication Systems, North Holland, 1990.

[5] Huang–Jen Chen, Thomas D. C. Little, *Storage Allocation Policies for Time–Dependent Multimedia Data*, to appear in IEEE Transactions on Knowledge and Data Engineering.

[6] Mon–Song Chen, Dilip D. Kandlur, Philip S. Yu, *Optimization of the Grouped Sweeping Scheduling (GSS) with Heterogenous Multimedia Streams*, Proceedings of the ACM International Conference on Multimedia, ACM Multimedia '93, Anaheim, California, 1993.

[7] Stavros Christodoulakis, Peter Triantafillou, *Research and Development Issues for Large–Scale Multimedia Information Systems*. ACM Computing Surveys 27(4): pp. 576-579, 1995.

[8] Ed Chang, Avideh Zakhor, *Variable Bit Rate MPEG Video Storage on Parallel Disk Arrays*, Proceedings of SPIE Conference on Visual Communication and Image Processing, Chicago, Illinois, pp. 47-60, September 1994.

[9] Ed Chang, Avideh Zakhor, *Cost Analyses for VBR Video Servers*, Proceedings of IS&T/SPIE International Symposium on Electronic Imaging: Science and Technology, San Jose, California, January 1996.

[10] Bharat Doshi, *Single Server Queues with Vacations*, In Hideaki Takagi, editor, Stochastic Analysis of Computer and Communication Systems, North Holland, 1990.

[11] D. James Gemmel, Jiawei Han, Richard Beaton, Stavros Christodoulakis, *Delay–Sensitive Multimedia on Disks*, IEEE Multimedia, pp. 57-67, 1995.

[12] Shahram Ghandeharizadeh, Seon Ho Kim, *Striping in Multi–disk Video Servers*, Proceedings of the SPIE High–Density Data Recording and Retrieval Technologies Conference, October 1995.

[13] Jim Gray (Ed.), *The Benchmark Handbook for Database and Transaction Processing*, 2nd edition, Morgan Kaufmann, San Mateo, 1993.

[14] D. James Gemmel, Harrick M. Vin, Dilip D. Kandlur, P. Venkat Rangan, Lawrence A. Rowe, *Multimedia Storage Servers : A Tutorial*, IEEE Computer, pp. 40-49, May 1995.

[15] Technical Reports ESPRIT Long Term Research Project Hermes (Foundations of High Performance Multimedia Information Management), No. 9141, [www.ced.tuc.gr/hermes/]

[16] Silvia Hollfelder, Achim Kraiß, Thomas C. Rakow, *A client–controlled Adaption Framework for Multimedia Systems*, Technical Report No. 1022, GMD–IPSI, Sankt Augustin, September 1996.

[17] Torben Hagerup, Christiane Rüb, *A Guided Tour of Chernoff Bounds*, Information Processing Letters 33, pp. 305-308, 1989.

[18] Raj Jain, *The Art of Computer Systems Performance Analysis*, Wiley, 1991.

[19] Leonard Kleinrock, *Queueing Systems. Volume 1: Theory*, Wiley, 1975.

[20] Kin K. Leung, Martin Eisenberg, *A single–server queue with vacations and non-gated time-limited service*, Performance Evaluation 12, pp. 115-125, 1991.

[21] Kin K. Leung, David M. Lucantoni, *Two vacation models for token-ring networks where service is controlled by timers*, Performance Evaluation 20, pp. 165-184, 1994.

[22] Randolph Nelson, *Probability, Stochastic Processes, and Queueing Theory : The Mathematics of Computer Performance Modeling*, Springer, 1995.

[23] Banu Özden, Rajeev Rastogi, Avi Silberschatz, *Disk Striping in Video Server Environments*, Proceedings IEEE International Conference on Multimedia Computing and Systems, June 1996.

[24] Yen–Jen Oyang, *A tight upper bound of the lumped disk seek time for the Scan disk scheduling policy*, Information Processing Letters 54, pp. 355-358, 1995.

[25] A. L. N. Reddy, Jim Wyllie, *I/O issues in a multimedia system*, IEEE Computer, 27(3), pp. 69–74, March 1994.

[26] Chris Ruemmler, John Wilkes, *An Introduction to Disk Modelling*, IEEE Computer, 27(3), pp. 17-28, March 1994.

[27] Nivo Randriam, Ulrike Wolf, *A Multimedia Storage Server for a News Archive* (in German), Diploma Thesis, Department of Computer Science, University of the Saarland, Saarbrücken, 1996.

[28] Abraham Silberschatz, Peter Galvin, *Operating System Concepts*, 4th edition. Addison–Wesley, New York, 1994.

[29] Peter Scheuermann, Gerhard Weikum, Peter Zabback, *Disk Cooling in Parallel Disk Systems*, IEEE Data Engineering Bulletin Vol.17 No.3, pp. 29–40, September 1994.

[30] Peter Scheuermann, Gerhard Weikum, Peter Zabback, *Data Partitioning and Load Balancing in Parallel Disk Systems*, Technical Report A/02/96, Department of Computer Science, University of the Saarland, 1996, submitted for publication.

[31] Hideaki Takagi, *Queueing Analysis : A Foundation of Performance Analysis, Volume 1 : Vacation and Priority Systems*, North Holland, Amsterdam 1991.

[32] Peter Zabback, *I/O Parallelism in Database Systems – Design, Implementation and Evaluation of a Storage System for Parallel Disks* (in German), Doctoral Thesis, Department of Computer Science ETH Zurich, 1994.

LH*$_S$: a High-availability and High-security Scalable Distributed Data Structure

W. Litwin[1], M-A Neimat[2], G. Levy[3], S. Ndiaye[3], T. Seck[3]

Abstract

LH$_S$ is high-availability variant of LH*, a Scalable Distributed Data Structure. An LH*$_S$ record is striped onto different server nodes. A parity segment allows to reconstruct the record if a segment fails. The insert or key search time is about a msec on a 10 Mb/s net, and about 100 µs at 1 Gb/s net, assuming the segments in the distributed RAM.   The file size depends only on the distributed storage available, i.e., a RAM file can reach dozens of GB in practice. Data security is enhanced, as every site contains only partial and typically meaningless data. The price to pay is 20 - 50 % more storage for the file than for an LH* file, and some additional messaging, especially for the scan search.*

1. Introduction

Multicomputers are collections of autonomous WSs or PCs over a network (*network multicomputers*), or of share-nothing processors with a local storage linked through a high-speed network or bus (*switched multicomputers*) [T95].   It is well known that multicomputers offer best price-performance ratio [T95], [M96]. Research on multicomputers becomes popular [C94], [G96]. The *Scalable Distributed Data Structures* (SDDSs), like LH* [LNS93], are new data structures designed for multicomputer files. An SDDS gracefully scales up with inserts over available distributed storage, the distributed RAM storage preferably. One problem that a designer of an SDDS may face is a site failure. Some applications require high-availability schemes, allowing data to remain available despite a site failure [M96]. Distributed data are also vulnerable to an unauthorized local or remote intrusion. This makes useful the high-security SDDS schemes, making an unauthorized access to the data difficult.

The LH* schemes with mirroring in [LNS96], called here LH*$_M$, are first SDDSs designed for high-availability. The schema proposed below, termed LH*$_S$, responds to the high-availability and the high-security needs.   A record in LH*$_S$ file is striped into $k > 1$ segments (stripes)

put on different nodes, and into distinct LH* files. There is also a segment with the parity bits, as in RAID schemes and others [PGK88], [HO95], [R94], [SS90]. The striping is basically performed at bit level, putting consecutive bits of the record into different segments. The schema supports any single bucket (server site) unavailability. It also supports any single-site intrusion without disclosing a record content. One can read at best one segment, typically meaningless, as containing 1 bit from every k in the record.

With respect to an LH* file, the LH*$_S$ file with the same records requires more storage, usually about $15 \div 25 \%$,   because of the parity segments. Access performance of LH*$_S$, in terms of network transfer time per insert or key search, is close to this of LH*. There is some deterioration for an insert, as the parity segment has to be sent out. Similarly the key search for a record can be somehow slower than for LH*, as it has to be sent out by the client to k buckets. There is also more CPU time involved as any record travels in at least two messages. Nevertheless, this price should be acceptable for many applications.

The bit-level striping affects more the scan search, where all the records are searched for some non-key values. A scan search in an LH* file is dealt with using a parallel query to every bucket. It requires in general a more costly processing in an LH*$_S$ file with the bit-level striping, as records have to be reconstructed on-the-fly. For applications where scan performance is of prime importance, LH*$_S$ allows for striping at the attribute-level. A segment contains then entire attributes of the record. Scan search performance becomes better, at the expense of the high-security, as an intruder to a site disposes at least of some attributes of a record.

Next section presents LH*$_S$. Section 3 discusses the performance of file manipulations. Section 4 discusses the security issues. Section 5 overviews the related work. Section 6 concludes the paper.

---

[1] Université Paris 9, litwin@etud.dauphine.fr

[2] Hewlet-Packard Laboratories, Palo Alto, California, neimat@hpl.hp.com

[3] Université de Dakar, ndiayesa@esp.esp.sn, seckm@ensut.ensut.sn

2. Overview of LH*s

2.1 Principles of LH*

We now recall the principles of LH* schemes [LNS93]. An LH* file resides on *server* computers (nodes), and is accessed by applications on *client* nodes. A server is always available for access from the clients. A client in contrast is autonomous, perhaps mobile, hence guaranteed to be accessible only when it is an initiator of the connection. The file consists of records identified by (primary) keys. Records are stored in *buckets* with a *capacity* of b records ; $b \gg 1$. Buckets are numbered $0,1,2..N$. There is one bucket of a file per server, although different files may share servers. Buckets are assumed in RAM. The file starts with bucket 0, and scales up with inserts, through bucket splits.

Bucket addresses are mapped to the network addresses of the servers using *physical allocation tables* at the clients, and the servers. Each element of a table contains an address. A table, let it be T, can be *static* or *dynamic*. In the latter case, the address for bucket n can be arbitrarily chosen, especially by the coordinator, and stored in $T(n)$. Different sites may have different tables. The coordinator refreshes T at every bucket, when it sends the request to split. The message contains then all the new addresses added to the file since the previous split of the bucket. The servers send T to clients with every IAM. A dynamic table can scale potentially to any length. Also, it allows for easier bucket migrations than if a static T.

The splitting and addressing rules of LH* are based on those of *linear hashing* (LH) [L80]. Every split moves about half of the records in a bucket into a new bucket at a new server, appended to the file. The splits are done in the order 0; 0, 1; 0, 1, 2; 0, ..., 2^i; 0, ... The next bucket to split is denoted bucket n, and is also called the *split pointer*.

The splits are triggered by bucket overflows. In LH*, a bucket that overflows reports the overflow to a dedicated node called the *coordinator*. The coordinator applies the *load control policy* to find whether the overflow should trigger the split. If so, the coordinator initiates the split of bucket n.

To perform the splits and the addressing, an LH* file uses a family of hash functions h_i, $i = 0,1..$ Each h_i hashes a key c into bucket address $h_i(c) = c \bmod 2^i$. A split results from the replacement of function h_i currently used for bucket n with function h_{i+1}. The i value is called the *bucket level*. At any time, an LH* file can only have buckets with level i or $i + 1$, $i = 0,1,..$ The coordinator is the only node in the file that knows the current values of n and i. The *correct address*, denoted a, of key c in an LH* file is the address where c should be, given n and i, i.e., where it should be *dynamically hashed*. The address a is defined by the LH addressing algorithm [L80]:

(A1) $a \leftarrow h_i(c)$;
      if $a < n$ then $a \leftarrow h_{i+1}(c)$;

To avoid a hot spot, LH* clients do not access the coordinator for the address computation. As for any SDDS, an LH* client has therefore its own *image* of the file. For LH*, it consists of values noted i' and n'; $i' = n' = 0$ for a new client. These values may vary among clients and may differ from the actual n and i. The client uses its image to calculate the address $a' = A(n', i')$ for key c, while issuing a (point-to-point) request for the search of c, or for an insert or a delete of the record identified by c. It then sends the request, and perhaps the record to server a'. LH* supports also multicast and broadcast queries addressing through one message all N buckets, [LNS93].

It might happen that $a' \neq a$. Hence, every server s receiving a request first tests whether $s = a$. For this purpose, every server keeps the current value of i. It can be proven that $s = a$ iff $s = h_i(c)$. If the test fails, the server forwards the request to another server. The LH* *test and forwarding algorithm* is as follows, [LNS93] :

(A2) $a' \leftarrow h_i(c)$;
      if $a' = a$ then accept c ;
        $a'' \leftarrow h_{i-1}(c)$;
      if $a'' > a$ and $a'' < a'$ then $a' \leftarrow a''$;
      forward c to bucket a' ;

The forwarding process could a priori create many hops. The major property of LH* is however that every request to an LH* file is delivered to the correct address after at most two hops, [LNS93].

As for any SDDS, the correct server finally sends a message back to the client, called an Image Adjustment Message (IAM). For LH*, an IAM contains the i value of server a'. The value of split pointer n is unknown to the servers, hence is not in IAMs. The client executes then the *IA-Algorithm*, [LNS93] :

(A3)   if $i > i'$ then $i' \leftarrow i - 1$, $n' \leftarrow a + 1$;
      if $n' \geq 2^{i'}$ then $n' = 0$, $i' \leftarrow i' + 1$;

The result of (A3) is a better image, with both i' and n' closer to the actual values. Also, as long as there is no new split, the same addressing error cannot occur. (A3) makes LH*-images converge rapidly [LNS93]. Usually, $O(\log N)$ IAMs to a new client (the worst case for image accuracy) suffice to about eliminate the forwarding. If a client already has a good image, but the file starts to scale-up, algorithm (A3) suffices to keep the incidence of forwarding on the access performance about negligible. In practice, the average key insert cost is one message, and both a successful and unsuccessful key search cost is two messages, regardless of the file size. The worst access performance of an insert or search corresponds to the case of two hops. These costs for LH* are of four messages, also regardless of the number of nodes of the file.

The principles of LH* led to many variants [LNS93a], [KLR96]. The schemes offer various trade-offs adapted to particularities of applications.

2.2 Principles of LH*ₛ

We now discuss the basic LH*ₛ using the *bit-level striping* (segmentation, scattering..). A *record R* is a key, usually denoted c, and a sequence of bits B, numbered from left to right $B = b_1,...,b_k b_{k+1}...b_{2k} b_{2k+1}...b_{mk}$. The size of B is mk, last bits being padded if needed in practice. When an LH*ₛ client should store R, then it proceeds as follows, Fig. 1:

• It produces *k segments*, $k > 1$. The i-th segment s_i consists from c and from all the bits s'_i :

$$s'_i = b_i\, b_{k+i}\, b_{2k+i} ...$$

• It produces the *parity segment* s_{k+1} that also contains c and the parity bits s'_{k+1}, let us say for the *even* parity:

$$s'_{k+1} = b'_1\, b'_2 .. b'_m$$

where bit b'_j is the parity bit for the string with the j-th bit of each segment ; $1 \le j \le k$. If some segment s of R cannot be read, the parity segment, allows to reconstruct s.

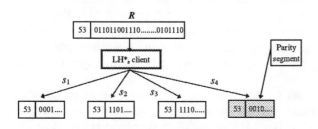

Fig. 1 LH*ₛ scattering of a record into k = 3 segments

An LH*ₛ file is created as a family Φ of $k+1$ LH* *segment files* $S_1..S_{k+1}$. File S_i stores all the segments s_i. The address of segment s_i is calculated from its key c that is, we recall, also the key of R. As in LH*ₘ , [LNS96], two segment files can be structurally-alike (SA). They have then the same parameters : the bucket size, the functions h_i, etc. They can also be structurally-different (SD) which means that these parameters differ. SD-files are *loosely-coupled* if they share functions h_i. Otherwise,

they are *minimally-coupled* [LNS96]. Fig. 3 shows the relationship between SA and SD files.

The basic constraint on Φ is that for every record R, all its segments are mapped to different nodes, or at least buckets. One way to achieve it is to provide each S with the physical allocation table T_S spanning over distinct nodes of the multicomputer. In other words, no node carries then a bucket of S_i and of S_j when $i \ne j$.

For SA segment files, every segment of the same record R is usually in the bucket with the same bucket address m within its segment file, as in Fig. 3. For instance, after some inserts into F, the segments of R with key $c = 100$, may be all in buckets 57 of their files. The client keeps a single LH* image with the (guessed) file level i' and the split pointer value n' for every S. For SD segment files, the segments' bucket addresses typically differ, Fig. 3. Hence, there is one image per S on the client and these images usually differ as well.

As usually for an LH* file, every S expands through splits, tolerates addressing errors, and sends IAMs to its clients. Splits among segment files are not synchronized, i.e., each S split autonomously. Hence, even in SA segment files, it may happen that bucket m in a segment file S_i splits before another bucket m in the segment file S_j ; $j \ne \iota$. One reason may be that S_j failed when it should split after a new insert. A segment of record R may then be in new bucket in S_i while another segment of R is still in bucket m in S_j. Hence, the addresses of the segments of a record within their SA segment files may sometimes differ as well.

The whole set Φ of LH*ₛ segment files S has a common component at some server called the *segment file coordinator*, SC in short. Its address is known to every server and every client. SC takes care of the LH* coordination for each S. This includes all the allocation tables, assumed dynamic, since easier to manage for a spare production. In addition, it has capabilities for the fault-tolerance of the whole collection that we'll introduce.

In particular, SC gets alerted when a bucket failure is detected. The alert may come from a client that failed with a file manipulation. It may also come from a server that could not forward a message or could not split. If a failure is confirmed, SC coordinates the creation of the spare.

2.3 File manipulation
2.3.1 Inserts

To insert record R, the client first produces the $(k + 1)$ segments. Then. it sends each segment s_i ; $i = 1..k + 1$; using a unicast message to bucket m_i , where m_i results from the LH* address computation (A1) executed on the client for each segment file S_i. Unlike for LH*, each message carries the value m_i for the reasons discussed more in depth in Section 2.4.2. The server addressed by the message usually carries bucket m_i. It might rarely happen that it carries another bucket. This occurs when bucket m_i failed and was recreated at another location. If it happens, the server that got the message forwards it to SC. SC determines from the allocation tables where bucket m_i actually is, and resents the message. An IAM comes later to the client, from bucket m_i, with its actual address.

Once bucket m_i gets the message, a forwarding may occur as usually for an LH* file. The forwarded message also carries the number, let it be m, of bucket m the message is intended for. If another bucket is found at the destination site instead, the message is resent to SC, as above, etc. Since in LH* there are at most two forwardings, SC can get the messages at most three time as well. Same process may occur for each segment file. It is however very unlikely that all this happens simultaneously for all the segments of the same insert. The typical case is that every segment is inserted without any forwarding.

Assuming nevertheless that a forwarding occurs at a segment file, the client receives an IAM. Up to $(k + 1)$ IAMs may therefore be triggered by an insert. The client of SD segment files adjusts each image. The client of SA segment files, has to proceed differently, since it has only one image. The basic strategy is that the client performs the IA-algorithm for an address a' only when all the $(k + 1)$ IAM messages with a' and (same) i' are received.

A client or a forwarding server may also find a bucket unavailable. It then alerts SC and forwards the segment to it. The client considers the insert successful if it encounters at most one failed bucket. Otherwise, the client waits for a message from SC, advising whether the insert is finally successful or not. The failed bucket can be indeed the correct bucket for the segment, or the intermediate bucket that should forward the segment. The insert basically fails if the SC finds unavailable more than one correct bucket for a segment. There can be in contrast several forwarding buckets unavailable. SC may bypass such buckets, as it has the actual image of the file. If only one bucket is unavailable, the segment that was passed to SC is finally inserted during the recovery procedure discussed below.

LH* supports also *bulk inserts*. A message with several records is then multicast to all the servers. Each server stores then the records whose keys correspond. LH*$_S$ file also supports the bulk inserts. A record can be sent entirely in a bulk message. Alternatively, one may spread its segments into several bulk messages. This strategy enhances the transfer security. Note that one should send also then the parity segment, computed by the client.

2.3.2 Splits

Splits of segment files are basically performed as for LH*. Especially, if the new bucket fails during the split, i.e., before the split is committed, the split restarts with a new target bucket. The new case is that a bucket can fail failure during the split. The split is stopped. The spare is created as for any failed bucket, using the other segment files to reconstruct all the unavailable segments, as described below. Then, the split is restarted from the beginning. Alternatively, the new bucket sends to the spare all its keys. The spare moves only the segments that should move and whose keys are not among the received ones.

2.3.3 Deletes

To (physically) delete $R (c)$, the client sends the key to all the corresponding $(k + 1)$ buckets. Every bucket deletes the corresponding segment, as discussed in [LN95]. Physical deletion being rare in practice, we do not discuss them more in what follows.

2.3.4 Search

2.3.4.1 Key search

The search for record R, given its key c, is performed basically through sending c to k servers, $S_1, S_2... S_k$. The client uses k unicast messages to the buckets whose addresses result from the LH* address computation for each segment file. For the SA segment files, the bucket address is computed once for every segment file. For SD segments, there are k calculus and the results may differ. If all the segments come, the clients synthesize the record.

As for the inserts, each message carries its intended bucket number. The servers may forward the messages, as usually for LH*, or to SC, if the actual bucket does not match the intended one. If a reply is missing, despite perhaps several attempts to get it by the client, the client alerts SC. If only one reply is missing, the client issues a message to S_{k+1}. If this segment comes, the client synthesize the record. Otherwise, the search fails.

The search can be unsuccessful. In this case, it is not necessary to have all the servers to reply. The buckets perform then the hashing $m = c \bmod k$. Only the bucket within S_m replies. An alternative strategy is that no bucket replies and the client declares the search unsuccessful by time-out. It is highly unlikely that if the search was successful, the replies from all k buckets were lost on the way, and the client incorrectly understood that the search was unsuccessful.

2.3.4.2 Scan search

LH* supports also the *scan search*, or the *scan* in short, where all records are searched for some non-key values. For records that are collections of attributes, the scan search criteria usually consist of a selection predicate on the attribute values. An LH* scan search is realized through a parallel search over each bucket using the selection expression got from the client. The results are returned to the client also in parallel. A scan may terminate using a *probabilistic* (time-out) *termination* where only the buckets that have sent records reply. One may alternatively request the *deterministic termination*, where any bucket replies, with its address, and selected records or a null message if the search is unsuccessful. The client may compute whether all the buckets currently existing in the file replied. If only a few records are to be selected and the file is large, then the time-out termination is much faster than the deterministic one.

A scan is sent by the client using either unicast messages or a multicast message. In the former case, the client may not know all the corresponding addresses. An algorithm propagating then the search to all the servers of the LH* file is defined in [LNS93a]. The drawback of a multicast message is that it is received by all the sites on the net. Hence it disturbs also those not serving the file.

A scan in an LH*$_S$ file is typically a more complex operation than in an LH* file with the same records. Each bucket contains indeed only some non-consecutive bits of each record. Such a content provides the high-security, but is about meaningless for evaluating selection predicates. The only practical way to proceed is to reconstruct all the records at some servers, where the parallel scan is performed as for an LH* file. The reconstruction is essentially a multiway equi-join on the key value between all the segments. The servers where it is performed are called *join servers*. It should be worth using all the available segment file servers as join servers and uniformly. This rationale leads to the following algorithm.

(A4) LH*$_S$ scan search

1. Using unicast or multicast, the client sends the scan search Q in parallel to every bucket m in its image(s) of each segment file S_i ; $i = 1,2..k$.
2. If unicast is used, then each server applies the LH* parallel search propagation algorithm.
3. For every segment s_i (c) with key c at every server, perform the hashing $h(c) = c \bmod k + 1$. Consider the server of segment $s_{h(c)}(c)$ as the join server of the record $R(c)$. If $i = h(c)$, then prepare for the reception of other

segments of R. Otherwise, send $s_i(c)$ to the corresponding address in file $S_{h(c)}$.
4. For every server, perform the join of all the segments received with the corresponding segments stored locally, to reconstruct every R.
5. If any expected segment is missing, alert SC and search S_{k+1}. Reconstruct remaining R's.
6. For each server, perform Q and send the result to the client.

Details of (A4) are discussed in [LN95]. The basic way for sending the results of Q back to the client is to simply to send all the selected records by every join server. Another possibility is to send from the server of a selected record the messages to the buckets with the corresponding segments requesting them to be sent to the client. Finally, the join server may send to the client only the keys. The client searches then the corresponding segments itself. The latter approaches are more costly in CPU and messages, but offer higher security.

The client may wish the parallel search to terminate in a deterministic or probabilistic way, i.e., by time-out. The deterministic termination is costly, as every bucket has to send a result, perhaps null. For a probabilistic termination it suffices that one sends only the selected records or segments. There is no guarantee that the client gets all the records that it should.

2.4 Failure management
2.4.1 Overview

We consider the following kinds of failures :
1. A search at an available server does not find a segment s_i ; $i \leq k$; while the client gets all other segments.
2. A bucket is unavailable for access.

In case (1), s_i is simply reconstructed by the client on the fly, after additional search of s_{k+1}. Then, s_i is reinserted, by the client or SC. If more segments are missing, the record and the segments cannot be reconstructed from s_{k+1}. The corresponding recovery is considered application dependent and beyond the scope of the basic LH*$_S$.

In case (2), the lack of access is due to the bucket failure, or to the network failure. Once the access is reestablished, the bucket restarts the service by contacting SC. The clients are served again by the bucket only if SC informs the server that no spare was produced in the meantime.

If a bucket fails, two strategies exist :
1. One continues, using the available segments, until the bucket recovers by itself. If $k \gg 1$, the difference in the workload on these segments should be negligible. If

updates occur, the corresponding segments are reconstructed when the bucket is up again.

2. A spare is produced, replacing instantly the failed bucket.

The choice between strategies (1) and (2) is application dependent. Strategy (2) clearly offers higher availability. This strategy is the basic one for LH*$_S$. The spare production algorithms depend on the structure, SA or SD, of the segment files. They are based on those for the LH* with mirrors [LNS96].

2.4.2 Creating a spare

Let it be bucket n_1 that failed in its segment file, let it be S_1. To create the spare, one should find the segment buckets of $S_2..S_{k+1}$ that contain the remaining segments of every record R whose segment s_1 was in the lost bucket. For each lost segment, the remaining segments of R have to be joined at some join server. The lost segment may then be recomputed at the join server, and inserted to the spare being created.

To determine the addresses of the buckets with the remaining segments, we consider at first the SA or SD segment files, except for the minimally coupled files. Let j_1 be the level of bucket n_1. Every S_i uses the same hash functions. Hence, for each S_i ; $i > 1$; two cases may happen:

1. The segments are all in one bucket. This will happen if there is not yet bucket n_2 in S_i such that $n_2 = n_1$ or level j_2 of bucket n_2 is $j_2 \leq j_1$. In particular, if $j_2 < j_1$, then bucket n_2 may contain more records than bucket n_1.

2. The records are in several buckets. This will happen if $j_2 > j_1$.

In case (1), n_2 is at the largest address n_2 such that:

$$n_2 = n_1 \text{ or } n_2 = n_{2,1} = n_1 - 2^{j_1-1} \text{ or } n_2 = n_{2,1} - 2^{j_1-2} \text{ or } ...$$
$$... n_2 = 0$$

In case (2), buckets to be read are bucket n_1 itself, its children, children of children, etc. Hence these buckets are :

$$m = n_1 \text{ or } m = n_{1,1} = n_1 + 2^{j_1-1} \text{ or } m = n_{1,2} = n_1 + 2^{j_1} ... \text{ or}$$
$$m = n_1 + 2^{j_2-1} \text{ or } m = n_{1,1,1} = n_{1,1} + 2^{j_1} \text{ or } m = n_{1,1,2} =$$
$$= n_{1,1} + 2^{j_1+1} \text{ or } m = n_{1,1,1,1} = n_{1,1,1} + 2^{j_1+1} ....$$

The first line corresponds to the addresses of the children of n_1. The next line corresponds to the children of the first child of n_1 (in some cases this line may if fact be a copy of the first line since one may have $n_1 = n_{1,1}$). Then, there are the children of the next child, etc. Fig. 2 illustrates the formulae.

Let b_i denote the bucket capacity of S_i. Let us assume that the load control policy is the same for both files. Then, typically, case (1) occurs if $b_i > b_1$ and case (2) occurs if $b_1 > b_i$. If $b_2 = b_1$, one has the case of SA segment files.

The following algorithm is executed by SC and the buckets' servers, to produce a spare for SA and SD files.

(A5) Spare creation for an LH*$_S$ file

Consider that the lost bucket is bucket n in file S_1.

1. For every segment file S_i; $i = 2..k+1$; SC determines as above the addresses m_i of buckets that could have the remaining segments of the record R whose segment s_1 was in bucket n. Let l be the total number of these buckets.

2. SC allocates a server for the spare and an empty new bucket n is created. This server receives from SC all the bucket addresses computed in Step 1.

3. For every m_i, SC sends the query with level j of bucket n. It requests every key c such that segment s_1 of R (c) was in bucket n, i.e., it requests to test for every c whether $n = h_j (c)$.

4. Every bucket server computes for each c found through Step (4) the hashing function $h (c) = 2 + c$ mod l. The server of bucket m with the segment $s_{h(c)}$ is assumed the join server for the record $R (c)$.

5. For every segment $s (c)$ from step (4), if bucket m is not at the server computing the function, then the server sends segment $s (c)$ to bucket m. To allow for that, the query of step (4) contains also the actual addressing parameters (i, n) of each segment file, and the physical addresses of all the buckets found through step (2).

6. For every bucket m, there is a terminating message with the number segments sent, expedited by every bucket from which bucket m expected or got segments.

7. Every record corresponding to the lost bucket is reconstructed on the join server. The lost segment is computed and sent to the spare bucket.

8. The spare server expects a termination message from each join server, containing the number of records that it should receive.

9. SC sends the physical address of the spare to the server with the parent of the lost bucket. The server updates its allocation table.

10. Through Step 4, the algorithm distributes the computation of the lost segments. A naive approach would be to centralize this computation on the spare, making it much less efficient. The goal of the terminating messages in Steps 6, 9, is the deterministic termination. Details of Step 5 - 9 are implementation depended. For slower nets, it may be advantageous send segments to the join server and from a join server to the spare in bulks.

146

The parent allocation table is the only one that points to the spare, as the parent might need to perform a forwarding, except for that of SC. Hence, it is the only bucket sever table that needs an update when the spare is built. Once SC commits the split, any query to the server of the failed bucket will be directed to the new one. This, after being forwarded by the server or the client to SC, as discussed in Section 2.3.1. The expected bucket number is necessary in every query to recognize the situation when the server of the failed bucket became a spare in turn and eventually got a new bucket. See [LN95] for further discussion of the algorithm.

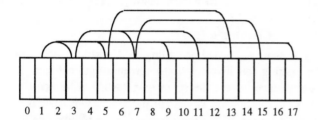

Fig. 2 Children and other descendants of bucket 1 in LH* file with level $j = 5$

3. Performance

3.1 Load factor

The load factor α of a file is defined as $\alpha = x\, R_s\, /b_S\, N$, where x is the number of records, R_s the record size, b_S the bucket size, and N is the number of buckets in the file. For an LH* file, one has in practice $\alpha \approx 70\ \% - 80\ \%$ [LNS93a]. For LH*$_S$ file, assuming the load of α for every segment file, one can show that the approximate value α' of the overall load factor is :

$$\alpha' = \alpha\ k\ /(k+1) - O\,[kf].$$

Assuming $k = 4$, one ends up with $a' \approx 55 - 64\ \%$, i.e., 15-25 % of more storage with respect to the LH* file, as the price for the high-availability.

3.2 Inserts

Splits, and forwarding should be infrequent with LH*$_S$, and the failures even more rare. An insert to an LH* file typically costs one message. Hence the typical, and the best, messaging cost of an insert into LH*$_S$ file is $(k + 1)$ messages. Small buckets for segment files make splits, and forwarding more frequent. This increases the average insert cost while building a file, up to 1.5 $(k + 1)$ messages per insert [LN95]. The insert cost increases on the other hand usually by three messages if a segment is sent to a bucket that failed in the meantime hence a spare was created. It may even triple in the worst case, thought

about impossible in practice, a discussed in depth in [LN95].

The messaging cost of an insert measured in the number of messages, is at least $(k + 1)$ times higher for an LH*$_S$ file than for an LH* file. Another performance aspect is the volume of data sent over the net. To insert a record of some length l_R, with the key length l_C, one transfers $(l_R - l_c\ )\ /\ k + k\ l_c\ ) \approx l_R\ /\ k$ more bytes over the net for an LH*$_S$ file than for an LH* file. For instance for $k = 4$, it represents only a 25 % increase.

The insert time is determined basically by the CPU time to send-out and receive the message, and by the transfer time. For longer records, over Kbytes, or slower nets, e.g., Ethernet, the transfer time almost entirely dominates [LNS94]. LH*$_S$ typical insert time should then be only 20 - 25% longer than the LH* insert time. For a 10 Mb/s net, and 1 KB record, this leads to the insert time of about 1.25 ms [LNS94]. For faster nets or shorter records, the CPU time begins to dominate. The insert time of LH*$_S$ becomes then closer to $(k + 1)$ /2 times LH* time, as the servers work in parallel, but the client basically serializes the received messages. The exact figures depends on the network speed and topology. For a 1 Gb/s net, 100 Mips CPU, and 1 KB record, the CPU time for an insert into an LH* file may be 51 µs and the transfer time 20 µs, leading 71 µs per insert [LNS94]. The same net would lead to the insert time of 140 µs for the LH*$_S$ file, i.e., two times greater, for, we recall $k = 4$. Note that this evaluation still neglects the time to segment the record that will add some µs.

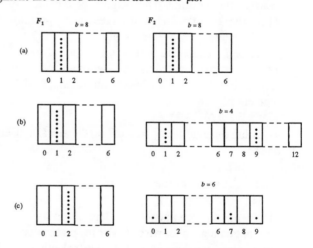

**Fig. 3 Types of LH*$_S$ segment files :
(a) SA-segments, (b) loosely-coupled SD-segments, and (c) minimally coupled SD-segments**

Observe finally that segment files can be on different nets, connected to the client through different controllers.

The transfer time decreases accordingly. It can become faster than for LH*.

3.3 Key search

The calculus similar to the one for inserts, shows that the typical successful key search costs $2k$ messages. An unsuccessful search costs typically 2 messages. In the theoretically worst case without a failure the cost of successful search is $9k + 1$ messages. A bucket failure costs typically an additional message to s_{k+1}, and the reply. It might cost up to 10 additional messages for a very unlucky client. If a failure is discovered during the search, it costs typically 2 additional messages to S_{k+1} and 1 message to SC.

With respect to the transfer time, it is about that of LH* assuming $l_c << R_c$, as only k segments are sent back. Hence for large records or slower nets, LH*$_S$ search time is about that of LH*. Otherwise, the successful search time grows towards $2 k t_m$, where t_m is the time to process a message at the client site. In the case of a Gb/s net dealt with for the inserts, the successful search time should be $4 * 56 + 31 = 255$ µs, instead of 87 µs for LH* [LNS94]. The unsuccessful search time is clearly about half of it, plus, perhaps the time-out.

3.4 Scan search

First component of a scan search price is the cost of query propagation the, let it be m_1. One has $m_1 = 1$, if the multicast is used. Otherwise, regardless of the client's image, one has $m_1 = N_S$, where N_S is the total number of buckets of k segment files, as every bucket is reached by exactly one message. The number of rounds is greater when the client's image diverges more, leading to a somehow larger propagation time.

Second component, let it be m_2, is the cost of merging all the records, according to Algorithm A4. This cost corresponds to all-to-all bucket messaging, and is for a segment file:

$$s = 0.7 \, b \, N \, (k - 1) \, / k,$$

assuming the load factor $\alpha = 0.7$ on the average. Hence one has :

$$m_2 = \Sigma \, s$$

and for SA segment files, one has :

$$m_2 \approx 0.7 \, b \, N \, (k - 1).$$

Finally the third component m_3 depends on the termination algorithm wished. For the probabilistic termination, one depends on the query selectivity and :

$$0 \le m_3 \le N_S.$$

Hence, for SA segment files, one has :

$$0 \le m_3 \le k \, N.$$

For the deterministic termination, one simply has $m_3 = N_S$, as all the buckets must reply.

A practical value of b is $b >> 1$, e.g., $b = 1000$. Cost m_2 is therefore dominant by orders of magnitude. For $k = 4$ for instance, and a large file, e.g., $N_S = 1000$, and, m_2 reaches 2.1M messages. Such messaging has to take at least a few seconds in practice.

Cost m_2 does not exist for LH*. Hence, scans in LH* file are cheaper and faster than in the LH*$_S$ file. This cost is the main price for the high-availability and high-security. If one needs the high-availability only, LH*$_M$ using mirroring allows for without this cost [LN96], but at much larger storage cost. On the other hand, if one segments the records without bit-level scattering, giving up some security, parallel queries may be executed more efficiently, as it will appear below, at the same storage cost as above.

3.5 Creating a spare

A spare is created according to Algorithm A5. The messaging cost involves first a few messages between SC and a server where the spare is created. Let this cost be c_1. One can assume $c_1 \approx 2$ in practice. Then RC has to contact servers where the segments used to compute the lost ones could be (Step 3 of Algorithm A5). For SA segments, the cost, let it be c_2 should typically be $c_2 = k$ messages. For SD segments, it can be $k < c_2 \le N_S$. One has $k = N_S$ for the minimally-coupled segment files where the segments for Step 3 has to be searched using parallel queries. Otherwise, one has $c_2 \le pk$, where p is an integer close to $max \, (b_s \, / \, b_i \,)$, where b_s denotes the bucket capacity of the lost bucket, and b_i is the bucket capacity of any other segment file, among the $k + 1$ files.

Next cost component, let it be c_3 corresponds to the join of the segments. One has thus on the average :

$$c_3 = 0.7 \, b \, k,$$

as there are on the average as many segments to reconstruct on join servers. Then the reconstructed segments are sent to the spare which leads to the cost component $c_4 = c_3$. Finally, the spare commits to SC, and SC sends the pointer to the spare's parent. All together this leads to the following typical costs :

- for SA files, one has:

$$c_S \approx 2 + k + 1.4 \, b \, k + 2,$$

- for SD files, one has:

$$2 + k + 1.4 \, b \, k + 2 < c_S \le 2 + max \, (b_s \, / \, b_i \,) + 1.4 \, b \, k + 2,$$

- and finally for minimally-coupled segment files, one has :

$$2 + k + 1.4 \, b \, k + 2 < c_S \le 2 + N_S + 1.4 \, b \, k + 2.$$

Hence the creation of a spare for minimally-coupled segment files can be by far the most expensive.

3.6 Multiple bucket failure

It is easy to see that any above discussed LH*$_S$ schema supports a single bucket failure. Resistance to multiple bucket failures depends on whether SA or SD segment files are used. For SA segment files, with bucket capacity of b segments, and no load control, a multiple bucket failure does not create any loss of records, as long as no failed buckets hold segments of the same record. This is an unlikely event. For any two segment files there are indeed only two such buckets. If this happens anyhow, than one looses $\alpha\, b$ records, on the average, i.e., $0.7\, b$ records in practice.

Loosely-coupled and minimally-coupled SD segment files, increase the probability of data loss in the case of a multiple failure, but decrease the amount of lost data. See [LN95] for the corresponding performance trade-offs.

4. High-security

4.1 Bit-level striping

The bit-level striping as used in an LH*$_S$ file provides naturally the *high-security* in the sense that no record becomes known to an intruder to a site or to a network. For every record R of the LH*$_S$ file striped at bit-level, each bucket has one of each k bits of R. If l is the length of R in bits, the key non-included, there are $s = l\,(1 - 1/k)$ bits of R missing from the any bucket. An intruder to a site has 2^s possibilities to complete a segment to the actual content. This is at least a very long computation in practice.

Next, even an intruder knowledgeable of LH*$_S$ principles, cannot find from the bucket where to find other segments. A bucket in one segment file does have the addressing parameters of other files (except when a scan is in progress). Hence, the intruder would need to search the missing segments anywhere in the multicomputer. One can reasonably expect such a task at least very long in practice.

Finally, LH*$_S$ protects against getting knowledge of the data through the listening on the net. Every message naturally carries only one from every k bits of the record. To reconstruct the intercepted segments with the same key, require $k!$ trials, assuming the intruder does not know the reconstruction order that is known implicitly only to the client. If this protection is not enough, one can easily scramble the same keys to different values for the transfer in different segments. For instance, the server can add the segment number to the key in the message, to be subtracted by the client. Finally, different segments of a record may come to the client through different sub-networks, making the intrusion through the network listening even more difficult.

Note that SA segment-files are somehow weaken from the high-security point of view than SD files. If an intruder to a bucket finds the addresses of other segments of a record, it knows the addresses of all other records in the bucket. Such correspondence is only partial for loosely coupled SD segment-files, and does not exist for the minimally-coupled files.

Note finally one more nice property of LH*$_S$. Even if an intruder learns the addresses of all the segments of a record at one time, these addresses change when the file scales.

4.2 Attribute level striping

LH*$_S$, as discussed above, enhances the high-security at the expense of scan performance. It makes segments meaningless through the scattering at bit level, in order to make data secure against intrusions. To make a scan efficient, through the parallelism, data should in contrast remain possibly entire. If efficient scans are of greater importance than the high-security provided by LH*$_S$ with bit-level striping, one should use the striping at the level of blocks of data.

One choice for LH*$_S$ is the *attribute-level striping*. Each of k segments of a record R (c) contains then c and some non-key fields of R. Each non-key attribute is entirely in one (and only one) segment. The attributes in a segment do not need to be the consecutive ones in R. The parity segment s_{k+1} contains the parity bits for the fault-tolerance. As the segments may be now of different length, s_{k+1} is of the length of the longest one.

The attribute level striping lowers the bucket security level. The intruder disposes of a meaningful part of a record, thought there is still no addresses in the bucket of the rest of R. In turn, one may process some scans without first reconstructing the records. This may lead to a substantial performance improvement [LN95].

Attribute-level striping also may lead to a better performance of updates and of the key search. An update to some attribute A (S) in segment S, requires access only to S and the parity segment. A search involving only the key and A (S) requires access to S only. LH*$_S$ with the attribute-level striping is more discussed in [LN95].

5. Related work

The ideas in LH*$_S$ originate in the RAID approach (Redundant Arrays of Inexpensive Disks) [PGK88]. However, LH*$_S$ scatters data over a distributed RAM of servers at a net, instead of a cabinet of disks. Another difference is that the LH*$_S$ stripes at the logical (record, and perhaps attribute) level, instead of physical page (sector) level, using the key as the identifier replicated in each segment. This allows LH*$_S$ to easily scale, unlike the RAID schemes.

The efficiency of the scan search as discussed for $LH*_s$ is not a part of RAID goals. The high-security goal of $LH*_s$ is not a part of RAID idea objectives neither. It follows the *Fragmentation-Redundancy-Scattering* (FRS) proposal for the data management over the networks, [R94]. One postulates in [R94] and its references that the FRS approach is among the most promising ones.

There were other attempts to use striping for network files. An overview of some of the proposed schemes is in [T95a]. Among earliest proposals, was the RADD (Redundant Arrays of Distributed Disks) schema [SS90]. The RADD schema is also *physical*, striping at page level. It is also static, designed for slow networks, and inefficient for the scans. High-security was not a concern for RADD design.

Between recent high-availability prototypes using a physical schema, there is the Zebra system, [HO95]. Zebra files are not SDDSs, e.g., since a centralized directory is required for the address computation. The system uses striped log-structured files with possibly large segments. It is not efficient for operating on individual records, e.g., in the database application context, [HO95]. In particular there is no provision in Zebra architecture for the scans.

6. Conclusion

$LH*_s$ appears an attractive SDDS providing the fault-tolerance and high-security of data. Both features are of interest to many applications. The price for new features is a fractional increase to the storage for the file, and some additional messaging, as compared to LH*. The additional cost is moderate, especially when most of file operations are key searches and inserts. Scans may affect the access performance more, especially if bit-level striping is used. One may trade-in some security for the attribute-level striping, improving the access performance.

Further research should concern performance analysis and experiments with various design issues. New ideas for RAID systems may give interesting result when transposed to the multicomputer environment [W96]. Given the commercial importance that multicomputers should have soon, [M96], another interesting alley should be to expand the Windows NT file striping capabilities to the $LH*_s$ capabilities. Finally, one should investigate high-availability variants using striping for other SDDSs, RP* schemes especially [LNS94], [LN96a].

References

[ASS94]   Amin, M., Schneider, D.and Singh, V., An Adaptive, Load Balancing Parallel Join Algorithm. 6th International Conference on Management of Data, Bangalore, India, December, 1994.

[C94]   Culler, D. NOW: Towards Everyday Supercomputing on a Network of Workstations. *EECS Tech. Rep. UC Berkeley*.

[D93]   Devine, R. Design and Implementation of DDH: Distributed Dynamic Hashing. *Int. Conf. on Foundations of Data Organizations, FODO-93. Lecture Notes in Comp. Sc.*, Springer-Verlag (publ.), Oct. 1993.

[G96]   Gray, J. Super-Servers: Commodity Computer Clusters Pose a Software Challemge. Microsoft, 1996. http:\\www.research microsoft..com\

[HO95]   Hartman J., Ousterhout, J. The Zebra Striped Network File System. ACM Trans. on Comp. Systems. 13, 3, 95, 275-309.

[KW94]   Kroll, B., Widmayer, P. Distributing a Search Tree Among a Growing Number of Processors. *ACM-SIGMOD Int. Conf. On Management of Data*, 1994.

[LNS93]   Litwin, W. Neimat, M-A., Schneider, D. LH* : Linear Hashing for Distributed Files. *ACM-SIGMOD Intl. Conf. On Management of Data*, 1993.

[LNS93a]   Litwin, W., Neimat, M-A., Schneider, D. LH*: A Scalable Distributed Data Structure. (Nov. 1993). To app. in ACM-TODS.

[LNS94]   Litwin, W., Neimat, M-A., Schneider, D. RP* : A Family of Order-Preserving Scalable Distributed Data Structures. *20th Intl. Conf on Very Large Data Bases (VLDB)*, 1994.

[LN95]   Litwin, W., Neimat, M-A. $LH*_s$: a high-availability and high-security Scalable Distributed Data Structure. U. Paris 9 Technical Report, 1995.

[LN96]   Litwin, W., Neimat, M-A. High-Availability LH* Schemes with Mirroring. Intl. Conf. on Cooperating Information Systems. Brussels, (June 1996), IEEE-Press, 1996.

[LN96a]   Litwin, W., Neimat. k-RP* : a High Performance Multi-attribute Scalable Distributed Data Structure. Intl. Conf. on Par. and Distr. Inf. Sys., IEEE-PDIS 96. IEEE-Press, 1996.

[M96]   Microsoft Windows NT Server Cluster Strategy: High Availability and Scalability with Industry-Standard Hardware. A White Paper from the Business Systems Division. Microsoft, 1996.

[PGK88]   Patterson, D., Gibson, G., Katz, R., H. A Case for Redundant Arrays of Inexpensive Disks (RAID). ACM-Sigmod, 1988.

[R94]   Randel, B. System Dependability. *Future Tendencies in Computer Science, Control, and Applied Mathematics*. Lecture Notes in Computer Science 653, Springer-Verlag, 1994. A. Bensoussan, J. P. Verjus, ed. .21-50.

[SS90]   Stonebraker, M, Schloss, G. Distributed RAID - A new multiple copy algorithm. 6th Intl. IEEE Conf. on Data Eng. IEEE Press, 1990, 430-437.

[T95]   Tanenbaum, A., S. *Distributed Operating Systems*. Prentice Hall, 1995, 601.

[T95a]   Torbjornsen, O. Multi-site Declustering Strategies for Very High Database Service Availabiity. Thesis Norges Techn. Hogskoule. IDT Report 1995.2, 176.

[VBWY94]   Vingralek, R., Breitbart, Y., Weikum, G. Distributed File Organization with Scalable Cost/Performance. *ACM-SIGMOD Int. Conf. On Management of Data*, 1994.

[W96]   Wilkes, J. & al.. The HP AutoRAID hierarchical storage system. ACM-TCS, 14, 1, 1996.

A Dynamic Migration Algorithm for a Distributed Memory-Based File Management System *

James Griffioen, Todd A. Anderson
Department of Computer Science
University of Kentucky
Lexington, KY 40506

Yuri Breitbart
Bell Laboratories
600 Mountain Ave.
Murray Hill, NJ 07974

Abstract

Conventional migration strategies attempt to evenly balance the load across all available server machines. This paper discusses why conventional migration approaches are not necessarily appropriate for distributed memory-based file systems and presents and alternative approach that spreads data (possibly unevenly) across as few machines as possible and involves other available machines only as needed. The main advantage of our approach is that it keeps the system minimally distributed thereby reducing the failure rate among servers, the communication overhead among servers, the time needed to compute data relocation, distributed addressing costs, and the probability of unanticipated migrations (e.g., caused by, and an inconvenience to, returning users).

1. Introduction

Database and file storage systems have historically suffered from high access latencies. In fact, I/O latency is one of the major reasons application performance has not improved at the same rate as processor speeds [15]. In our previous work [11], we introduced a distributed memory-based file system (MBFS) that used the idle memory and processor cycles of a network of workstations to provide persistent storage with read and write latencies more than an order of magnitude faster than conventional disk-based storage systems. Other researchers have proposed similar systems that improve read latency (as opposed to read/write latency) by treating remote memory as additional file cache space [2, 6, 3, 7, 12].

This paper builds on our past work by examining the issue of data migration in a distributed memory-based storage system. We introduce a new data migration algorithm that differs drastically from conventional migration algorithms used to load balance processes in a distributed system [19] or file accesses in a disk-based distributed storage system [21, 22].

Conventional process migration algorithms and load balancing algorithms attempt to (1) spread the load across all available machines, and (2) balance the load as evenly as possible. Failure to use all machines means wasted CPU cycles. In addition, if one processor is more heavily loaded than another processor, performance may suffer. Thus balancing is important. The same goals apply to disk-based file systems that allow file migration. For example, the snowball disk-based distributed file system [21, 22] showed the importance of balancing, noting that a highly balanced load (e.g., a maximum imbalance of 0.5%) performs three times better than a slightly imbalanced load (e.g., a maximum imbalance of 5%). Achieving a carefully balanced load is computationally expensive and keeping the load balanced typically means frequent migration.

Our previous work [11] illustrated two unique characteristics of distributed memory-based storage systems that differentiate them from their disk-based counterparts. These differences significantly affect the goals we set for a memory-based migration algorithm.

First, disk-based file server performance is primarily determined by client request rate. An increased request rate means longer disk queuing delays at the server resulting in higher response times. Although memory-based servers are affected by client request rate, the amount of data stored on a server also influences a server's performance. If the amount of data being accessed exceeds the server's memory capacity, page swapping increases and as a result, the server's performance can degrade by an order of magnitude or more. Consequently, memory-based servers are characterized by two loads rather than one. *CPU load* represents the number of requests processed per second by the

---
*This work supported in part by NSF grant numbers IRI-92121301, CCR-9309176, CDA-9320179, and CDA-9502645.

CPU and *memory load* represents the amount of *active data*[1] stored at the server. If the CPU is busy 100% of the time or if the server's memory space is 100% utilized we say the server has "reached its capacity" and is "saturated". Exceeding the memory capacity is potentially more dangerous than exceeding the CPU capacity because CPU overloads only cause performance to degrade slowly while memory overloads cause disk paging that can degrade performance by an order of magnitude or more.

A second finding from our previous work is that if two different servers are both executing below their capacity, both servers will have approximately the same average response time, regardless of their specific loads. When a server is executing below its capacity, CPU queueing delays and memory access times are insignificant compared to the network latency. Because network latency dominates a server's response time, the specific load on the server has little impact on performance. This is not true of disk-based systems. In disk-based systems, disk latency and disk queuing delays dominate server response time. Thus, small changes in request rate can severely affect a disk-based server, even if it is lightly loaded.

Memory-based storage systems can, of course, use disks for additional storage space if necessary. However, if the active file system data exceeds the aggregate physical memory capacity of the system and disk swapping ensues, queuing delays caused by high disk latencies will begin to dominate server response time just like disk-based storage systems. To differentiate disk-based models from memory-based models, we assume that memory-based storage systems have sufficient aggregate memory capacity to hold a file system's active data. Because the active data is primarily memory-resident, the number of disk faults will not be sufficient to affect average server response time.

A final characteristic of our memory-based system that impacts the migration algorithm is the fact that the system uses *idle* memory and processing power. The location of idle resources in the system will change (over time) for various reasons (e.g. users returning to their machines after an absence). If a machine undergoes a transition from idle to active, MBFS must relinquish the resources it has borrowed on that machine and find alternate idle resources. Anticipating transitions is difficult because user behavior is typically unpredictable. Consequently, transitions should be avoided if at all possible. When they do occur, other idle resources must be found quickly to minimize the inconvenience to the users and applications.

In light of our two previous observations and the goal to avoid inconvenience to client applications, this paper presents a new migration algorithm that attempts to keep the system minimally distributed while allowing load imbalances. Keeping the system minimally distributed reduces the failure rate among servers, the communication overhead among servers, the distributed addressing costs, and the chance of a migration occurring because of unanticipated transitions from idle to active. Despite the minimal distribution and load imbalances, the system exhibits performance similar to that of a maximally distributed fully balanced system.

2. Related Work

Remote memory systems have been investigated in a variety of contexts. The following briefly comments on related remote memory systems, and, when possible, describes the migration mechanism used. We also briefly mention past work in the area of load balancing.

2.1. Remote Memory Systems

Comer and Griffioen [2] introduced the *remote memory model* in which client machines accessed the memory resources of one or more dedicated *remote memory servers*. Client machines that exhaust their local memory capacity move virtual memory data to a remote server's memory and retrieve data on demand. Only dedicated remote server memory was accessible to clients. Each client's memory was private and inaccessible even if it was idle. Data migration between servers was not supported.

Felten and Zahorjan [5] enhanced the remote memory model to use idle client machines for backing store instead of dedicated memory servers. Idle client machines advertise their available memory to a centralized registry. Clients needing more space contact the centralized registry and randomly pick one of the idle clients returned by the registry. Like [2], data was not migrated among servers.

Dahlin et al. [3] describe an algorithm called N-Chance Forwarding that manages a cooperative cache. N-Chance Forwarding tries to keep as many different pages in global memory as it can by showing a preference for *singlets* (single copies of a block in some client's memory) over multiple copies. Duplicate pages, chosen for replacement, are simply discarded because the cache only stores *clean* (unmodified) pages. A singlet is forwarded from machine to machine N times before being discarded. Since the forwarding destination is picked randomly, forwarded pages could be sent to heavily loaded clients or even non-idle machines with no available memory.

Feeley et al. [7] describe the Global Memory Service (GMS) system that uses per node page age information to approximate global LRU on a cooperative cache. Like N-Chance Forwarding, GMS's page replacement algorithm only stores *clean* pages and does not consider a client's CPU

---

[1] *Active data* refers to the file data being actively accessed by the current set of applications. Section 3 provides a more detailed description.

or memory load when deciding the movement or replacement of pages.

Hartman and Sarkar [16] present a *hint-based* cooperative caching algorithm. Previous work such as N-Chance Forwarding [3] and GMS [7] maintain *facts* about the location of each block in the cooperative cache. Although block location hints may be incorrect, the low overhead needed to maintain hints outweighs the costs of recovering from incorrect hints. Should hints be missing or incorrect, a client can always retrieve a block from the server, to which all write requests are sent. Using hints, block migration is done in a manner similar to that of GMS [7].

The Harp file system [12] runs on a set of dedicated server nodes and uses memory, UPS, and replication to ensure persistence and availability. MBFS uses UPS in a similar fashion. However, MBFS also supports server expansion and contraction and data migration.

Franklin et al. [6] use remote memory to cache distributed database records and move data around using an algorithm similar in nature to that of N-chance forwarding. Client load was not considered by the data migration mechanism. Several other researchers have proposed non-distributed memory-resident database designs [8] which do not have to deal with data migration.

2.2. Load Balancing

Distributed process scheduling and load balancing have been studied by many researchers [19, 18]. All of these systems focus on placing processes on machines in such a way that all processors are continuously busy and the load on each processor is roughly equivalent. For most distributed applications, maintaining a balanced load is crucial in order to optimize performance. Even the slightest imbalances can severely degrade performance. Other systems treat tasks as a work heap with processors seeking-out tasks. This assumes that any processor can service any task. In MBFS, each server is responsible for only a portion of the storage space and cannot serve an arbitrary request. For each client request, MBFS uses a dynamic addressing scheme [11, 22, 13] to find the address of the server that can satisfy the request.

The topic of *disk balancing* was addressed in Snowball [22], a distributed disk-based database. Snowball demonstrated that small load imbalances (disk utilization across servers differed by only 5%) increased average server response time by a factor of three over highly-balanced loads (disk utilization differences of 0.5%). As we will show in the following sections, balanced loads that are crucial for disk-based systems are not crucial for memory-based systems.

3. A Memory-Based Storage Model

The Memory-Based File System (MBFS) uses the idle memory found in a network of workstations to store file data. In the following, we briefly outline the architecture of the MBFS system. Details of the system can be found in [11].

The MBFS system consists of general purpose workstations connected via a high-speed network. Although the network can be arbitrarily large, made up of one or more local area networks, we assume the latency between any two machines in the network is small (e.g., at least one order of magnitude faster than typical disk latencies). Users execute general purpose programs at random times on the network of workstations. We call any application executed on a workstation a *client application*. Although MBFS provides basic file storage, we will assume in this paper that the primary client application is a distributed database that needs high-performance file storage. An MBFS *server* process executes on every machine that has idle capacity. Together the servers provide the storage space for the MBFS memory storage system. MBFS servers have the lowest priority and are essentially "guests" of the machine they borrow resources from.

At any given time, each workstation operates as an MBFS client, server, neither, or both, and may change roles over time. When clients need the local machine's resources, the server component will shrink or disappear. When no clients are active, the server will acquire the idle resources. In this way, the system dynamically adjusts to alternating periods of activity and inactivity.

The primary role of the MBFS servers is to keep all active file data memory resident, and to respond to client requests without incurring any disk accesses. MBFS stores both modified and unmodified data. Servers ensure long-term persistence of modified data by propagating newly written or modified records to their disk in the background. To ensure short-term persistence without accessing disks, MBFS temporarily writes modified data to a limited number of special server machines equipped with Uninterruptable Power Supplies called *WUPS* (Workstations with UPS). In the event of a power failure, the UPS gives the workstation adequate time to write the memory contents to disk and shutdown, ensuring that all data is reliably stored and can be recovered. Recovery from server crashes are handled with techniques such as those proposed in [1].

MBFS assigns each file to exactly one server. A server where the file is stored is called the *primary location* of the file. To find the primary location of a file, MBFS uses an addressing function that allows the address table to be dynamically expanded or contracted. Each entry in the table maps a "bucket" of file block IDs to the server where the block is stored. Our current addressing algorithm is based on dynamic hashing with multiple hash-levels [11, 22, 13].

Our dynamic addressing algorithm has several advantages. First, it minimizes the table size. Second, it allows the table size to grow or shrink in response to the addition or removal of new servers. Third, buckets in the table can be split to create smaller buckets in order to obtain a more reasonably balanced load. Finally, timestamps can be used to merge address tables on different machines to create a more up-to-date copy of the address table. Note that the primary location of a file may change over time as a result of migration. In our original MBFS system, migrations occurred only as a result of server overload. The system had no ability to expand or contract the number of servers. The migration algorithm described in this paper addresses the issue of workstations that alternate between active and idle periods, thereby causing servers to come and go over time. Our new algorithm dynamically adds new servers to the system as machines become idle and migrates data off of machines whose client applications reclaim previously idle resources.

A fundamental difference between the MBFS architecture and other remote memory systems is the fact that MBFS assumes the file system's "working set" (i.e., *active* file data) fits easily within the aggregate idle memory space of the system. All other file data (i.e. *inactive* data) is placed on disk. We base our assumption on the rapid proliferation of PCs and workstations and the decreasing cost of memory. Many industrial and academic settings already have a significant number of networked computers, the majority of which sit idle most of the time [4, 14]. In such settings, machines with hundreds of megabytes of physical memory are becoming common. Consequently, we expect that distributed systems with aggregate memory capacities of tens or hundreds of gigabytes will be common in the very near future.

To differentiate between active and inactive data, MBFS currently uses a simple time-based mechanism. If data has not been accessed within a predefined amount of time Δ, we assume the data is no longer active and does not need to be stored in memory. The parameter Δ is can be defined using an updated version of Gray and Putzolo's 5 minute rule [9], but other active data definitions based on concepts like file system working sets [20] could be used as well. When inactive data is accessed again, hopefully via MBFS's automatic prefetching mechanism [10], the data will again be marked as active and placed in memory storage.

4. Migration Algorithm

The fact that MBFS assumes a massive distributed memory storage space (i.e., memory is the primary storage media) has several implications that are not valid of other remote memory systems [7, 16, 3]. These differences played an important role in the design of our migration algorithm.

First, because MBFS can differentiate between active and inactive data, it reports space used to store inactive data as available memory instead of viewing it as "used memory". This increases the perceived available memory. Second, assuming the active data fits easily into idle memory implies that we do not expect all memory to be in use storing active data. If a machine becomes overloaded, idle resources can be found elsewhere in the system to absorb the load. Third, the system does not need to go to great lengths to ensure that memory is used efficiently. For example, the system does not need to develop complex/costly algorithms that remove duplicates or eliminate fragmentation in order to save space. Fourth, we do not need to use all available memory in the system, but instead can afford to leave some memory idle (i.e., unused and unmanaged) until it is needed.

Given these differences, we developed a set of design objectives specific to migration in a memory-based file system. The following sections outline our design goals and present our dynamic migration algorithm.

4.1. Design Goals

We identified the following design goals for our memory-based migration algorithm:

1. A server should only migrate data when saturation is imminent or when triggered by an unexpected decrease in idle resources on the machine.

2. The cost of achieving a perfectly balanced load should be considered in the light of expected performance improvements resulting from a better balance.

3. The algorithm should migrate data to as few machines as possible.

4. The algorithm should migrate data to machines least likely to be used in the near future.

5. Load redistribution should not result in migration thrashing.

6. The algorithm must consider both memory and processor load when migrating.

Our primary objective was to design a migration algorithm that prevents memory servers from becoming saturated. As described in section 1, the performance of a saturated server degrades rapidly, in some case by an order of magnitude or more. Consequently, the algorithm must ensure that server saturation does not occur. Note, this means a server does not need to get rid of load if it is not saturated or about to be saturated (goal 1).

Balancing the load among servers and keeping the load balanced is not crucial to memory-based systems. In a disk-based system, imbalances of as little as 5% can result in a 200% difference in response time between servers [22], whereas imbalances of 50% only produce differences of 11% between servers in memory-based systems [11]. Moreover, achieving a perfectly balanced load will add overhead that in turn affects system performance. In memory-based systems, the response time improvements resulting from a balanced load are typically so small that they hardly justify achieving a perfectly balanced load. Thus, it is important that MBFS consider the cost/benefit ratio when deciding whether the load balancing algorithm should continue searching for a better solution (goal 2).

In a disk-based storage system, spreading the load across the maximal number of disks (servers) produces the best response times. In a memory-based system, a subset of servers will perform approximately as well as the maximal number of servers as long as no server becomes saturated [11]. This means that the migration algorithm can select a minimal number of servers and achieve performance similar to a system that uses the maximum number of servers (goal 3). To prevent migrations from occurring in the future, the algorithm should avoid sending data to machines that are likely to become active in the near future or to machines that are already near their capacity (goal 4).

Systems that attempt to constantly keep the load balanced often result in frequent (albeit small) migrations with data ping-ponging between machines (goal 5). Finally, unlike conventional load balancing systems that only consider CPU load, a memory-based migration algorithm must consider both the CPU load and the memory load (goal 6).

4.2. Determining When To Migrate

Conventional load balancing algorithms attempt to keep the load evenly distributed among all machines and thus invoke the load balancing algorithm whenever unacceptable load imbalances arise. Keeping the system balanced at all times is not one of MBFS's design goals. Instead, MBFS only wants to prevent servers from reaching such imbalanced loads that it could affect the average response time. This only occurs when a server reaches either its CPU or memory capacity.

Consequently, the MBFS migration algorithm introduces the concept of a *danger level* to indicate that server saturation is imminent. To identify potential server saturation, the system defines two dangers levels: one for the CPU load and one for the memory load. If either load reaches its danger level, migration is invoked to remove the overload.

The CPU danger level is defined as a percentage of the CPU's capacity. Although performance will degrade if the CPU exceeds its capacity, CPU loads slightly greater than 100% of capacity do not significantly affect the server's response time because network latency, not CPU queueing delays, still dominates a server's response time. Thus, we typically set the CPU danger level to be 100% of the CPU's capacity.

Unlike CPU overloads, memory overloads result in high latency disk accesses and queuing delays that can quickly degrade a server's performance by several orders of magnitude. Given the enormous performance penalty for memory overload, we must ensure that memory load never approaches its capacity. On the other hand, setting the danger level too low wastes valuable memory space and can also degrade performance. To avoid these two extremes, MBFS sets the danger level as high as possible such that the server is still able to migrate data off before the growth rate causes saturation. We define the memory danger level and other parameters below.

$$MemDangerLevel =$$
$$TotalMem - (\alpha \times (TimeNeededToMigrate \times GrowthRate))$$

$TimeNeededToMigrate$: the amount of time it takes to migrate data off of the server

$TimeNeededToMigrate \times GrowthRate$: the expected number of bytes that will be added during the migration

α: a padding constant to provide additional time ($\alpha >= 1$).

To prevent thrashing, MBFS uses a *safe level* in conjunction with the danger level. If the load is below the safe watermark we assume the machine is underloaded and can handle additional load. The danger level represents an overloaded state while the safe level represents an underloaded state. The migration algorithm will not push any machine over its safe level. This ensures that the new load on the receiving machine will remain sufficiently below the danger level preventing any migrations in the near future.

4.3. Selecting Servers To Take The Load

Although, MBFS allows any machine to play the role of client or server, we expect future distributed systems will still categorize some machines as "servers only" for reasons of protection, security, centralization, resource sharing, and guaranteed performance. Consequently, MBFS classifies every machine as either a *restricted access* machine (which will primarily act as a server) or a *general access* machine (which will act as a client, server, both, or neither). MBFS assumes that restricted access machines are more reliable and have minimal general client application activity.

Machines acting as MBFS servers will be functioning in one of the three modes: *active* mode (the server currently stores file data), *idle* mode (the server's memory is not currently used to hold file data), or *inactive* mode (the server cannot hold file data). Thus the set of machines capable of accepting additional load are:

Restricted Access Servers: A restricted access machine with an active MBFS server.

Restricted Access Idlers: A restricted access machine with an idle MBFS server.

General Access Servers: A general access machine with an active MBFS server.

General Access Idlers: A general access machine with an idle MBFS server.

The system obtains load information from other machines at runtime via a receiver-initiated approach [18] and classifies each machine according to the above definitions.

In keeping with our design goals, the MBFS migration algorithm migrates data to as few servers as possible and selects machines that are unlikely to be used in the near future. That is, restricted access machines are preferred over general access machines, and fewer machines are preferred over many.

The migration algorithm selects server machines as follows. First, the system calculates the load that must be migrated off of the overloaded server. The algorithm then adds machines to a list until the amount of unused resources in the list can absorb the overload (i.e. unused memory space and CPU cycles below the safe levels). The algorithm adds machines to this list in the order (1) Restricted Access Servers, (2) General Access Servers, (3) Restricted Access Idlers, and (4) General Access Idlers. A parameter M defines the number of Idler machines to add each time through the loop. Setting $M = 1$ results in a minimal set of servers while settings of $M > 1$ cause servers to be added in groups, hopefully producing lower loads on all servers and increasing the time period between migrations. The server selection algorithm is shown in Figure 1a.

The above selection approach has several advantages. First, although a user's personal workstation will volunteer its unused resources, MBFS's migration algorithm will not use the resource unless absolutely necessary. Algorithms that spread data across all machines increase the probability that a newly started client application will have to wait while data migrates off the machine. The increased probability of migration also implies an increase in the processing and network load used to handle the migrations. Using fewer servers reduces the number of migrations as well as the likelihood that a client application will have to wait. Second, file data has an affinity for restricted access machines because they tend to be more reliable and predictable. In particular, they are less susceptible to accidental power cycles, crashing, or load variations resulting from client applications. Third, spreading the data across fewer machines lessens the likelihood that some part of the file storage system will be inaccessible. Tending towards a more centralized approach reduces the mean-time-to-failure of the overall storage system. Fourth, spreading the load across many machines produces larger address tables because the data is

```
SelectServers {
  calculate Overload
  add all Restricted Access Servers to ServerList
  if (available resources in ServerList > Overload) {
    compute data placement
    migrate data
    return
  }
  add all General Access Servers to ServerList
  if (available resources in ServerList > Overload) {
    compute data placement
    migrate data
    return
  }
  while (Restricted Access Idlers Remain) {
    add M largest Restricted Access Idlers to ServerList
    if (available resources in ServerList > Overload) {
      compute data placement
      migrate data
      return
    }
  }
  while (General Access Idlers Remain) {
    add M largest General Access Idlers to ServerList
    if (available resources in ServerList > Overload) {
      compute data placement
      migrate data
      return
    }
  }
}                          1(a)
```

```
ComputeDataPlacementSchedule {
  while (no migration schedule has been found) {
    Revert to original machine load info
    Sort bucket list (by appropriate load metric)
    For each bucket (largest to smallest) {
      Find the server (X) that would have the
          smallest load after the addition
          of this bucket
      if (X's load over its safe-level)
        goto SPLIT
      else
        add bucket to X's load info
    }
    Compute Max and Min Server loads
    if (Max load - Min Load < split tolerance)
      return migration schedule

    SPLIT:
    Remove largest bucket (Y) from bucket list
    Split Y into L_SPLIT sub-buckets
    Add sub-buckets to bucket list
  }
}                          1(b)
```

Figure 1. (a) The selection algorithm used to identify servers with available capacity. (b) The algorithm used to compute a data placement schedule.

partitioned into many smaller pieces. Finally, our previous work showed that a few highly loaded servers offer similar performance as many lightly loaded servers [11]. Consequently, a minimal number of servers has approximately the same performance as the maximal number of servers.

4.4. Computing a Data Placement Schedule

Although load balancing is not a goal of the MBFS migration algorithm, balanced loads do give the best server response times and can decrease the frequency of migration occurrences. Consequently, the MBFS migration algorithm attempts to achieve an approximately balanced load whenever migration is necessary. To regulate "how balanced the load should be", we introduce a *tolerance* parameter, T, that defines the maximum allowable difference between the maximum server's load and the minimum server's load. Note that the tolerance parameter T does not determine when migration occurs, nor does the migration algorithm guarantee that it will keep the load balanced within tolerance T. It only defines how close the migration algorithm should come to finding a balanced load when migration is necessary, and thereby defines the amount of effort the algorithm is willing to expend achieving a balanced load.

The objective of the tolerance parameter T is to limit the amount of effort spent balancing the load in light of the benefits obtained from a more balanced load. Small T (e.g., 0.1%) result in well-balanced loads that will hopefully increase the amount of time before another migration is needed. A tolerance of 100% provides no balancing guarantees. When T is 100% the algorithm only guarantees that each machine involved in the migration will remain below its safe level.

The data placement algorithm is given in Figure 1b. To minimize the size of the address table used by MBFS's dynamic addressing algorithm, the data placement algorithm begins by selecting entire buckets for migration to other servers. If no distribution of the existing buckets satisfies the tolerance parameter T, the largest bucket is split into L_SPLIT buckets, where L_SPLIT is defined as a parameter of MBFS's addressing algorithm. After splitting the largest bucket, the process is restarted and continues until an acceptable data placement schedule is achieved.

During each iteration, the entire list of buckets managed by the migrating server is sorted by memory load if memory saturation has occurred or by CPU load if processor saturation has occurred. The algorithm begins by setting the load on the migrating server to zero and then tries to distributed the entire list of buckets (likely placing some buckets back on the migrating server). Each bucket from the list is successively placed on the machine with the smallest resulting load, assuming that the machine's safe levels are not exceeded. This continues until the entire load has been dis-

tributed or until the current bucket cannot be placed. If the load was distributed and the tolerance was satisfied, the algorithm is done. If the tolerance was not satisfied or the current bucket cannot be placed, the algorithm splits the largest bucket (creating L_SPLIT smaller buckets) and starts over.

L_SPLIT is an important parameter to the algorithm because it allows us to define how quickly the address table size grows and also how fast the placement algorithm converges. Our results, described in section 6, show that the L_SPLIT level has a significant effect on how fast the data placement algorithm converges at low split tolerance values (5% and below) but has little effect on system performance at higher split tolerance values (10% and above).

5. Simulation Model

We incorporated the MBFS file system and migration algorithm into the SunOS kernel and ran some small-scale experiments on a real system of workstations. Although the prototype provides proof of concept for the design of a real system, the limited nature of our experimental environment prohibits us from experimenting with larger number of machines and machines with different memory and processing capabilities. For these reasons we developed a simulation model to evaluate the performance of MBFS in a wider range of potential environments. The following only reports on results obtained from our simulation model.

The simulation model begins with an "empty system" in which each client starts with an address table that directs all file accesses to a single MBFS server. The initial MBFS server is a restricted access machine and is part of a simulated network of N machines with memory capacities ranging from 16 MB to 512 MB. A simulation configuration file defines the number of machines N, how many machines will be restricted access machines, how many will be general access machines, and how much idle memory each machine has. Table 1 lists the simulation parameters used in our tests.

The simulator consists of two parts: a file access generator and a migration system. To generate migrations resulting from memory overload, a file access generator simulates insert and delete operations on file blocks (the only operations that affect the memory load imposed on a server). The file access generator runs until a server's memory becomes overloaded. While the results reported here use file accesses taken from a normal distribution [17], we have simulated several other synthetic file access distributions and compared these with traces from our prototype. The nature of the distributed hashing algorithms is that it distributes accesses evenly across the MBFS storage space. Consequently, the file access distribution, whether a simulated distribution or a real file access trace taken from our prototype, had little effect on the system's performance.

When a server becomes overloaded, the simulator invokes the migration component of the simulation model to migrate the load. The migration component invokes the *SelectServers* algorithm and the *ComputeDataPlacementSchedule* algorithm to produce a data placement schedule. The simulator then transfers the load from the overloaded server to the other servers and updates the addressing tables accordingly. At this point, the file access generator is invoked again and the cycle continues. Consequently, each simulation involves a long series of insert-migrate iterations. The simulation ends after a fixed number of inserts or if the inserted data exceeds the aggregate memory storage capacity of the system currently being simulated.

The simulator maintains several statistics including the number of migrations, the cost of each migration, final address table sizes, the precision of load balancing, etc. The following section presents these results.

Algorithm parameter	Value(s)
M - Number of idlers to add	3
T - Load tolerance	0.1% - 100%
L_SPLIT - # of sub-buckets in a bucket	3 - 7
Environment parameter	**Value(s)**
N - Number of machines	100
Big memory machines (256-512 MB)	5% of N
Medium memory machines (64-128 MB)	70% of N
Small memory machines (16-32 MB)	25% of N
# of restricted access machines	10% of N
# of general access machines	90% of N

Table 1. Simulation Model Parameters

6. Simulation Results

The migration algorithm trades balancing precision for faster computation of the data placement schedule. Intuitively, it would appear that if the algorithm generates a less balanced load, the frequency of migrations could increase. The more unbalanced the load, the sooner another server may become overloaded. Therefore, the balancing precision should be selected in such a way as to avoid the side effect of additional migrations.

To quantify this tradeoff, we measured the average time needed to compute a data placement schedule and the frequency of migrations that occur during a fixed interval. We only report warm-start results that were recorded after the system had been sufficiently primed and all start-up effects were eliminated. We measure the computation time as the number of bucket operations (i.e., the number of iterations of the *for* loop in Figure 1b) that occur while computing the migration schedule. The compute times for various tolerance settings are shown in Figure 2.

As expected, computing a well-balanced load (0.1%) is an order of magnitude more costly than computing a slightly

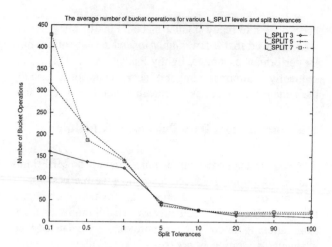

Figure 2. Average time needed to compute a data placement as measured in iterations of the for loop in Figure 1b.

or totally imbalanced load (10% - 100%). However, imbalanced loads do not increase in any meaningful way the frequency of migrations the system experiences (see Figure 3). In fact the number of migrations is occasionally

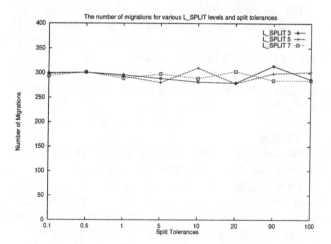

Figure 3. The number of migrations during the test period.

higher for balanced loads than unbalanced loads. This is due in part to the fact that well-balanced loads are more inclined to squeeze into existing servers and keep the server count low than their imbalanced counterparts. Despite the inclination to squeeze into fewer machines, our results show that, on average, well balanced machines (low T values) end up spreading the load across the same number of servers as systems that are not perfectly balanced (high T values).

Figure 4 illustrates how migrations are distributed in time

158

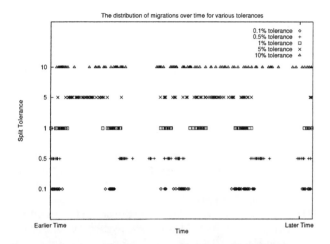

Figure 4. Migration distribution. Each point represents the time at which a migration occurred.

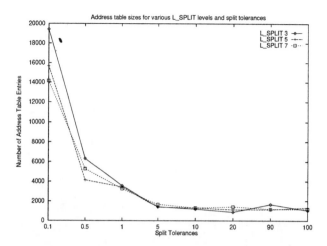

Figure 5. Address table size. Each point represents the size of the address table at the end of the simulation.

for various tolerance settings. Low tolerances produce a rapid succession of closely-spaced migrations followed by a long period without any migrations (resulting from the addition of a new server). In this case, servers are well-balanced and become saturated at roughly the same time, triggering a rapid series of migrations that impose a significant load on the system. These heavy migrations periods consume a significant amount of network bandwidth and server CPU cycles solely for the purpose of migration. To prevent two (or more) overloaded machines from simultaneously migrating too much data to the same underloaded machine, the system must ensure that migrations are synchronized and coordinated. The synchronization overhead and partial serialization of migrations affects performance when many migrations occur simultaneously. As a result, the average server response time during such heavy migration periods often increases dramatically. On the other hand, when the servers are not perfectly balanced, the servers reach their danger levels at different times and thus spread the cost of migration more evenly over time.

Our results also show that the safe/danger watermark technique used by the algorithm prevents the system from thrashing. That is, the system does not migrate data to machines that are already near their danger level. On average, the machine undergoing migration last received data from another server 26 migrations earlier.

Small address table sizes are desirable for space reasons, but also because fewer hash levels improve the dynamic hashing algorithm's performance. In addition, the delay associated with an addressing error (which involves the transmission of one or more address table correction messages) is typically less. Figure 5 shows the final size of the address tables for various split tolerances.

Note that the tolerance T only represents the maximum "allowable" difference between a heavily loaded server and a lightly loaded server. In practice, the "real" difference will be significantly less than the tolerance T. Figure 6 shows the average load difference the migration algorithm actually achieved at various tolerance levels. Although high tolerance settings could theoretically result in large imbalances, the actually load differences observed at high tolerance settings are quite low ($< 8\%$). In fact, our results show that on average the system can achieve a 10% tolerance with just two iterations of the migration algorithm and fewer than 30 bucket operations (see figures 2 and 6).

Our algorithm tries to minimize the number of servers in an attempt to increase the mean-time-between-server-failures and to reduce the possibility of migrations caused by newly active client applications. Because we take a non-conventional approach, we wanted to compare the performance of our system against an unrealistic system where machines do not crash and client applications do not start on idle workstations. In such an environment, optimal performance is achieved by spreading the load across all machines. Consequently, we modified our simulator to spread data across all machines during the first migration. While the modified simulator performed an order of magnitude fewer migrations than the original, the minimal server approach had average server response times at most 12% higher than the modified simulator.

7. Conclusions

We described a dynamic migration algorithm that limits server involvement and trades poorer precision for better compute times without affecting overall system perfor-

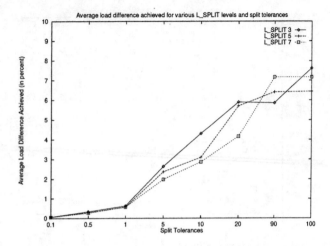

Figure 6. Average load difference achieved.

mance. We show that the algorithm's potentially imbalanced loads do not significantly affect the system's response time, can be computed an order of magnitude faster than balanced loads, do not significantly affect the number of migrations that occur, and reduces addressing costs. The use of a saturation prevention method combined with the ability to expand to other servers keeps the migration algorithm from thrashing.

References

[1] P. M. Chen, W. T. Ng, S. Chandra, C. Aycock, G. Rajamani, and D. Lowell. The Rio File Cache: Surviving Operating System Crashes. In *1996 International Conference on Architectural Support for Programming Languages and Operating Systems*, 1996.

[2] D. Comer and J. Griffioen. A New Design for Distributed Systems: The Remote Memory Model. In *The Proceedings of the 1990 Summer USENIX Conference*, pages 127–136. USENIX Association, June 1990.

[3] M. D. Dahlin, R. Y. Wang, T. E. Anderson, and D. A. Patterson. Cooperative Caching: Using Remove Client Memory to Improve File System Performance. In *Proceedings of the First Symposium on Operating Systems Design and Implementation*, pages 267–280, November 1994.

[4] K. Efe and V. Krishnamoorthy. Optimal Scheduling of Compute-Intensive Tasks on a Network of Workstations. *IEEE Transactions on Parallel and Distributed Systems*, 6(6):668–673, 1995.

[5] E. W. Felten and J. Zahorjan. Issues in the Implementation of a Remote Memory Paging System. Technical Report 91-03-09, Department of Computer Science and Engineering, University of Washington, March 1991.

[6] M. Franklin, M. Carey, and M. Livny. Global Memory Management in Client-Server DBMS Architectures. In *18th International Conference on Very Large Data Bases*, 1992.

[7] M. Freeley, W. Morgan, F. Pighin, A.Karlin, and H. Levy. Implementing Global Memory Management in a Worksta-tion Cluster. In *Proceedins of the 15th ACM Symposium on Operating Systems Principles*, December 1995.

[8] H. Garcia-Molina and K. Salem. Main Memory Database Systems. *IEEE Transactions on Knowledge and Data Engineering*, 4(6):509–516, December 1992.

[9] J. Gray and F. Putzolo. The 5 Minute rule for Trading Memory for Disk Access and 10 Byte Rule for Trading Memory for CPU Time. In *Proceedings of the SIGMOD Conference*, pages 395–398, 1987.

[10] J. Griffioen and R. Appleton. Reducing File System Latency Using a Predictive Approach. In *The Proceedings of the 1994 Summer USENIX Conference*, pages 197–207. USENIX Association, June 1994.

[11] J. Griffioen, R. Vingralek, T. Anderson, and Y. Breitbart. Derby: A Memory Management System for Distributed Main Memory Databases. In *The Proceedings of the IEEE 6th International Workshop on Research Issues in Data Engineering (RIDE '96)*, February 1996.

[12] B. Liskov, S. Ghemawat, R. Gruber, P. Johnson, L. Shrira, and M. Williams. Replication in the Harp file system. In *Proceedings of 13th ACM Symposium on Operating Systems Principles*, pages 226–38. Association for Computing Machinery SIGOPS, October 1991.

[13] W. Litwin, M.-A. Niemat, and D. Schneider. Rp*: A Family of Order-Preserving Scalable Distributed Data Structures. In *Very Large Data Bases Conference, Santiago, Chili*, 1994.

[14] M. W. Mutka and M. Livny. Profiling Workstations' Available Capacity for Remote Execution. In *Proceedings of the 12th IFIP WG Symposium on Computer Performance '87*, December 1987.

[15] J. K. Ousterhout. Why Aren't Operating Systems Getting Faster As Fast as Hardware? In *Proceedings of the Summer 1990 USENIX Conference*, pages 247–256, June 1990.

[16] P. Sarkar and J. Hartman. Efficient Cooperative Caching using Hints. In *Proceedings of the Second Symposium on Operating Systems Design and Implementation*, pages 35–46, October 1996.

[17] H. Schwetman. *CSIM Reference Manual (Revision 16)*. Microelectronics and Computer Technology Corporation, 1992.

[18] M. Singhal and N. Shivaratri. *Advanced Concepts in Operating Systems: Distributed Databases and Multiprocessor Operating Systems*. McGraw Hill, 1994.

[19] J. M. Smith. A Survey of Process Migration Mechanisms. *ACM Operating Systems Review*, 22(3):28–40, July 1988.

[20] C. Tait and D. Duchamp. Detection and Exploitation of File Working Sets. In *Proceedings of the 1991 IEEE 11th International Conference on Distributed Computing Systems*, pages 2–9, May 1991.

[21] R. Vingralek, Y. Breitbart, and G. Weikum. Distributed File Organization with Scalable Cost/Performance. In *ACM SIGMOD Conference*, 1994.

[22] R. Vingralek, Y. Breitbart, and G. Weikum. SNOWBALL: Scalable Storage on Networks of Workstations with Balanced Load. Technical report, Department of Computer Science, University of Kentucky, 1995.

PANEL :

OLAP AND DATA WAREHOUSING

Author Index

Notes

IEEE COMPUTER SOCIETY

http://computer.org

Press Activities Board

IEEE Computer Society Press Publications

The world-renowned Computer Society Press publishes, promotes, and distributes a wide variety of authoritative computer science and engineering texts. These books are available in two formats: 100 percent original material by authors preeminent in their field who focus on relevant topics and cutting-edge research, and reprint collections consisting of carefully selected groups of previously published papers with accompanying original introductory and explanatory text.

Submission of proposals: For guidelines and information on CS Press books, send e-mail to cs.books@computer.org or write to the Acquisitions Editor, IEEE Computer Society Press, P.O. Box 3014, 10662 Los Vaqueros Circle, Los Alamitos, CA 90720-1314. Telephone +1 714-821-8380. FAX +1 714-761-1784.

IEEE Computer Society Press Proceedings

The Computer Society Press also produces and actively promotes the proceedings of more than 130 acclaimed international conferences each year in multimedia formats that include hard and softcover books, CD-ROMs, videos, and on-line publications.

For information on CS Press proceedings, send e-mail to cs.books@computer.org or write to Proceedings, IEEE Computer Society Press, P.O. Box 3014, 10662 Los Vaqueros Circle, Los Alamitos, CA 90720-1314. Telephone +1 714-821-8380. FAX +1 714-761-1784.

Additional information regarding the Computer Society, conferences and proceedings, CD-ROMs, videos, and books can also be accessed from our web site at www.computer.org.